"Although the Russian-American Christian University has now closed, its history as told by its president John Bernbaum is both important and fascinating—and a riveting read. The university's twenty-five-year existence is a story of Russia's fraught transition out of communism and of extraordinary feats of international cooperation, a nearly unbelievable record of perseverance through official roadblocks and of unanticipated achievement by Russian students, and a moving account of deep person-to-person friendships. It is hard to imagine a more illuminating narrative of recent Russian history and Christian-inspired cooperation."

Mark Noll, author of *A History of Christianity in the United States and Canada*

"It seemed unimaginable, during seventy years of officially atheistic communism, that a Russian-American Christian University (RACU) would ever exist in Russia. With the vision and courage of its founder/president, John Bernbaum, and the RACU faculty, board, and other supporters, in 1995 a Christian liberal arts university became a reality. RACU was cherished by its Russian students and increasingly challenged by the Russian government. Now its legacy lives on in the lives of hundreds of RACU graduates, who were prepared for their future work and Christian service. *Opening the Red Door* is not only a captivating story but also a well-documented historical narrative and inspiring tribute to the ways of God in the world."

Anita Deyneka, Mission Eurasia board member emeritus

"*Opening the Red Door* is a splendid, well-written book, filled with tragic insights into the failure of post-communist Russia to escape the dark shadows of its past. (The last chapter is particularly outstanding.) John Bernbaum is revealed not only as a first-rate historian but as an inspirational figure of immense faith—whose steadfast attempts over a quarter of a century to establish a private Christian university in Russia take shape against the backdrop of historical and contemporary forces destined to sweep it aside. In the end, the book is a testimony to the power of doing the right thing and leaving the results to God, trusting in the seeds of good that are planted through graduates whose influence is yet to be measured."

Kent R. Hill, Senior Fellow for Eurasia, Middle East, and Islam at the Religious Freedom Institute, Washington, DC

"What a book for such a time as this! John Bernbaum, a friend and longtime Christian educator, has given us something special in this volume. Academically trained in international relations and experienced in diplomacy, he shows himself to be a gifted writer with keen insight into recent Soviet and Russian history as well as one who understands the hard work of Christian education. Moreover, John writes about the country and its people from the inside. He shares with us his experience of both high hopes and heartbreaking dismay for Russia and his beloved colleagues and friends there. The dark door may have closed, but it will not extinguish the light from Christ's transcendent lordship."

James W. Skillen, president (retired), Center for Public Justice, Washington, DC

"This is the story of a remarkable man with a remarkable dream. In establishing Russia's first Christian-based liberal arts university, John Bernbaum came to know key players in the Russian government and the Russian Orthodox Church. His gripping account provides a unique perspective on the new Russia—and on the challenges to Christian witness as Russia seeks its way into the future."

John P. Burgess, author of Holy Rus': The Rebirth of Orthodoxy in the New Russia

"How do Christians enable sustained expressions of faith for their cultures? This special narrative of the Russian engagement with American Christian higher education describes the struggle for such a space over the twenty-some years that the red door was open. It is a true tale of committed Christians from two continents in an unexpected higher education partnership that reshaped many callings, including my own. The book's lessons abound for educators in every country as we internationalize faith-based higher education and engage the surprises of other regions. Profoundly, this tome urges Christians to walk through global doorways when open and, before the face of God, to foster worldwide strategies for Christian higher education."

Shirley J. Roels, executive director of the International Network for Christian Higher Education

"This astounding tale of Russia's sudden openness to Christian higher education, John and others' tireless work to build a Christian liberal arts college, and then the unrelenting pressure of those who sought to undermine this beacon of light provides an inspiring lesson in Christian creativity, perseverance, and integrity in the midst of struggles. For those wanting to learn about Christian culture making and innovation in action, this book provides a fantastic example."

Perry L. Glanzer, professor of educational foundations, PhD graduate program coordinator, resident scholar, Baylor Institute for Studies of Religion, Baylor University

"Christian higher education is expanding around the world, often in the face of political and religious opposition. *Opening the Red Door* is a fascinating story of one determined attempt to establish an academically rigorous, spiritually vibrant Christian university in postcommunist Russia. Though it was established during a thaw in United States and Russian relations in the 1990s, the Russian-American Christian University ultimately could not survive the deterioration of that relationship following the terrorist attacks of September 11, 2001. But it was not for naught. Seeds were planted. John Bernbaum's firsthand account of the rise, decline, and enduring legacy of the Russian-American Christian University serves as a vivid window into the momentous years between the end of the Cold War and the formation of new global alignments following 9/11. It is also a testament to the incredible dedication of Christians who believe that the growth of the global church needs to be supported and guided by Christian academic institutions. As such, it will inspire as well as instruct readers interested in international politics and the complex relationship between Christian universities and their social context."

Shirley V. Hoogstra, president, Council for Christian Colleges and Universities

"Many people write about history, but few actually live through and play a part in shaping those historically significant events. John Bernbaum is one of those few. After the fall of communism, the former Soviet Union experienced a social, economic, spiritual, and educational vacuum never seen before in modern times. Into that vacuum God sent John Bernbaum, his family, and his team to provide not just a solid educational model, not just a Western-style institution of higher education, but the very hope and truth found in Christ alone. This is not just a story about a university; this is a story about a universe in which biblically epic faith and tenacity changed a nation and continues to have a ripple effect through the former Soviet world today. This is a well-written book about a remarkable and seismic shift in history."

Teri McCarthy, writer, speaker, and educational consultant

"As John Bernbaum's longtime colleague, who watched the unfolding development of the Russian-American Christian University in Moscow, I am thrilled to see this new book capture the story of God's work in the arena of higher education through decades of visionary leadership, collaboration, and dogged hard work. At a pivotal time in world history, Christian higher education stepped up to the plate and into the fray during the demise of the Soviet Union with the goal of providing student exchange programs and establishing a Christian liberal arts institution in Russia—despite facing numerous trials and roadblocks that offer leadership lessons in and of themselves. While we often think of nineteenth-century spiritual giants who poured their lives into bringing the Gospel to certain countries or people groups, this book tells of a contemporary "hero" who brought a dream to fruition, benefitting hundreds and thousands of people on the journey that he shares in these pages. Phillip Yancey's foreword affirms that this book reads "like a spy novel," yet the narrative that unfolds is true and worthy of capturing along with other "stones of remembrance" as we share the journey of faithful proactive response to God's call on our lives."

Karen A. Longman, professor at Azusa Pacific University

"This book recounts an amazing opportunity: an invitation from Russian reformers at the end of the Cold War to found a Christian liberal arts university in Moscow. John Bernbaum was at the center of that adventure, and in *Opening the Red Door* he shows, in frank and colorful prose, what made this enterprise possible and what brought it down in the end. Christian higher education today is a global endeavor, but it is not just about growth and success. It is a risky business, and we can learn much from our struggles and failures. I commend this highly instructive account to all who engage in Christian higher education."

Joel Carpenter, Nagel Institute for the Study of World Christianity, Calvin College

JOHN A. BERNBAUM

FOREWORD BY PHILIP YANCEY

OPENING THE RED DOOR

THE INSIDE STORY OF RUSSIA'S
FIRST CHRISTIAN LIBERAL
ARTS UNIVERSITY

ivp
Academic

An imprint of InterVarsity Press
Downers Grove, Illinois

InterVarsity Press
P.O. Box 1400, Downers Grove, IL 60515-1426
ivpress.com
email@ivpress.com

InterVarsity Press® is the book-publishing division of InterVarsity Christian Fellowship/USA®, a movement of students and faculty active on campus at hundreds of universities, colleges, and schools of nursing in the United States of America, and a member movement of the International Fellowship of Evangelical Students. For information about local and regional activities, visit intervarsity.org.

Cover design and image composite: David Fassett
Interior design: Jeanna Wiggins
Images: graduation hats: © CGinspiration / E+ / Getty Images
　　　Kremlin complex: © Bloomberg Creative Services / Getty Images
　　　speckled paper background: © Zakharova_Natalia / iStock / Getty Images Plus

ISBN 978-0-8308-5261-1 (print)
ISBN 978-0-8308-6517-8 (digital)

Library of Congress Cataloging-in-Publication Data
A catalog record for this book is available from the Library of Congress.

P	22	21	20	19	18	17	16	15	14	13	12	11	10	9	8	7	6	5	4	3	2	1
Y	39	38	37	36	35	34	33	32	31	30	29	28	27	26	25	24	23	22	21	20	19	

To a wise counselor who gave me

many good ideas over the years,

who read every word of this manuscript

and helped to make it better,

and who is my lifelong partner and closest friend,

MARGERY SUSAN BERNBAUM.

CONTENTS

FOREWORD
Philip Yancey

THE YEAR 1989 SAW A REVOLUTION as earthshaking as the one that had occurred in France two hundred years before. Without a shot being fired, the hated Berlin Wall fell, and as the world watched in amazement, one by one countries such as Czechoslovakia, Hungary, Poland, and Romania threw off the shackles of communism. Even more shockingly, client states within the USSR began declaring their independence, and within two years the superpower known as the Soviet Union ceased to exist.

I visited Russia in November 1991, while the revolution was still sorting itself out. Soviet hard-liners had recently attempted a coup, kidnapping Mikhail Gorbachev in Crimea and sending troops and tanks into the streets of Moscow. In response, Boris Yeltsin led courageous street protests and turned the tide toward democracy, becoming a national hero in the process. Gorbachev returned to the city, and by the time I arrived he was engaged in a power struggle with Yeltsin. No one knew who would prevail.

I went to Russia as part of a group of nineteen, the first delegation of Western Christian leaders ever invited to Moscow by the government. The letter of invitation, signed by the chairman of the Supreme Soviet, could have been written by an evangelical about the United States. It began, "In the difficult, often agonizing transitional period that our country is experiencing . . . spiritual and moral values acquire a great, if not paramount, significance in their ability to guarantee us against confrontation, civil conflicts, the erosion of moral foundations, and the lowering of standards."

These words were remarkable in view of Russia's hostile attitude toward all religion during most of the twentieth century. The zealously atheist government had shuttered ninety-eight of every one hundred churches and killed forty-two thousand priests; scholars estimate that at least ten million martyrs died for their religious beliefs. Now Russian leaders were anxiously looking for spiritual renewal. Gorbachev himself had written in his book *Perestroika*, "Today our main job is to lift the individual spiritually, respecting his inner world and giving him moral strength and help."[1]

As guests of the president, those of us in the Christian delegation were treated like VIPs, meeting with Gorbachev and the Russian Duma (parliament) as well as officials of the KGB. For a journalist like me, however, the most memorable meeting took place at the office of the renowned communist newspaper *Pravda*.

The newspaper occupied a five-story building in the heart of Moscow's printing district, though many of the offices in that building now sat vacant. *Pravda's* circulation had fallen off a cliff—from eleven million subscribers to seven hundred thousand—and to survive the newspaper had reduced its staff by two-thirds. It soon became clear why *Pravda* was hosting our delegation: we were being recruited for a kind of reverse propaganda. In an act of desperation, the official organ of the Communist Party was reaching out to its antithesis—evangelical Christianity—as a way of gaining credibility, or at least gaining sales. "Perhaps we could reprint from the Bible?" suggested the editor, "or could one of you write a regular column on religion?"

The editors were shaken to the core, so much so that they were now seeking help from emissaries of religion, which Karl Marx had famously called "the opium of the people." The editor in chief of *Pravda* admitted that "Christian values may be the only thing to keep our country from falling apart." He seemed genuinely puzzled by the recent turn of events. "We went to the best Marxist schools. We learned about equality and justice, about the need to overcome poverty and racism. You Christians share so many of the ideals we were committed to. Yet, with the best of intentions, we communists ended up creating the greatest monstrosity the world has ever seen."

Some in our group, such as Peter Deyneka Jr. and Alex Leonovich, had a hard time believing the words we were hearing. They had lived through the era of persecution, when their radio broadcasts were jammed by the government and when Christians were sent to Siberia for possessing a Bible. Credibility was stretched further the following day, when the head of the KGB used the word *repentance* while apologizing for the nation's treatment of Christians.

---

[1]Mikhail Gorbachev, *Perestroika: New Thinking for Our Country and the World* (New York: Harper & Row, 1987), 30.

The next morning, while jogging, I came across visual proof of the revolution underway. My running path led to a park in which I found huge statues of Stalin, Marx, Lenin, and other communist heroes. They had been toppled from their pedestals and ignominiously deposited in a kind of dumping ground. Russia's gods had failed them, and the nation was now looking for a new god.

ıIı

Over the next few years, representatives of every religion and cult flooded into Russia. One cooperative project created a curriculum based on the Ten Commandments for Russian schools. Storefront churches appeared beside stately old Orthodox cathedrals. Street preachers declaimed alongside vendors hawking their wares.

John Bernbaum, one of the nineteen guests of the president on our visit, was energized with a longer-term vision. As the executive vice president of the Christian College Coalition, he represented some seventy-six faith-based colleges and universities. When he was asked by Russia's minister of science and education to come to Moscow and establish a Christian liberal arts college, he sensed that Russia needed a foundational shift that could integrate faith with such fields as science, the humanities, psychology, history, politics, and business—exactly the goal of the US institutions he represented.

After hosting the first delegation of Soviet educators who came the States to learn about private faith-based education, he told an inquiring journalist, "This is truly one of those rare moments of truth in a nation's history when basic decisions are being made that will set the future course for millions of people." Little did he know that he would make 103 trips to Russia over the next twenty-five years.

This book tells the story of Bernbaum's quest to establish the first Christian liberal arts university in the Republic of Russia, in partnership with business and education leaders in the States and Russia. It was truly a leap of faith. As his daughter put it, "Dad, you have had opportunities to accept college presidencies in the States. Why would you become the president of a college with no students, no faculty, no campus, and no funding?"

"A good question," Bernbaum mused, one he often revisited. "I will never forget standing for the first time in Red Square near the famous, often-pictured St. Basil's Cathedral and the Kremlin. I kept asking myself, *What am I doing here?*

What is a guy from the West Side of Chicago doing in the capital of our Cold War rival by invitation of its government?"

The history of establishing a university could be dry and boring. However, in light of the upheavals taking place in Russia during that time, a word such as *boring* does not apply to this book. *Opening the Red Door* reads more like a spy thriller. As Bernbaum and his team were working through the tasks of recruiting faculty, seeking accreditation, devising textbooks, and finding classrooms, Boris Yeltsin ordered an armed attack on the legislature, a war raged in Chechnya, the ruble's value fell like a meteor, and the country's gross domestic product shrank by 50 percent.

It seemed at times as if economic problems would scuttle the entire project. During the formative years of the Russian-American Christian University, Russia went through two economic downturns similar in impact to the Great Depression of the 1930s. Due to soaring inflation, a student who missed a tuition payment by one day might owe 20 percent more the following day.

Bernbaum, an educator from the American Midwest, also had much to learn about crosscultural differences. Christian students openly cheated and plagiarized each other's papers; "We're a communal society," they rationalized. Russian faculty domineered their students, shaming them into submission. And every contractor, inspector, and bureaucrat expected bribes.

Somehow, despite all these challenges, in September 1996, just six years after Bernbaum's initial trip to Moscow in October 1990, the Christian university opened. Educational freedom in Russia had entered a new era.

Robert G. Kaiser, a *Washington Post* correspondent stationed in Moscow, described the revolution that began in 1989 this way: "In just over five years, Mikhail Gorbachev transformed the world. He turned his own country upside down. He woke a sleeping giant, the people of the Soviet Union, and gave them freedoms they had never dreamed of. He tossed away the Soviet Empire; he ended the Cold War. These are the most astounding historical developments that any of us are likely to experience."[2]

Sadly, Bernbaum's saga—and Russia's—does not end there. As we now know, a red door that swings open can also close tight. Vladimir Putin rose to power and began reversing many democratic trends. His nationalism found a ready ally

---

[2]Robert G. Kaiser, "Gorbachev: Triumph and Failure," *Foreign Affairs* (Spring 1991): 160.

in certain leadership groups in the Russian Orthodox Church, which successfully lobbied for laws against "foreign" religious organizations. Finally, just a year after moving into a beautiful new building, the university (now called Russian-American Institute) had to close its main programs. Three years later the board of trustees decided to sell the building and use the assets from the sale to set up a foundation to continue its ministry in Russia and Ukraine in different ways.

Other visionaries might look back on the experience as a failed venture, a massive investment that bore little tangible return. An optimist by nature, Bernbaum prefers to focus on the students and faculty affected during the years when the door was open and through the ongoing programs of the foundation.

▮▎▮

In October 2018, I participated in some of those ventures supported by RACU's foundation. First, I met with students in Ukraine and Belarus who were studying in a School Without Walls led by Mission Eurasia, the organization founded by Peter Deyneka. In Belarus, one of Russia's closest allies, I also spoke at a conference attended by six hundred young professionals from fourteen different nations that were previously part of the Soviet Union, including Kazakhstan, Azerbaijan, Armenia, and Georgia. The conference was conducted in a language everyone understood, Russian, a holdover from Soviet days.

Belarus summoned up flashbacks to the Cold War era. Even to this day, the KGB occupies one of the largest, most imposing buildings in the capital city of Minsk, and no one has dared remove statues of Soviet heroes. "Choose your words carefully," my hosts advised, "for KGB agents will certainly be present, monitoring what goes on."

The attendees had gathered to learn how they could best use their Christian influence within societies steeped in a tradition of atheism. I heard thrilling stories of transformation from young people raised under atheism who felt adrift after the collapse of communism—until they found meaning and purpose as followers of Jesus.

John Bernbaum spoke at the same conference. I had not seen him in twenty-seven years. He was the same jovial, irrepressible, humble man I had first met in 1991 on the way to Moscow. We swapped stories, and I heard firsthand the details of his arduous work in putting together a distinctive university, only to see it undermined by an increasingly repressive government.

Naturally, we discussed recent developments too—the growing hostility between Russia and the United States, the investigations into Russian meddling in elections, armed conflicts in places such as Crimea and Georgia. From his insider's vantage, John had prescient observations about the past and the future.

In some ways, the aftermath of 1989 is as surprising as the revolution itself, for the upheaval barely made a dent in the Russian soul. I puzzled over John's lack of regret over all that had transpired—puzzled, that is, until John and I met the six hundred eager young professionals, who represented countless more affected by his work during the years when the red door yawned open.

ACKNOWLEDGMENTS

THE IDEA OF BUILDING A CHRISTIAN liberal arts college in Moscow was not my idea. It was a vision that Peter and Anita Deyneka (Peter Deyneka Russian Ministries) developed together with their colleagues, particularly Ivan Fahs, a sociologist at Wheaton College (Wheaton, Illinois). They laid the groundwork and, when President Boris Yeltsin's minister of science and education invited the Christian College Coalition to establish this school, I was asked to make the plan a reality. What subsequently emerged was an amazing network of Russians and Americans who decided it was an idea worth doing.

The story of the Russian-American Christian University (RACU) is the story of a partnership between Russians and Americans supported by a relatively small but generous group of donors committed to an educational project designed to equip young Russian Christians for future leadership roles in their country. It was also designed to be a cultural bridge between Russian and American Christians— a bridge separate from bilateral political and economic pressures.

With the help of key advisors, we were able to assemble an impressive Board of Trustees with a passion to support this vision. These trustees and their spouses became deeply involved in RACU's ministry, and the American trustees made repeated trips to Moscow for board meetings and graduations—trips that nurtured their friendships with RACU's Moscow team and students as well as with Russian trustees.

The list of those whom I would like to thank for their dedication to RACU is a long one and their names are listed in the various appendices at the end of this book: trustees, advisors, provosts, faculty, and staff who were all part of this exciting undertaking.

The idea for the book came from conversations with Anthony J. Diekema and Richard L. Gathro, two of RACU's trustees, who wanted the story of this adventure shared with others. The Board approved their proposal and asked me to write the book, which I agreed to do on a part-time basis over two years. Dennis J. Kuester, chair of the Board of Trustees, was a constant source of encouragement, and his support proved to be very valuable as the research and writing of the manuscript developed.

In addition to my wife, Marge, who edited every chapter and offered wise advice on how to improve the narrative, Gladys S. Lewis served as manuscript editor. Her impressive experience as a professional helped to shape the structure of the book and the quality of the text. She proved to be a wise counselor, and her expertise was invaluable.

Ralph Veerman, a friend for many years, served as my literary agent with considerable energy and drive. He had played a role in RACU's development and helped mentor me in fundraising, so he was already substantially involved. In addition, others helped us locate a publisher and served as encouragers, including Bob Hamrin, Anita Deyneka, Paul Elliott, Phil Burgess, John Burgess, Doug and Nancy Greenwold, and David Renwick, as well as my family.

When IVP Academic agreed to publish the book, it was exciting news since this publisher was at the top of my list of potential publishing houses. Jon Boyd, academic editorial director at InterVarsity Press and the designated editor for *Opening the Red Door*, has proven to be a valuable partner because of his years of experience and wise counsel. Special thanks are due to IVP's Ashley Davila, who went above and beyond to help focus the narrative along its essential threads.

To the participants in the story of RACU, I am deeply grateful for all you contributed. Together we planted seeds that I believe have and will bear much fruit.

ABBREVIATIONS

ARO   Anti-RACU Opposition, RACU Archives

CMC   Christian Ministry Center files, RACU Archives

MC   Moscow Communications, RACU Archives

PresR   President's Reports, RACU Archives

ProvR   Provost's Reports, RACU Archives

RA   RACU Archives

RBM   RACU Board of Trustees Minutes, RACU Archives

SL   RACU Support Letters, RACU Archives

The records of the Russian-American Christian University are available at Asbury Theological Seminary Library in Wilmore, Kentucky, along with the archives of other Russia-related ministries and private organizations. A visual history of RACU can be found at BEAM, Inc.'s website—BEAM-inc.org—which includes videos and photographs of various events in the university's history, including several graduation ceremonies, the dedication ceremony for the new campus, and other highlights.

When I sat in the run-down office of one of President Yeltsin's cabinet ministers on October 26, 1990, during my first— and unanticipated—trip to Moscow, I had no idea that an invitation the minister of science and education would propose to me would dramatically change my life and that of many others, both Russian and American. This is the story of that invitation and its development over twenty-five years.

THE RED DOOR SLOWLY OPENS

THE COLD WAR DRAGGED ON FOR DECADES following the end of World War II, seeming to have no end. But then, on March 11, 1985, Mikhail Gorbachev became general secretary of the Central Committee of the Communist Party of the Soviet Union, and slowly some dramatic changes began to occur with America's Cold War rival. After several general secretaries who were old party officials, the fifty-four-year-old Gorbachev was a leader representing a younger generation, as he was the first general secretary of eight who held this position who was born after the October Revolution in 1917.[1]

During the 1970s, while in his thirties and serving as a provincial party official, Gorbachev traveled to Belgium, the Netherlands, Germany, France, and Italy, and these experiences profoundly affected his life. As he wrote in his *Memoirs*, "The most significant conclusion drawn from journeys abroad: people lived in better conditions and were better off than in our country. The question haunted me: why was the standard of living in our country lower than in other developed countries?"[2]

When Gorbachev took this position, he believed his mandate was clear; he had to revive the Soviet economy after years of stagnation under Leonid Brezhnev and his immediate successors. One month after his selection, Gorbachev announced a program of reform, which we now know was only vaguely formed in his mind. The Soviet economy was stalled, modern technologies were needed from the West, and industrial and agricultural production required significant

---

[1] For a comprehensive biography of Mikhail Gorbachev, see William Taubman, *Gorbachev: His Life and Times* (New York: Norton, 2017).

[2] Mikhail Gorbachev, *Memoirs* (New York: Doubleday, 1995), 102-3.

increases. He also knew that the Soviet Union was ailing from a moral and spiritual malaise, an insight that many observers in the West completely overlooked.

GORBACHEV'S REFORMS

Evening news broadcasts around the world began to use unfamiliar Russian words to describe the changes underway in the USSR, words that soon became familiar to those interested in world politics. Gorbachev introduced his new policy of *perestroika* ("restructuring") in 1986, which called for dramatic changes in the Soviet economy, changes that began to alter the centralized planned economy that had characterized the communist regime from its inception. His book *Perestroika*, published in November 1987, summarized what he intended to achieve as general secretary.[3] Gorbachev held the firm conviction that the USSR must initiate fundamental changes, but he had no long-term plan with specific steps in mind. He wanted to reform the Leninist system, not destroy it, but he also knew "we cannot continue living in the old way."[4]

He faced extraordinary challenges without precedents or processes to follow. No leader of any country had successfully changed a Stalinist-style command economy into a market economy. In addition, he had a conservative majority in the Politburo, the top ruling council of the Communist Party leadership, who could block any reforms viewed as threatening. Gorbachev also had to be sure that his reforms did not make the Soviet people desirous of even more radical changes. As a result, his reform efforts moved forward by fits and starts.

In his modest first reforms, Gorbachev called for fast-paced technological modernization and less government interference in the economy, plus an anti-alcohol campaign to combat widespread alcoholism. He soon realized that even these reforms required political changes in order to make them meaningful. Within one year of his appointment as general secretary, Gorbachev replaced one-third of the country's provincial and local Communist Party leaders and also added a group of new members to the Central Committee of the Communist Party. Then, in January 1987, he proposed multicandidate elections, followed by other changes designed to reduce Communist Party control of the government.

---

[3]Mikhail Gorbachev, *Perestroika: New Thinking for Our Country and the World* (New York: Harper & Row, 1987).
[4]Martin Malia, *The Soviet Tragedy: A History of Socialism in Russia, 1917–1991* (New York: Free Press, 1994), 445-52.

In March and April 1989, the first free election in the Soviet Union since 1917 took place to choose members for the newly formed Congress of Peoples' Deputies. A year later, Gorbachev was elected as the first president of the Soviet Union, a position for which there were no other candidates on the ballot.[5]

A SECOND SURPRISING INITIATIVE: *GLASNOST*

Even more remarkable changes soon followed. In 1986, Gorbachev introduced a policy known as *glasnost* ("openness"), which gave Soviets freedom of speech and assembly that were previously unknown in the Soviet Union. Radically reduced press censorship came into effect, and thousands of political prisoners were released, beginning with Andrei Sakharov, who was freed after six years of exile in Gorky. Gorbachev described his policy of *glasnost* in this way: "We want more openness about public affairs in every sphere of life. People should know what is good, and what is bad, too, in order to multiply the good and combat the bad. That is how things should be under socialism. . . . Truth is the main thing."[6]

When Gorbachev came to power, he knew it was important for the Russian people to understand their country's past; without that knowledge, no significant reforms could be made. Nikita Khrushchev's "secret speech" in 1956 that denounced Stalin was a beginning, but this thaw was extremely limited; Gorbachev decided to take on this challenge of historical truth telling. After two years of hesitation, Gorbachev decided to use the seventieth anniversary of the Bolshevik Revolution in October 1987 to "open the door to history." He did not anticipate what followed. As David Remnick, the *Washington Post's* correspondent during this time, observed, "Once the Soviet regime eased up enough to permit a full-scale examination of the Soviet past, radical change was inevitable. Once the system showed itself for what it was and had been, it was doomed."[7]

While historians and foreign-policy experts in the West hoped that Gorbachev would reveal the true character of the history of communism and were disappointed with what he said, Gorbachev did reveal some remarkable admissions, such as "the guilt of Stalin and those close to him . . . for the mass repressions and lawlessness that were permitted [and were] immense and unforgivable."

---

[5]For an analysis of Gorbachev's early political reforms, see Fred Coleman, *The Decline and Fall of the Soviet Empire: Forty Years That Shook the World, from Stalin to Yeltsin* (New York: St. Martin's, 1996), chaps. 11-12.
[6]Gorbachev, *Perestroika*, 75.
[7]David Remnick, *Lenin's Tomb: The Last Days of the Soviet Empire* (New York: Random House, 1993), xi, xxx.

David Remnick described his revelations this way: "Gorbachev's speech opened the gate. And the lion of history came roaring in."[8]

Previously forbidden books were now available for the first time, beginning in 1988. Boris Pasternak's *Doctor Zhivago*, Mikhail Bulgakov's *Heart of a Dog*, and Vasily Grossman's *Life and Fate* were the first of the anti-Soviet classics to be released to the public.[9] Monthly literary journals, weeklies, and even daily newspapers were filled with reports on how many people had been shot and imprisoned; how many churches, mosques, and had been synagogues destroyed, and their leaders murdered or put in gulags; and even how much plunder and waste was previously hidden from view. Soviets could now read what they knew from their own experience; there was an "equality of poverty" in the USSR.[10]

FREEDOM OF RELIGION

This policy of openness had clear implications for the role of religion in the Soviet Union. Beginning in 1917, Communist Party leaders attempted a radical experiment never considered by earlier rulers to create the first secular state in which religious institutions would be eliminated as well as all daily expressions of spirituality or belief in the supernatural realm. They created a "plot to kill God."[11]

The first target of the Bolsheviks' antireligion campaign was the Russian Orthodox Church, which suffered persecution on a scale not previously known. By the end of Stalin's Great Terror in 1939, the Marxist government had almost completely eliminated the institutional church. Every Russian Orthodox monastery and theological school had been closed.[12] For Protestants, the first ten years was a golden age, but by 1929 Stalin directed his severe repression at all religious groups, including Jews and Muslims. Decades of harsh persecution of Christians—Orthodox, Catholics, Protestants, and other religious communities, with the number of martyrs estimated to be twenty million—came to an abrupt end in 1988 when Gorbachev decided to support the one thousandth anniversary

---

[8]Remnick, *Lenin's Tomb*, 49-51.

[9]Remnick, *Lenin's Tomb*, 264-67.

[10]Here's an example of these revelations: "Only 2.3 percent of all Soviet families can be called wealthy, and about 0.7 of these earned that income lawfully. . . . About 11.2 percent can be called middle-class or well-to-do. The rest, 86.5 percent are simply poor." Remnick, *Lenin's Tomb*, 203.

[11]See the insightful study by Paul Froese, *The Plot to Kill God: Findings from the Soviet Experiment in Secularization* (Berkeley: University of California Press, 2008).

[12]John Burgess, *Holy Rus: The Rebirth of Orthodoxy in the New Russia* (New Haven, CT: Yale University Press, 2017).

of Christianity in Russia and spoke about the importance of religious and moral values for the life of his country.[13] This dramatic move, which many in the West simply ignored, severed the link between Marxism-Leninism and atheism. The Law on Freedom of Conscience, passed in October 1990, granted complete religious freedom to all people of faith in the USSR. A remarkable law, it opened the door for American Christians to become engaged actively in the reform programs of Gorbachev.[14]

GORBACHEV'S NEW FOREIGN POLICIES

Gorbachev surprised everyone with the extent of his economic and political changes in the USSR as well as initiatives in foreign and military policies that resulted from the changing domestic issues. Shortly after his election as general secretary of the Communist Party, he initiated what appeared to be a unilateral withdrawal from the Cold War. In order to focus all of his energies on reform at home, he determined to lower tensions with foreign opponents, especially the United States. He had no cultural hostility toward the West, liked Westerners, and came to regard some of them as personal friends.[15]

Gorbachev boldly set out to establish a relationship with the American president, a remarkable change for Soviet leaders. He met with President Ronald Reagan five times between 1985 and 1988, and then seven times with President George H. W. Bush between 1989 and 1991. While the primary topics of these summit meetings were nuclear-arms control and substantial reductions in weapons of mass destruction, negotiators for both the general secretary and the president also discussed a wide range of issues, including joint educational programs.

In February 1988 Gorbachev announced the full withdrawal of Soviet forces from Afghanistan, a painful war that had lasted for ten years and cost the lives of many young Soviet soldiers. Later that year, Gorbachev clarified his repudiation of the Brezhnev doctrine, which justified continued Soviet domination of Eastern Europe, and replaced it with a policy that allowed countries that were a

---

[13]Todd M. Johnson, "Christian Martyrdom: A Global Demographic Assessment" (presentation, University of Notre Dame, Notre Dame, IN, November 2012), www.gordonconwell.edu/ockenga/research/documents /TheDemographicsofChristianMartyrdom.pdf.

[14]For a comprehensive history of Russia's religious policies after 1990, see Geraldine Fagan, *Believing in Russia: Religious Policy After Communism* (New York: Routledge, 2013).

[15]Vladislav M. Zubok, *A Failed Empire: The Soviet Union in the Cold War from Stalin to Gorbachev* (Chapel Hill: University of North Carolina Press, 2007), 316.

part of the Warsaw Pact to make their own decisions about their internal political and economic systems. Western journalists referred to this change as the Sinatra doctrine ("I want to do it my way").[16]

In a rapid and totally unexpected series of events in Eastern Europe in 1989 and 1990—events that began with a ten-year struggle in Poland, then another of ten months in Czechoslovakia, followed by two more radical changes that occurred in ten weeks in East Germany and then ten days in Romania—communist regimes were toppled.

For most people who witnessed these remarkable events in the Soviet Union's empire in Eastern Europe, the collapse of the Berlin Wall in November of 1989 was the highlight. Some scholars argue that 1989 will become as significant in world history as the French Revolution of 1789 or the Reformation in the early sixteenth century. In rapid succession, communist regimes lost power in Eastern Europe, and two years later the implosion of the USSR followed, a totally unanticipated event.

THE CHANGING CONTEXT: NEW OPPORTUNITIES

Rapid-fire political and cultural changes set the context for Western educational leaders who wanted to participate in the reform of Russian higher education. Gaining an understanding about the traumatic changes in the USSR was essential in terms of explaining both the opportunities and the challenges for faculty and administrators who decided to take advantage of the possibilities for educational exchanges. Gorbachev and his successor, Boris Yeltsin, attempted to reshape a nation that was struggling to survive. Its top-down autocratic leadership was being tested, and the drive to remake Russia into a normal country proved to be a difficult task.

One sign of the changing, tumultuous times took place on the evening of December 31, 1989. A longstanding Soviet custom called for the leader of the Communist Party to address the nation just before the stroke of midnight and the start of the New Year. Unlike previous speeches, which usually were self-congratulatory, Gorbachev acknowledged that 1989 had been "the most difficult year of *perestroika*," and he admitted that his economic reforms had encountered "heavy weather." He ended his speech by pleading for "reason and kindness, patience and tolerance."[17]

---

[16]Coleman, *Decline and Fall of the Soviet Empire*, 297-305.

[17]Jack F. Matlock Jr., *Autopsy on an Empire: The American Ambassador's Account of the Collapse of the Soviet Union* (New York: Random House, 1995), 295-96.

For the first time, Lenin's name was not mentioned in the traditional address; Lenin was out, and religion was in. One of the principal television channels featured a roundtable of clergymen discussing the human values of faith and a sermon by a metropolitan of the Russian Orthodox Church. As US Ambassador Jack Matlock noted, the contrast with the past was striking because previously the mass media only mentioned religion to attack it. A week later, when the Russian Orthodox Church observed Christmas according to the Gregorian calendar, the entire three-hour service in one of Leningrad's cathedrals was televised.[18] Changes within the USSR in politics, economics, and religion marched ahead, while outside the borders of the USSR, Eastern European members of the Warsaw Pact were declaring their independence.

When the wall came down in Berlin, a number of member institutions of the Christian College Coalition (CCC) asked the coalition staff to organize a strategy session to discuss opportunities for faculty and student exchanges with Soviet universities. The coalition was established in 1976 by thirty-eight faith-based liberal arts colleges and universities and grew to seventy-six institutions by 1990.[19] This initiative, the first of its kind for the CCC, was launched with a sense of urgency, since no one knew for sure how long this window of opportunity would last. In response, coalition President Myron Augsburger agreed that the coalition would host a strategy session on "Initiatives in the Soviet Union" in Washington, DC, on December 21, 1989. Delegates from nine coalition colleges and universities attended the session, along with leaders from other evangelical student ministries engaged in educational exchanges.

The consensus of the participants called for the coalition to take the lead in setting up a study program in the Soviet Union that would be available to students from schools that were too small to organize their own program, and also for the coalition to serve as a coordinator for member institutions committed to starting their own "sister" relationships with Soviet universities. By serving as a networker, the coalition could collect information on existing exchange programs and share lessons learned from their experiences.[20]

---

[18]Matlock Jr., *Autopsy on an Empire*, 295-96.

[19]James A. Patterson, *Shining Lights: A History of the Council for Christian Colleges & Universities* (Grand Rapids: Baker, 2001).

[20]Christian College Coalition, "Strategic Session on Initiatives in the Soviet Union," December 21, 1989, 5, RA.

No one knew what lay ahead. In my years of work with the CCC, dating back to 1976, I had the growing conviction that Christian colleges were not considered major players in the world of higher education in America, but now we were being given an opportunity to engage in educational exchanges with America's Cold War rival, the Soviet Union.

Because many coalition schools had graduates working with various mission agencies and student ministries in Eastern Europe and the USSR and therefore had relations with church leaders in this region, we had advantages in terms of building networks with contacts in this part of the world. While we did not know what would happen in terms of political and economic changes, we could sense that extraordinary opportunities were opening up, and we had a passion to pursue them.

EDUCATIONAL REFORM: A LOW PRIORITY

Of all the spheres of Soviet life to be reformed, education was the last to be addressed. The enormous size and magnitude of the education establishment in the Soviet Union may explain why Gorbachev postponed any reform efforts affecting education. With 105 million students, 3 million teachers, 130,000 elementary and secondary schools, and 900 universities and institutes, the scale of the enterprise was overwhelming. The first challenge was simply to manage it; the second challenge was to reform it.

From 1985 to 1990, Gorbachev paid little attention to education. But in May 1990, pressure from below began to build for educational reform, and Gorbachev was confronted by university rectors (presidents), many of whom were democratically elected to their positions for the first time in the Soviet period. They expressed deep concern that education was a low priority and argued against the inadequate funding that prevailed.

At this pivotal meeting, Gorbachev stated that "we need a new system of higher education" in the Soviet Union, and he called for *perestroika* in education. His education minister, Gennady Yagodin, who accompanied him to the meeting with the rectors, went on to state that educational institutions need to be "relieved of the chains" of government control. These were strong words and signaled the beginning of radical changes in Soviet higher education.

Two months later, the newly appointed chairman of the Russian Republic's State Committee for Science and Higher Education, Nikolai Malyshev, announced bold plans to pull the Russian academic system away from the control of Moscow bureaucracies. He called for the decentralization of all higher education institutions in the Soviet Union and said, "Everything must be done from below." This sentiment for radical reform in education was reflected in Gorbachev's first major educational initiative, in October 1990, five months after his meeting with the university rectors. This decree allowed all higher education institutions to disengage from centralized governmental control and assume greater independence.[21]

THE DOOR OPENERS

In this context, Peter and Anita Deyneka and their staff at Slavic Gospel Association were able to launch an effort to establish cooperative relations with Soviet educators and to build student and faculty exchange programs between Soviet universities and Christian colleges in the United States. The Slavic Gospel Association had over 140 missionaries working in countries under Soviet rule and six hundred monthly evangelistic broadcasts directed at the USSR. As a result, the Deynekas had not been permitted to enter the Soviet Union since 1976.

Gorbachev's policies of *perestroika* and *glasnost*, together with his support of religious freedom, particularly his participation in the one thousandth anniversary of the Russian Orthodox Church, provided an opening for the Deynekas, who successfully applied for visas in 1989 to attend the annual Moscow Book Fair. When Anita Deyneka attended the meeting of coalition educators in December 1989, she saw their enthusiasm and went to work on finding a way to build connections with key Soviet education officials.

In January 1990, the Deynekas, making their first trip to the Soviet Union in fourteen years, met with the first deputy minister of higher education of the USSR, Evgeny Kazantsev, who represented 178 Soviet universities and was enthusiastic about educational exchanges with Christian colleges and universities in America. In a subsequent meeting with a Soviet government official from the Council of Religious Affairs, a government agency that formerly was instrumental in persecuting Christians, the Deynekas were told, "It is important for nonbelieving Soviet students to come to America to be exposed to other values."

---

[21]John A. Bernbaum, memorandum to the coalition board of directors, "Update on the Feasibility Study for the Russian-American Christian University (RACU)," January 12, 1994. It is noteworthy that in Mikhail Gorbachev's lengthy *Memoirs* (New York: Doubleday, 1995), there is no mention of educational reform.

Another unidentified Soviet intellectual who met with them emphasized the urgency of creating opportunities for American students to enter the USSR and for Soviet students to go to America. He said, "Our nation is in turmoil. We need exposure to the values of democracy." After talking with him and other educators, Anita Deyneka reported that many Soviet proponents of Gorbachev's *perestroika* believed that an exchange of Soviet and American students and faculty "could help to promote peaceful change toward democracy and stabilize their country." She underlined that there was "not only a receptivity to such educational exchanges" but also "an eagerness that they be arranged as swiftly as possible at this critical time."

Before they left Moscow, Kazantsev persuaded Peter Deyneka to sign a nonbinding protocol of intentions that highlighted the need to develop an exchange of student groups from the USSR and the United States "with the purpose of acquainting them with culture and education" in both countries and "to begin as soon as possible." He also proposed teaching the Russian language to interested students and faculty and expressed a desire to have American textbooks translated into the Russian language.[22]

The Deynekas contacted the CCC staff on their return from the USSR in late January 1990 and asked whether the coalition would be willing to take the lead in arranging educational exchanges, since Kazantsev had made it clear that he wanted to work with an association of colleges and universities rather than individual schools.

When I received the letter from the Deynekas, I immediately referred it to the coalition's president, Myron Augsburger, with this note: "Myron: Read this, my friend, and you will sense the incredible opportunities that exist." Augsburger was a leader with a global vision, and he enthusiastically responded, "What an opportunity!" The Deynekas recommended that the coalition send one of its vice presidents to the USSR in March, accompanied by Dick Scheuerman, a colleague from the Slavic Gospel Association. Karen Longman, a coalition vice president, was asked to represent the coalition on this trip.

MEETING LEADING SOVIET EDUCATORS

Longman and Scheuerman's trip in March 1990 coincided with Gorbachev's election by the Congress of Peoples' Deputies as the first president of the Soviet

---

[22]The report on the Deynekas' trip to Moscow in January 1990 is described in Anita Deyneka's letter to me, January 22, 1990, RA.

Union.[23] Although Gorbachev continued to serve as general secretary of the Communist Party, his efforts at radical reform were creating significant opposition by right-wing party leaders. Because the Communist Party did not share political power with any other party, the rising discontent by ordinary Russians with all of the changes in the USSR was targeted at the communist system itself. By spring and summer 1990, surveys indicated that only 14 percent of the Russian people "fully trust[ed]" the Communist Party. Other polls reported that between 80 and 90 percent rejected socialism, although many older citizens feared the loss of the social welfare benefits.

While there was excitement about the USSR's new sense of national self-discovery and relief from the culture of lies propagated by Soviet authorities, the collapse of the economy was creating great alarm among the people. In early 1990 only the most basic food items were available in state stores, and rationing of food was instituted for the first time since the Second World War. Talk about a possible famine circulated. The Soviet economy was sliding into depression, and the rate of economic growth, which had begun to slow down dramatically in 1988, approached zero. The USSR was in turmoil.[24]

On one of their first days in Moscow, Longman and Scheuerman met with leaders of the Department of Foreign Languages at Moscow State University. Its impressive architecture struck them as a metaphor for Soviet society: externally imposing but internally decayed. They walked past many seminar rooms with no more than a dozen students in each. They also noticed that none of the chairs matched other chairs in the room. In one of the hallways they saw a whiteboard that was used for announcements had just been painted. Someone angry with the government's refusal to honestly deal with the challenges facing the people on the street had written in large letters across the board, "You cannot paint over the truth."

The Russian foreign-language faculty members told them that "people here are dying to go abroad," but the problem was lack of hard currency. "We don't have a single Xerox machine for the humanities faculty. To make copies, you have to make a reservation a year in advance."

---

[23]The summary of this trip is based on two documents: Karen Longman's memorandum for the record, "Soviet Trip Notes, March 9-20, 1990," May 1990, and Richard D. Scheuerman's report, "March 1990 USSR Trip Notes," March 1990, RA.

[24]For a comprehensive analysis of Gorbachev's efforts to reform the Soviet economy, see Chris Miller, *The Struggle to Save the Soviet Economy: Mikhail Gorbachev and the Collapse of the USSR* (Chapel Hill: University of North Carolina Press, 2016).

Moscow State University was the USSR's premier university, and it included seventeen schools with eighty English-language teachers at that time. Departmental leaders told them, "There is practically no limit to the number of people waiting to learn English. The demand is huge for the English language."

Of the various educators they met, discussions with Mikhail Matskovsky, a distinguished sociologist from the Academy of Sciences, were the most remarkable. Matskovsky described his work on the Ten Commandments Project as an effort to rebuild the moral and spiritual base of Soviet society. The collapse of communism had left a spiritual void, in his judgment, and he was convinced the Ten Commandments could fill this void.

Matskovsky was also very supportive of student and faculty exchanges. He expressed concern that American students would find it dull to visit the USSR because there was no good shopping, no swimming pools, and only a few sports, but he wanted to give them insights so they would value their experience. He explained that he wanted these Christian college students and faculty to talk with "our people who think about their spiritual problems and dream about our new society."

On the last day of their trip, Longman and Scheuerman met Deputy Minister Kazantsev, who viewed their meeting as a direct follow-up to his time with the Deynekas in January. Kazantsev told them that twelve Soviet universities had asked him to help them establish exchange programs with colleges and universities in the United States. He wanted to move forward with the exchange initiative. He noted that only Soviet students who mastered English would be selected for the program. He asked Longman and Scheuerman to identify six to twelve coalition schools to start the project, and they agreed to identify five as a start. Kazantsev then proposed that a delegation of Soviet educators visit the United States as guests of the coalition and promised to invite a delegation of coalition educators to visit Soviet universities in reciprocity. If the coalition would cover the costs of the Soviet delegation in the States, he added that he would do likewise when the coalition delegation paid a return visit.

PLANNING THE FIRST EDUCATIONAL EXCHANGE

Karen Longman reported on her trip upon returning to the States; with the approval of President Augsburger, I immediately sent a letter to the presidents of coalition-member institutions informing them of the opportunities for exchange programs in the USSR and sister relationships between coalition schools and Soviet universities. Coalition presidents were told that the Soviet Ministry of Education wanted to begin with at least five sister relationships and that plans were under way for a trip in the fall to pursue this opportunity. In the next two weeks, thirteen member schools expressed an interest in these exchange programs, and detailed plans began to coordinate the exchange of delegations.

President Augsburger asked me whether I would be willing to direct the USSR Initiative of the coalition on a part-time basis while continuing to serve as vice president and director of the American Studies Program. The opportunity to do so thrilled me. My colleagues described me as an educational entrepreneur because I enjoyed the challenge of starting new programs. This opportunity loomed as irresistible. I dug out my graduate school notes on Russian history and reshelved my Russian history and literature books. My passion centered on international work in crosscultural contexts, so this opportunity seemed to be an ideal fit for my gifts, talents, and desires.

What would happen next? Could we mobilize our member schools to get involved? We did not have any answers, but in less than one month we saw an opening develop.

2

THE RUSSIANS ARE COMING! THE RUSSIANS ARE COMING!

AFTER MONTHS OF NEGOTIATIONS, made complex because of the enormous difficulty communicating with Soviet educators, who had little access to fax machines and international phone connections, a delegation of Soviet educators arrived in Washington, DC, on September 25, 1990, for a ten-day visit. This distinguished group comprised three categories of people: Ministry of Education officials from the Russian Republic, including the deputy minister for higher education, Evgeny Kazantsev, who served as head of their delegation; six Soviet presidents and vice presidents (rectors and vice rectors) of universities and technical institutes; and several representatives from cultural and art institutions.[1] I assumed that there were also one or two KGB officials who were a part of this delegation, since this was a known Soviet practice, but they remained unidentified, of course.

The Christian College Coalition staff prepared a ten-day schedule for the Soviet visitors, which included briefings on American higher education, with a special focus on Christian liberal arts education; visits to member institutions of the coalition that were closest to the Washington, DC, area and whose leaders had expressed an interest in these initial exchange efforts; and a general exposure to American culture and family life.

---

[1]Rectors and vice rectors of the following Soviet institutions were members of this delegation: University of Gorky (Nizhni Novgorod State University), Tula Polytechnic Institute, Yaroslav Polytechnic Institute, Ivanov Chemical-Technological Institute, Moscow Automotive-Fabrication Institute, and Russian Peoples' Friendship University.

Figure 2.1. Soviet educators arrive in Washington, DC (September 1990).

INTRODUCING SOVIET EDUCATORS TO PRIVATE HIGHER EDUCATION

One of our first tasks involved explaining to these Soviet educators that in the American system of education, private colleges and universities played an important role. When we took our guests to various educational associations in Washington, where officials talked with them about private liberal arts education, it immediately became clear that when they heard the words "private education" they were quick to dismiss it as an insignificant feature of American higher education. In the USSR, state universities dominated the landscape, and private educational institutions were relatively unknown.

Learning that 56 percent of American colleges and universities were private was a surprise to them. Of the more than 3,535 colleges and universities in America in 1990, 1,972 were private, including the Ivy League schools and many well-known universities and colleges, both large and small.[2] We gave them a list of coalition-member schools and pointed out that a number of them were nationally and regionally ranked as selective, quality institutions. Another immediate challenge

---

[2]"Almanac," *Chronicle of Higher Education*, September 5, 1990, 3.

arose from how to translate "liberal arts" into Russian. The delegation's translator struggled with this and eventually decided to define it as "humanitarian" or "humanizing" education. The coalition staff also explained to our guests that faith-based higher education was another distinctive feature of American higher education as represented by the member colleges and universities of the CCC. While 77 colleges and universities were members of the coalition at that time, there were 100 to 125 other Christian colleges as well. Little did we know that it was this distinctiveness that would really capture their attention.

CAMPUS TOURS

We divided our guests into two groups and took one group to the campus of Messiah College in Grantham, Pennsylvania, and the other group to Eastern Mennonite College in Harrisonburg, Virginia. They met with the leadership of these colleges, toured the campuses, and attended classes, where they watched faculty-student interaction. It was fascinating to see that these rectors and vice rectors especially wanted to see dorm rooms and the kitchens where food was prepared for the students, but the coalition staff was not sure why this was a priority for them.

During the visit to Messiah College, our guests entered a classroom where a biology professor had his feet on the desk at the front of the room, and one of the rectors said, "In the Soviet Union, I would lose my job for doing that!" The class started, and the professor engaged his students in discussion and demonstrated his obvious interest in their well-being. The Russian educators kept talking about that experience afterwards.

We did not realize how surprised they were by the way in which faculty and students enjoyed each other's company, were supportive of each other, and enjoyed the give-and-take conversations before and after class. Nothing like this happened in Soviet educational institutions, we were to learn later from firsthand experience.

Early the next week, we drove the delegation to St. Davids, Pennsylvania, to visit the campus of Eastern College. In addition to meeting with the college's leadership and touring the campus facility, the delegates attended a class in the MBA program in which the professor and graduate students were discussing ethics and moral issues related to the development of capitalism. Our guests were intrigued by this conversation; afterwards they said to us that this was the kind of discussion that must take place in Russian society because of all the corruption that they saw happening around them. They clearly understood that liberal arts education had a humanizing impact, and this distinctiveness captivated them.

HOSTED BY AMERICAN FAMILIES

When they were leaving us to return to Moscow, the Soviet delegation told us that their most memorable experiences occurred during the time they spent with American families, staying in their homes, and learning about lives and communities in the United States. The first weekend they were in town, our guests were invited into the homes of various host families for two nights. Their hosts took them shopping and to the various tourist sites in the nation's capital, but shopping was clearly the favorite activity.

Marge and I had three guests in our home, including the delegation's translator, which was very helpful. When we took them to the grocery store, they told us that they were sure these places were especially created for their trip, like

Figure 2.2. The Bernbaums host their first Russian guests. Pictured left to right: John Bernbaum, Yevgenii I. Nikulishev, Marge Bernbaum, Aleksander F. Khokhlov, and Yevgenii N. Kunitsyn. The door to the Bernbaums' home was red.

Potemkin villages, fake places built in czarist days. They were stunned by the variety of food products and the vast array of choices. The same reaction came when they entered a large hardware store with its enormous layout and aisles of products, which they thoroughly enjoyed exploring.

Attending church on Sunday morning provided another activity that made an intense impression on our Russian visitors. All of our host families were Christians, and church involvement surprised many of our guests. They assumed that religion was for uneducated people, but they quickly learned that this was not true in the United States. Alden and Lorna Johanson, a top budget official at the Department of Transportation and a nurse, respectively, hosted two rectors at their home, and one of them was Nikolai Trofimov, a distinguished geologist and vice rector of Russian Peoples' Friendship University. He became a close friend of the Johansons and us as a result of this trip. Kyle Royer, the CCC's vice president for finance, also hosted two guests, and Kyle and Karen told us that their guests took walks around their neighborhood with one of their young daughters. They held hands with the little girl, talking to her in Russian while she responded in English, each without understanding what the other was saying. The personal bonding was priceless.

HAMMERING OUT THE PROTOCOL

On the final day of the Soviet visit, delegates from participating coalition institutions joined our Soviet guests at the Dellenback Center in Washington, DC, for a day of consultations about potential cooperative programs. This day of negotiations resulted in the formal signing of a Protocol of Intentions, which proposed the following five areas of cooperation: (1) to encourage student exchanges and foreign study opportunities for academic credit and cultural enrichment; (2) to develop opportunities for faculty exchanges and visits for teaching courses, faculty development, and cultural enrichment; (3) to facilitate and promote exchange and joint development and production of instructional materials; (4) to assist in the development of programs in Russian- and English-language instruction; and (5) to promote joint humanitarian projects, scientific research, and other programs in areas of mutual interest.

These negotiations and the drafting of the protocol were not easy. With little experience on the part of coalition staff and strong-willed leadership on the

Soviet side, the day proved to be exhausting. One of the difficulties we experienced was the great sense of urgency on the part of the Soviet educators. One of our advisers said to us, "We need to imagine the Soviets on the ground floor of a house which is on fire with their children on the second floor in serious danger. They are trying to observe all of the rules of protocol, but desperately asking for help *right now*."

This urgency became evident to us within the first forty-eight hours of the Soviets' arrival. They twice confronted the coalition staff with demands for the immediate negotiation of exchange agreements between Soviet and coalition institutions. In the face of these demands, we could only respond that we were interested in exchange agreements but were not sufficiently familiar with the institutions represented by the Soviet delegation to be confident that they were the right partners who could best benefit from the assistance we could give.

Four sets of difficulties faced us. The first related to matching Soviet institutions with coalition universities. Because a number of the Soviet delegates came from technical institutes, their institutions did not seem to us to be a good match for the coalition's four-year liberal arts colleges and universities. We soon learned that these institutes were selected because of the large commercial enterprises affiliated with them, which meant they had financial support, while many better-known Soviet universities were basically bankrupt. In addition, many of these technical institutes had quickly converted to university status since they had the power to make these decisions in this period of educational reform.

The second difficulty related to the tumultuous events going on within the Soviet Union. The radical changes occurring in the country, particularly the struggle for power between Mikhail Gorbachev and Boris Yeltsin, created conditions of upheaval in which no one could be certain who was in charge. In the months before this delegation arrived, the newly elected Congress of Peoples' Deputies of Russia issued the Declaration of State Sovereignty for the Russian Republic; this declaration meant Russian political authorities were in charge and no longer took their orders from the ministries of the USSR.

In addition to all of the political changes, the Russian Ministry of Education, one of the last of the bureaucracies to experience *perestroika* (restructuring), was slowly reforming. Even while the Soviet delegates were in the States, significant changes were occurring in Soviet higher education. I had the impression that the ground was shifting constantly for them as well, and no one was certain whether Soviet or Russian officials were in charge. It appeared that for the first time rectors could negotiate contracts with American institutions without going through the government bureaucracy or getting its preapproval.

The third difficulty was a practical and obvious one: working through poor communication systems. Not only was there the issue of translating all messages and materials, plus the reality of needing to channel all coalition and Soviet written communication through the Deynekas' Slavic Gospel Association network, but also the lack of reliable contacts in the Soviet Union who had access to copiers and fax machines.

The final complicating factor concerned the composition of the Soviet delegation itself. Deputy Minister Kazantsev had a good understanding of the uniqueness of coalition-member institutions because of three lengthy conversations with the Deynekas and meeting with students from Wheaton College who visited him in Moscow. In fact, he said several times during the trip that he was particularly interested in our schools because of their emphasis on spiritual and moral values and because of the moral quality of our students. He explicitly said that he wanted coalition students to come to the Soviet Union "bringing their faith in Christ with them." He also said, "We understand that [religion] has made great contributions to our nation and to the world. . . . We are finding that there is enormous interest in the study of religion [among Soviet youth]."[3]

For most of the Soviet delegation, however, their interest was initially targeted at pursuing educational exchange programs with quality institutions in the United States. They were not prejudiced against church-related colleges, but neither were they attracted to them because of their Christian emphasis. By the time the trip was over, this had changed. They seemed positively attracted to a relationship with CCC institutions, and they came around to sharing the views of their delegation leader, Evgeny Kazantsev. Several Soviet rectors explicitly noted that their exposure to the way in which coalition faculty discussed moral and spiritual values in their courses challenged them to rethink how spiritual values could penetrate their curriculum as well.

---

[3]John A. Bernbaum, "Soviet Officials Explore Spiritual Values in Higher Education," *Christian College Coalition News*, November 1990, special section, 1.

FINAL THOUGHTS ON THE FIRST DELEGATION VISIT

Our first experience of hosting a Soviet delegation exhausted us by the time it was done. Many such visits followed, which made clear to us the importance of building personal friendships with these leaders. Russian culture is a relational one, and developing personal relationships was key to getting anything done in Russia. Two educators became close friends: Nikolai Trofimov, vice rector of the Russian Peoples' Friendship University, and Aleksander Khokhlov, rector of Nizhni Novgorod State University, one of the bright young leaders in Russian education and also a newly elected member of the Congress of Peoples' Deputies. We did not know when we met them how important their friendships would prove to be.

When I was asked by a journalist at the conclusion of this first visit from a Soviet delegation to summarize the significance of our negotiations with them, I responded,

This is truly one of those rare moments of truth in a nation's history when basic decisions are being made that will set the future course for millions of people. Our desire is to be witnesses of Jesus Christ to our Soviet friends and to help them restructure their educational system so that moral and spiritual values are integrated into all facets of their educational programs. The roots of Russian spirituality lie deep in their collective history and must be rediscovered. We also hope to challenge our own students to gain a vision for their lives that might include building bridges between our two cultures.[4]

---

[4]*Christian College Coalition News*, November 1990, special section, 3.

3

ENTERING THE SOVIET HEARTLAND

AFTER THE SOVIET DELEGATION'S VISIT to the States in September 1990, the CCC delegation selected to travel to the USSR experienced both excitement about this opportunity and apprehension. As departure time approached, my adrenaline was flowing. After studying about Russia in graduate school but never having visited the country, my imagination was piqued. Little did I know that this trip would be the first one of 103 over the next twenty-five years.[1]

Made up of ten college representatives and two staff members from the Slavic Gospel Association, the coalition delegation had worked hard to prepare for the trip. Because of my position as vice president of the coalition and part-time director of the USSR Initiative, I served as the designated head of the CCC delegation, and that responsibility worried me. While traveling to the USSR was an adventure, serving as chief coalition negotiator with Soviet education leaders more than thirty years older than I cost me lots of sleep. After a long but comfortable flight to Moscow, the plane landed with a jolt in the Soviet Union. Our crosscultural education began with learning the meaning of patience, and the term "waiting in line" was redefined by this trip.

Deputy Minister of Education Evgeny Kazantsev, accompanied by a large delegation of Soviet officials, enthusiastically greeted us at the airport. I considered him a friend after his time in Washington, DC, although he could be a tough negotiator. We were driven to the Hotel Rossiya, a large, five-star hotel with thirty-two hundred rooms adjacent to Red Square. Shortly after we settled into

---

[1]This chapter is based on my twenty-one-page single-spaced trip diary and my five-page executive summary report to the coalition's board of directors, "Coalition Delegation Visit to the Soviet Union (October 20-28, 1990)," December 6, 1990.

our rooms, our hosts took us to a luncheon at a cultural center across the Moscow River, which previously served Communist Party elites. After we entered a beautiful private dining room, a light lunch was served, beginning with long-winded introductions and greetings by the deputy minister. I responded with similar words of greeting, though much shorter in length, and introduced the American delegation. Kazantsev then introduced new officials from the State Committee of Science and Higher Education—an indication that major changes had happened and new leaders held key positions.

Following the luncheon, we learned that our delegation had been divided into small groups to visit Soviet universities in six cities within 250 miles of Moscow, departing that very evening by train. Our hosts instructed the coalition delegation to prepare for three-day visits to the Soviet universities selected by the Ministry of Education: Yaroslavl Polytechnical Institute, Tula Polytechnical Institute, Ivanovo Chemical-Technological Institute, University of Gorky, Leningrad Pulp and Paper Institute, and Stavropol Polytechnical Institute, the last of which was located in Gorbachev's home district in the Crimean region. While visiting technical universities was not a surprise by now, a pulp and paper institute seemed to be an odd choice.

THE OVERNIGHT TRAIN TO GORKY

We headed back to our hotel and began packing for three-day trips to cities we knew nothing about—a tough way to get started since most of us had hardly slept on the plane and were already quite exhausted. We wondered how we would handle this trip in terms of physical stamina. How could we engage our hosts, represent our campuses, and make clear, wise decisions when we were all ready to fall asleep at any time and still faced hours of additional travel by train?

Three of us were invited to visit the University of Gorky; my travel partners were Stephen Hoffman from Taylor University and Orval Gingerich from Eastern Mennonite College. This location was chosen for me because the rector of this university, Aleksander Khohklov, had stayed at my home in September, and we had quickly established a warm friendship.

While we were excited about the invitation to visit Gorky, a city made famous because it served as the place chosen to exile dissident Andre Sakharov, we did not realize that this city had been closed to all foreigners since 1932 due to its large number of military research and production facilities. Because of our lack of familiarity with Gorky, we slowly realized that this visit was a remarkable indication that radical changes were under way in the USSR. Not only were we foreigners, but we were Americans—Cold War enemies of the USSR—so the warm reception we received amazed us. Later we learned that the city of Gorky had been officially renamed Nizhni Novgorod, its original name, on October 20, 1990—two days before we arrived there.

We arrived in Gorky at exactly 7:00 the next morning and soon learned that trains in Russia are remarkably punctual. Khokhlov and other leading university officials met us at the train station; he warmly greeted us, photographers snapped pictures, and off we went to our hotel, located on a high riverbank overlooking the city. With ten floors, the hotel was clearly the nicest guest facility in town. The other guests in the hotel all seemed to be Russian military officers. We were grateful to have an hour to unpack in our single, nicely furnished rooms and to refresh ourselves after the overnight train ride.

OUR CAMPUS VISIT

After breakfast at the hotel, we went to the campus, where we met fifteen to twenty department chairs and vice rectors of the university. Cameras and flashbulbs popped everywhere. Khokhlov handled this event well and with good humor. As department chairmen dutifully waited in the hallway until we arrived, he commented with a twinkle in his eye, "They would never enter my office until I told them they could." The Soviet educators greeted us warmly, and we appreciated the gracious introductions by the rector. Khokhlov clearly decided he was going to make this a high-profile experience for his university community.

After initial introductions to the university leadership, we headed downtown to visit with the vice mayor and his staff as well as Communist Party officials from the Gorky region. We spent thirty minutes in formal conversation, with much talk of opportunities for cooperation between the United States and the USSR. Following the session with the vice mayor, television journalists insisted on holding an interview with us on the steps of the mayor's office building, a new experience for American educators like us.

After a short driving tour through Gorky and then a four-hour boat tour down the Volga River, we had dinner with our hosts and then met with numerous representatives of several departments of the university. During conversations with them, the question of student exchanges was openly discussed, and we explored how exchanges might work in ways that would benefit both Russian and American students.

Our second day in Nizhni Novgorod, we had a delightful luncheon in the apartment of the rector. We were surprised to find his apartment located in a poorly maintained building, but once inside we found an attractive suite of rooms. We thoroughly enjoyed meeting Khokhlov's wife, Galena, who became our good friend in the years that followed. At the end of the meal, an exchange of gifts took place, a common practice in Russia. I gave the rector's son, Dema, who also had lunch with us, a Michael W. Smith cassette tape and asked him to give his sister, who was not able to join us for the luncheon, an Amy Grant tape. I told him that my kids enjoyed this Christian music and hoped they would also like it.

TALKING WITH THE STUDENTS

One of the highlights of our trip to Gorky took place during an afternoon session with students in the main auditorium of the campus. I had been told in advance to prepare a few comments concerning Soviet and American education but had no idea what lay ahead. Much to our surprise, our hosts ushered the three of us into the largest auditorium on campus jammed with more than five hundred students and faculty members. Brought up onto the stage to a table set in a panel format, we found ourselves flooded with bright lights and cameras. After an introduction by Khohklov, he asked me to make a few opening remarks. I spent approximately twenty minutes, with the help of an excellent translator, Alexander (Sasha) Lubavsky, sharing observations about American higher education and particularly about the nature of liberal arts education. I also talked honestly about some of the problems American higher education faced. Among other things, I discussed the provincial character of North American education and faculty who did not train students to live in a global world, joking that most of our students would have no idea where Nizhni Novgorod was located. I then asked if the students knew where the states of Indiana and Virginia were in the United States, where Taylor University and Eastern Mennonite College were located. This brought lots of laughs about how students in both countries needed to learn more about each other. Finally, I discussed the uniqueness of Christian higher education, with its goal of graduating students who desired to make a difference in the world motivated by a love for Jesus Christ.

Khokhlov then invited the students to submit questions in a written format to us, with the expectation that I would answer their questions as head of the delegation, although I would have liked my two colleagues to also participate in this dialogue. I decided to use this opportunity to have some fun with the Russian students, and sometimes while Sasha translated my remarks I teased him for taking so long to say in Russian what I said, which the students really enjoyed.

We then began a ninety-minute question-and-answer session. Questions included:

- What are the major life values for an average American?
- Are there any Russian Orthodox colleges in your association?
- What is your attitude toward communists in the USSR and the United States?
- Is it necessary to believe in God to study at your colleges?
- We understand you are here to talk about student exchange programs. Please tell us about your plans in as much detail as possible!

The only frivolous question was, "What can you say about Soviet Pepsi-Cola? Why don't you drink it?" This student noticed the bottles of soda and water in front of us and that none of us had tried the Soviet Pepsi-Cola. A number of questions dealt with the issues of homelessness and hunger in America, since I had referred to these issues, and I told them that our schools worked hard to equip students to help the poor and vulnerable.

When this extraordinary session neared an hour, the vice president received a question and then started to laugh when he wrote the translation in English and gave it to me to read: "How do you do? You are a beautiful man!" The audience erupted in laughter. My response: "Wait until my wife hears about this!" I got teased about this, of course, for the remainder of my time in Nizhni Novgorod.

CONCERTS WE NEVER EXPECTED

At the conclusion of our question-and-answer session, the rector invited everyone to remain seated for a concert. We were in for a treat! First up: four Russian students with guitars, two men and two women, sang several songs in English, including a rousing rendition of "When the Saints Go Marching In" and "Ain't

Gonna Study War No More." They were followed by the Gorky Academic Choir, a group of thirty to forty formally dressed men and women who sang a brief concert of three songs. The first was a song of praise from the Russian Orthodox liturgy, the second an American Negro spiritual titled, "Who's Knocking at the Door?" and then they concluded with the famous "Song of the Volga Boatmen." I had to pinch myself to believe what we were experiencing.

Following the concert, we had another remarkable experience. In the Kremlin in downtown Nizhni Novgorod, we attended a concert of the Moscow Patriarchal Choir. The concert, which lasted for almost three hours, was one of Russian Orthodox worship music, sung by a somber-looking choir of fifteen Russian Orthodox priests. We returned to our hotel at 10 p.m. exhausted but exhilarated. The music and the level of interest in spiritual things had been very exciting to experience and gave us much to ponder.

DRAFTING EXCHANGE AGREEMENTS

Our third and final day in Gorky proved to be a workday, essentially spent drafting protocols regarding student and faculty exchange programs. We gradually worked our way through various draft proposals—a tedious process, but also a remarkable learning experience about negotiating with Russians and the difficulties of using words in different languages that mean very different things. These negotiating sessions, broken up by coffee breaks, radio and television interviews, and many photo opportunities, went on for hours. By early afternoon, a draft protocol with Eastern Mennonite College was completed with translations in Russian and English.

Later that afternoon, Orval Gingerich and I had a chance to meet with fifteen carefully selected students from each of two departments, history and literature. Stephen Hoffmann, the third member of our party on this trip to Gorky from the United States, could not join us as he continued to iron out issues in a similar protocol for Taylor University. We had an impressive discussion with these bright Russian students. They asked questions about Christianity and wanted to know how it related to higher education. The students seemed intensely interested in what we had to share with them and did not want the meeting to end, and neither did we.

After a brief tour of the university's dormitories and health-care facilities, we returned to the administration building and finalized the protocol with Taylor

University. After a farewell banquet, accompanied by several of our Russian hosts, we departed the hotel for the train station and at 10:20 p.m. left for Moscow. This was now our fifth night in the Soviet Union, and it was our third night spent trying to sleep while bouncing either on a plane or a train.

I will never forget the experience of visiting this university and the historic city of Gorky, now Nizhni Novgorod, and can still picture the faculty, students, and various sites in the city. To a person, they had a genuine interest in us as people and in our colleges and a great curiosity about our knowledge of Russian history and culture. Orval noted, "The fact that we were given permission to visit a city which is officially on the list of closed cities illustrates that *perestroika* is real. Even though this is a difficult time economically, I sensed a very optimistic spirit and a sense of hope that the future holds good things for the Soviet people."[2] Steve offered this insight: "After some seventy years of serious effort to integrate atheism into its educational curriculum, Soviet authorities have evidently decided in favor of Christian values as a more desirable basis."[3]

Our university hosts tried very hard to be sensitive to us. They often asked us to lead in prayer before a meal. Limited use of alcohol took place during formal dinners, not a typical experience in the USSR. On two occasions we had a special brandy offered to us, but generally alcohol was not present. The three of us also agreed that while the physical facilities and grounds of the campus were surprisingly poor and not well-maintained, the quality of the faculty was impressive.

That no courses at the university were currently taught in English presented a difficult issue for us, because we did not know how our American students would survive in this context. Although we noted that few faculty members and students had English-language competence, the rector, vice rector, and a number of faculty members reported that our presence on their university campus generated a tremendous excitement on the part of students and faculty to further develop their knowledge of the English language. When talking with those who knew English, we quickly learned which illegal radio broadcasts they heard. Those who secretly listened to the British Broadcasting Company (BBC) spoke English with a British accent, while those who listened to forbidden broadcasts from the Voice of America spoke American English, Midwestern style.

---

[2]*Christian College Coalition News*, December 1990, special section, 4.
[3]*Christian College Coalition News*, December 1990, special section, 4.

Our first campus visit in the USSR amazed all three of us because of the warm receptivity shown to us. The university was located in a secret military-industrial city where the Soviets had been building armaments to counter their Cold War rival, the United States, and yet our hosts welcomed us like long-lost friends. In addition to their gracious hospitality, the interest of the Russian students and faculty in spiritual matters was encouraging. The students especially wanted to talk about the meaning of life and what had lasting value. They wanted to know what America's experience had been with the connections between religion and politics and how this might apply to them. A spiritual and intellectual hunger existed on this campus, and we left this city feeling a strong need to come back and work with these new friends now that the red door was wide open.

EXPERIENCING MOSCOW FOR THE FIRST TIME

Although we had begun our trip in Moscow on October 20, 1990, our entire delegation had left the capital city that same day to visit universities in various regions of the USSR. When we returned to Moscow early in the morning on October 25, the opportunity came to see Moscow for the first time.[4] The three of us who visited Nizhni Novgorod returned to Moscow by the overnight train and arrived at 6 a.m.; although we enjoyed the train trip, we arrived tired and red-eyed. Our Soviet hosts from the State Committee of Education met us on the platform and took us by van to the Hotel Orlenok, our lodging site for the remaining days of our stay and conveniently located near Moscow State University. When we entered the lobby of the large, run-down hotel, we saw it was filled with sleeping people who appeared to be internationals. Unlike the Rossiya Hotel, where we rested and changed clothes the day we first arrived in Moscow, this hotel was not an impressive place. My single room was just big enough to turn around in once I got out of bed.

After eating a quick breakfast in the cafeteria, Steve, Orval, and I used our free time for sightseeing, once again escorted by our affable hosts. We enjoyed the ride through downtown Moscow, with our Soviet guides pointing out many of the highlights, such as Gorky Park and other memorable places in the city. I will never forget standing for the first time in Red Square near the oft-pictured

---

[4]This first visit to Moscow is also based on my twenty-one-page single-spaced trip diary and my five-page executive summary report to the coalition's board of directors, December 6, 1990, RA.

St. Basil's Cathedral and the Kremlin. I kept asking myself, *What am I doing here? What is a guy from the West Side of Chicago doing in the capital of our Cold War rival by invitation of its government?*

By early afternoon, the other members of our delegation rolled into Moscow from five different Russian cities. We had all had positive experiences, having been warmly greeted and hosted, and yet all returned to Moscow exhausted from very full schedules and very little sleep.

CAMPUS VISITS IN MOSCOW

Our introduction to Soviet higher education continued when our American delegation was once again divided into smaller groups and taken to several universities and institutes in Moscow. We quickly understood that Soviet higher education was highly specialized and job focused. That night, after the visits during the day, the delegation squeezed into one of our hotel rooms to share our experiences on the various campuses where we had spent the last three days. Certain themes came from every report: the warmth with which we were received, the enthusiasm for exchange agreements, the interest in learning English, and the desire for education in the history of Christianity and Christian ethics. We also discussed the advantages of establishing exchange programs with universities that were located away from Moscow, in cities where there weren't many Americans or other foreigners. Each of the delegates spoke about Soviets they met who had great pride in their communities and local history, and how each identified their city as the heartland of the Soviet Union. These remarkable experiences provided lots of laughs in our subsequent conversations with our Soviet hosts, who were residents of Moscow and considered these other cities second-rate locations.

The next day we were brought back to the Moscow Automotive Fabrication Institute and, after meeting with students and faculty of the Economics Department, we were taken to an impressive cultural center located near the factory. This beautiful marble cultural center had an auditorium, art galleries, a library, dance and ballroom floors, and a number of cafeterias. Clearly the employees of the automobile factory, who might have felt hemmed in by their small apartments, could get out and enjoy a nice luxurious environment.

An academic forum was set up for the afternoon, and our small delegation was seated at a table in the middle of the room across from a delegation of Soviet guest academics, including faculty members in sociology from Moscow State University, an economist, the first secretary of the Soviet Philosophical Society, and a Russian Orthodox priest who lectured at Moscow State University on the history of Christianity. The meeting began when the Russian Orthodox priest turned toward us and said, "For seventy years, Russian citizens have been denied access to the Bible. For the last seventy years, American citizens have had free access to the Bible, but I suspect our problems are very similar despite this difference."

I immediately indicated to our host that I wanted to respond as head of the American delegation. I thanked the priest for his remarks and told him that I agreed with his analysis and shared with him that everywhere we had traveled in the Soviet Union we had seen signs of the richness of the Russia's spiritual heritage. The most impressive buildings were cathedrals and monasteries, and everywhere we looked we saw the importance of the Christian tradition over the centuries of the history of the Russian nation. I agreed that it was a tragedy that the Russian people had been denied education and knowledge of their own religious roots, but I shared that the same thing was happening in the United States, not because of the power of a repressive government but because of the process of secularization. We agreed that both societies were in need of spiritual renewal.

This experience, together with our visit to the University of Nizhni Novgorod, provided a helpful introduction to Soviet higher education. We met Soviet educators, learned about their academic programs, saw the dynamics between Soviet faculty and students, and noted the poor campus quality of their educational institutions. As we grew in our understanding of the USSR's educational system, we were helped in our planning for student and faculty exchange programs.

RUSSIA'S NEW HIGHER EDUCATION LEADER

As our time in Moscow rushed onward, I felt increasing tension because I was being pulled in many different directions. A number of Russian rectors were asking me to come to their campuses, because I was head of the delegation, but I could not respond affirmatively to all of the requests. To my surprise, the Soviet hosts informed me that I had a meeting at the State Committee of Science and Education. While not anxious to meet these government officials, because it seemed wiser to work with university leaders and avoid any political interference, I soon learned I had no choice.

The office of the State Committee on Science and Education, located in an old, poorly kept office building with a dirty yellow exterior, had hallways jammed with used furniture. It was not an attractive facility. The room where the meeting took place had everything imaginable that could be props and settings for Hollywood's Cold War movies. It was a communist, bureaucratic headquarters, 1930s-style room with photographs on the walls of top education officials and, of course, Lenin.

Deputy Minister Kazantsev and several members of the staff of the committee greeted us warmly and told us that we would soon be joined by the first vice chairman of the committee, Vladimir Kinelev, a physicist whom Boris Yeltsin had recently appointed to this leadership role. I did not understand at that time that a major shift was taking place between Soviet education officials and leaders newly appointed by Yeltsin, who were pushing the "old guard" to the side as they exerted their leadership. Yeltsin, elected chairman of the Supreme Soviet of the Russian Republic in May 1990, made clear that Russia was now in charge of its own affairs, and Soviet executives from the Gorbachev administration no longer dictated policy in Moscow.

As soon as he arrived, Kinelev, a handsome young man wearing a Western-style business suit with a brightly colored tie, apparel not often seen in Moscow, asked me whether I had any questions about proposed academic exchanges. Then he began to tell me what he intended to do as the new leader in Russian higher education. He said he planned to give the leaders of the universities and institutes the power to make decisions to improve their schools without waiting for approval of the state committee. In addition, he granted them the legal right to make their own arrangements for passports and visas, and he intended to remove Communist Party offices from the campuses of the universities and institutes in the Soviet Union to allow these schools to develop more democratic methods of operation. The recital of his projected program stunned me. Kinelev emphasized that creating educational exchanges with universities in the United States and Western Europe was of critical importance to make these reforms happen. He also said to me that Khokhlov, rector of the University of Gorky, told him about "the atmosphere on your coalition campuses because of their humanitarian values and high moral standards, and this is very attractive to us."

THE INVITATION

After asking a number of questions about the Christian College Coalition, its member institutions, and its funding, he totally surprised me when he said, "We hope a time will come when you will found one of your colleges on our soil, a college that would become a member of the Christian College Coalition."[5] I was shocked by this invitation. Two years before, Christians were not allowed to attend universities and institutes in the Soviet Union, but we were being asked to start a Christian college in the capital city of our country's Cold War rival, the first time any foreign country ever asked the coalition to establish a college on their soil.

Immediately Peter Deyneka's urgent advice flashed through my mind, "Do not make any promises to Russians that you cannot fulfill. Americans have been doing that in this country for the last few years, and the Russians are tired of false promises!" As a result of that advice, I told Kinelev that I would tell the president and board of the coalition about this invitation but was not sure how they would respond. I suggested that we begin with a series of student and faculty exchanges and then, once we saw how they developed, attempt to move on to more complex programs. He agreed with my proposal and thanked us for coming to his office and participating in our productive conversation.

OUR FINAL DAY IN RUSSIA'S CAPITAL

On our last full day in Moscow, our Soviet hosts arranged a tour to the Zagorsk Monastery, which is approximately an hour and half from Moscow. The visit to the Zagorsk Monastery, rich in the history of the Russian Orthodox Church, was an impressive experience despite the cold, overcast day. After several hours, we returned to the bus for our trip back to the hotel. Our Soviet hosts decided not to take us back to the hotel where we were staying but directly to the Hotel Rossiya for our farewell dinner.

The farewell meal took place in a beautiful restaurant with a spectacular view of the Kremlin. Without any warning, Deputy Minister Kazantsev invited me to begin our meal with prayer, and I was stunned. After recovering from the surprise

---

[5]My trip diary information was supplemented by my colleagues. The meeting with Kinelev was recorded in detail by Elaine Stahl's seven-page report on the meeting. I also wrote one of my *Chronicles from Russia*, titled "The Invitation," about this meeting, dated October 1990, RA.

of this request, I used the opportunity to explain to our Soviet hosts that the reason we pray is that we believe in God, who is transcendent, cares for us, created us with a purpose, and gave us life, health, food, and friends.

After my opening comments, as I was getting ready to begin my prayer, I noticed an amazing thing happening in the room. Vice Rector Nikolai Trofimov, who had been to the States in September and had stayed with Christian friends of ours who held hands while praying before dinner, reached out and took the hands of the other people at his table. Because he is a distinguished scientist and a respected older leader among educators in Russia, people at the surrounding tables decided to do what he did and, before I knew it, everyone in this room, including Communist Party officials, were all holding hands. What an amazing sight!

We spent our final afternoon and evening after the farewell dinner walking around the Kremlin, which was illuminated at night, taking photographs of the delegation in front of St. Basil's or Lenin's Tomb, and sharing insights about our experiences together. The entire delegation treasured its time in the USSR, and hopes were high that this was the beginning of important relationship building between Christian colleges and Soviet universities.

ASSESSING THE TRIP'S ACHIEVEMENTS

As a result of the Soviet delegation visit to the States in September 1990 and the subsequent coalition delegation visit to the Soviet Union in October, we achieved two primary goals. First, our delegation had signed a number of bilateral agreements for student exchange programs beginning in 1991 and 1992. Never before had we anticipated the creation of exchange programs with our Cold War rival. For example, two preliminary educational exchange agreements signed with the University of Gorky involved Taylor University and Eastern Mennonite College.

Two other coalition institutions, Tabor College and Fresno Pacific College, which (like Eastern Mennonite College) had links to Mennonite communities located in Russia since the early 1800s, worked out draft agreements with Tula Polytechnic Institute. Other schools represented in the delegation left without making firm commitments but expressed a genuine interest in developing programs for themselves. By the time we boarded the airplane for home, we anticipated that at least eight, if not ten, of the institutions represented by our delegation would establish exchange agreements and would begin moving Russian and American students between our two countries in the next academic year.

The second major result of our trip involved the building of personal relationships with key leaders in higher education in the Russian Republic. We not only established personal contacts with leaders of numerous Soviet universities and institutes but also had the opportunity to deepen our friendship with leaders of the State Committee on Science and Higher Education. In conversations with university and institute administrators, we were repeatedly asked to send teams of faculty members who could guide their institutions during these critical times of transition. Faculty members would be asked to help with the restructuring of their economic and business curriculums as the Russian Republic attempted to move from a centrally planned economy to a free-market economy. This meant that the entire curriculum in the business and economics fields had to be fundamentally restructured.

We also received repeated requests for faculty members who could lead seminars or teach courses on the history of Christianity and Christian ethics. Apparently the courses offered in these subjects at Soviet universities in recent years were filled to capacity, and the great demand for these courses could not be met by Soviet faculty. In talking to my delegation colleagues, most of us did not anticipate Soviet educators being so attracted to the "humanizing elements" of our Christian liberal arts curriculum. They repeatedly asked us to help them integrate moral and religious values throughout the curriculum of their institutions. None of us expected such a response when we left for the USSR.

The most amazing opportunity that emerged from our visit, one that was completely unanticipated, was the invitation by the state committee to establish a Christian college in Moscow. Soviet education leaders repeatedly asked us, "When can you begin?" We had the challenge of going back to our home institutions and sharing with them our excitement and our sense of the strategic importance of this moment in history.

What a challenge. What an opportunity. But were we going to be able to respond constructively and quickly, since no one knew how long this transition period of openness to the West would last?

4

GETTING STARTED

After returning from our trip to Moscow, the American participants excitedly shared the insights we had gained from our experience with anyone who would listen. For most of us, our first trip to the Soviet Union was a wonderful educational experience. The openness and receptivity of Soviet leaders about educational reform surprised us, especially the benefits that the Soviet educators saw in Christian liberal arts education.

Myron Augsburger, president of the CCC, enthusiastically received our trip report, and we heard the same response from other delegates who reported to the leadership on their campuses when they returned home. When I had a chance to report to the coalition's board of directors about my trip, the directors expressed excitement about exchange programs for faculty and students but not about the request to build a Christian college in Moscow. Many of the directors, who were presidents of member institutions, argued that the coalition operated as a service organization for member institutions, and its responsibility did not include founding Christian colleges overseas. While very disappointed with this decision, I decided to continue to work with the board, hoping that they would change their position over time.

THE RUSSIAN-AMERICAN MBA PROJECT

One of the first substantive projects to grow out of the trip to the States by the delegation of Soviet educators in September 1990 originated during their visit to the campus of Eastern College. In the conversations that took place following their attending a class in Eastern's MBA program, they discussed how ethical and moral values shape the development of a country's economic system. They asked how they could encourage this type of discussion in their business and economics programs.

Linwood Geiger and several of his faculty colleagues at Eastern College decided to respond by proposing that a joint Russian-American MBA curriculum be developed by a team of Russian and American professors, a curriculum that had a distinctive moral and ethical component built in. After securing a grant from the Psalm 103 Foundation to support this initiative, Geiger contacted the coalition and asked whether its staff would be willing to partner with Eastern College to implement this project.[1]

Geiger and his colleague James Engel traveled to Moscow in January 1991 to follow up on the coalition delegation's visit and to find Soviet partners for this MBA initiative. Their trip experiences immediately made it clear to them that changes in Russia were taking place very quickly and that the new leadership emerging in Russia, under Yeltsin's direction, had different perspectives from the Soviet leaders allied with Gorbachev. However, the weakness of the Soviet economy made it difficult for either of the rival leaders to secure funding for new reform efforts in education. When Geiger returned home, he contacted me and reported on his trip, noting in particular his conversation with Vladimir Kinelev, the head of the Russian State Committee on Science and Higher Education, the highest-ranking Russian official whom we had befriended. Kinelev had asked Geiger to inform me that the committee had received approval to work with us on the establishment of a Christian college in Moscow, and he wanted the leadership of the coalition to know about this important decision.

THE USSR INITIATIVE

In the spring of 1991, the coalition staff invited member colleges and universities to join the USSR Initiative, as the project was labeled, in response to the interest by member colleges and universities to develop programs in this previously inaccessible part of the world. I was assigned direction of the program on a part-time basis, and this new role was much more exciting to me than my existing job as executive vice president of the coalition. Fifteen schools immediately agreed to participate, and exciting new programs blossomed all across the United States.

---

[1]John A. Bernbaum, memorandum to the coalition board of directors, "The MBA Consultations in Moscow in August–September, 1991," October 7, 1991, 1-2.

In 1989 only one coalition member institution (Seattle Pacific University) offered courses in the Russian language. Campus leaders quickly made plans to initiate Russian languages courses in ten member schools in the next two years, aided by Russian-language teachers who eagerly agreed to come to the States to start these programs. Numerous student and faculty exchanges were organized between the two countries.

In the months that followed, five student exchanges—previously impossible— started, and American and Russian students had the opportunity to study on campuses in their respective countries. Deputy Minister Kazantsev, the head of the Soviet delegation that came to Washington, DC, in September 1990 and our primary liaison up to this point, was invited to be the commencement speaker at Spring Arbor College in May 1992—a bold initiative resulting from a friendship made during the delegation's visit.

Mennonite educators from Fresno Pacific College (Fresno, California), Tabor College (Tabor, Kansas), and Goshen College (Goshen, Indiana), all coalition member institutions, volunteered to teach in a summer English-language institute in Lithuania, designed to be a pilot project leading to the goal of establishing a Christian college in that country that would serve both Eastern European and American students. This initiative was independent of the coalition's work and resulted in the establishment of Lithuania Christian College, which is still in operation and thriving under a new name—LCC International University.[2]

RADICAL CHANGES AND POLITICAL CONFLICTS IN THE USSR

The emergence of so many new initiatives with the coalition's Russian partners surprised all of us, since we could not have even imagined these programs only a year earlier during our first visit to Russia. The complicating factor, however, was how the political and economic tumult in the USSR would affect these initiatives. Building bridges to Russia seemed daunting, clearly a difficult task even in normal times because the political animosities of Cold War rivals did not quickly disappear. In addition, the stereotypes both countries had of the other loomed large and hindered trust on both sides.

---

[2]"USSR Initiative," *Christian College Coalition Update* (Spring 1991). The invitation to serve on the board of advisers of Lithuania Christian College proved to be an important part of my education in terms of how to build a college from scratch in this part of the world. While the context was different, the insights I gained were significant.

President Dwight Eisenhower began exchange programs with the Soviet Union in 1955, and his initiative was renewed and expanded in 1988 when President Ronald Reagan and Mikhail Gorbachev signed an agreement for their two countries to grow this earlier program in 1989–1991. Four years earlier President Reagan had said, "It may seem an impossible dream to think there could be a time when American and Soviet citizens of all walks of life travel freely back and forth," but we were now witnessing this impossible dream.[3]

Gorbachev's foreign policy initiatives also encouraged countries in Eastern Europe to set their own future course, and this meant the replacement of Communist Party officials by reformers. Between 1989 and 1991, Poland, Estonia, Latvia, Lithuania, Moldova, and Ukraine declared their independence from the Soviet Union. The USSR became the UFFR—the Union of Fewer and Fewer Republics.

Gorbachev's domestic reforms, highlighted by *perestroika* and *glasnost*, led to major changes in Soviet society, but his intention seemed focused on reforming communism through controlled liberalization rather than replacing the Soviet system of governance. He did not intend to grant full cultural freedom, to create a constitutional government, or to build a market economy with private property. By the spring of 1991, Gorbachev's reform efforts had run out of time. He faced political opposition from hardline conservatives, economic challenges with escalating inflation, and increased challenges from Soviet republics that declared their sovereignty from control by Moscow.[4]

By 1989 Gorbachev's chief political rival was Boris Yeltsin, although he had been appointed by Gorbachev in 1985 to be first secretary of the Communist Party in the capital city, which meant he was basically serving as mayor of Moscow. Early on Yeltsin became dissatisfied with the pace of reform. He fired top Communist Party officials who were not willing to reform the government and showed his rebellious nature by refusing to use chauffeurs to drive him to work, choosing instead to ride the trolley bus.

A few years earlier, Yeltsin made a bold move when he resigned from the Politburo, the chief ruling council in the USSR. No one in Soviet history had ever voluntarily resigned from this prestigious position, yet Yeltsin's decision helped

---

[3]Yale Richmond, *Cultural Exchange and the Cold War: Raising the Iron Curtain* (University Park: Pennsylvania State University Press, 2003), 226-27.

[4]Fred Coleman, *The Decline and Fall of the Soviet Empire: Forty Years That Shook the World, from Stalin to Yeltsin* (New York: St. Martin's, 1996), 323-24.

him to gain enormous popularity among Moscow residents who were frustrated by all the changes under way in their country that were accomplishing very little. Two years later, elected to the Congress of Peoples' Deputies, he was clearly emerging as the leader of those who wanted major reforms in the Soviet Union and who doubted that Gorbachev was going to dismantle the decrepit Soviet system. Yeltsin had a record as an emerging Communist Party leader and then shifted his stance to become a major leader of the democratic movement, and this combination gave him credibility that attracted widespread support. His energy and charisma empowered him.[5]

When Yeltsin visited the United States for the first time in September 1989—three months before the meeting of coalition educators—he emphasized the same view Gorbachev had expressed about educational exchanges. From his contacts with Americans, he realized that his views of Americans, shaped by decades of Soviet propaganda, were incorrect. Americans, he noted, were not "aggressive, ill-mannered, nasty and pushy," but "wonderfully open, sincere and friendly, industrious and intelligent" people. He was also impressed by their optimism and belief in themselves and their country. When he came back home, he became an ardent advocate of US-Soviet educational exchanges.[6]

Yeltsin increasingly became convinced that the communist system could not be reformed and had to be dismantled. He began to exert leadership when he was elected chairman of the Supreme Soviet in May 1990, and utilizing this position in the highest legislative body in Russia, he mobilized Muscovites as his supporters. On the Saturday evening before Orthodox Easter in 1991, Yeltsin appeared in Moscow's Yelokhovsky Cathedral for the Easter service, conducted by Patriarch Alexii II. As US Ambassador Matlock noted, the emerging leader of Russia "had come to terms with the traditional Russian church," which previously had been vilified by the Communist Party.[7]

Similarly, when he defeated Gorbachev's candidate for the presidency of the Russian Republic on June 12, 1991, Yeltsin took his oath of office in the Palace of Congresses and asked Patriarch Alexei II to bestow blessings on him. For the first

---

[5]Lilia Shevtsova, *Yeltsin's Russia: Myths and Reality* (Washington, DC: Carnegie Endowment for International Peace, 1999), 9-10.

[6]Leon Aron, *Yeltsin: A Revolutionary Life* (New York: St. Martin's, 2000), 324-27.

[7]Jack F. Matlock Jr., *Autopsy on an Empire: The American Ambassador's Account of the Collapse of the Soviet Union* (New York: Random House, 1995), 506.

time in its history, Russia had a leader elected by the people. And for the first time since Czar Nicholas II was crowned in 1894, a Russian leader sought the blessing of the Orthodox Church.[8]

Yeltsin's election marked a new phase in the Russian revolutionary movement. Like the solidarity movement in Poland, Yeltsin and his supporters renounced the reform of communism as an illusion and set out to build a so-called normal posttotalitarian society. Yeltsin's first decree as president concerned education, and he announced that education would be a superpriority of his new administration. A deputy of the Supreme Soviet in Moscow, commenting on Yeltsin's Decree Number 1, stated: "A resurrection of education will be followed by a resurrection of culture and spiritual values of our people." While a vigorous renewal of interest in spiritual issues did emerge, the promise of making education a top priority never materialized because of the overwhelming conflicts that accompanied all of the political and economic changes in Soviet society.[9] After the election, Russia had a noncommunist government run by Yeltsin that was forced to coexist with a reformed but still standing communist regime headed by Gorbachev. Obviously, this dual power structure could not last for long, any more than it did in Poland or in Russia in 1917.[10]

Yeltsin clearly did not back down in his confrontation with Gorbachev as the two struggled for political leadership. These dramatic changes created such confusion that we often did not know whether Gorbachev's team or Yeltsin's was in charge.

THE MBA PROJECT AND RUSSIA'S FUTURE ECONOMY

While struggles between Gorbachev and Yeltsin dominated the news reports from Moscow, our work focused on the proposed MBA project—a major educational bridge-building operation—even though the future direction of Soviet society was unclear and created lack of certainty in our planning. Although the goal of rebuilding the curriculum of business and economics departments in the Russian Republic seemed too ambitious, Yeltsin's educational team adamantly argued that it had to be done. Stanislav Shatalin, a well-known Russian economist and the principal author of the "500 Day Plan" to restructure the Soviet

---

[8]Matlock Jr., *Autopsy of an Empire*, 522.

[9]Bernbaum, "MBA Consultations in Moscow in August-September, 1991," 3.

[10]This insight was made by Martin Malia at this time in his article "A New Russian Revolution?" *New York Review of Books*, July 18, 1991, 29.

economy, traveled to the United States during this period of Yeltsin's beginnings and observed that his country needed "the intellectual help of the West" through exchanges of students, professors, and businessmen. He also noted, "Our economics education is really at a barbarian level," and this highlighted the challenges facing the American MBA delegation.[11]

The staff of the coalition's USSR Initiative, together with faculty from Eastern College, turned their primary attention in spring 1991 to the joint Russian-American MBA program, an ambitious project that was unique in design and potentially of great significance at this point in the reform movement in the USSR. While Soviet officials struggled with decisions about the future of the Soviet economy, the educators we worked with were more concerned with the ethical and moral foundations on which the new Soviet economy would be built. Increasingly Yeltsin's appointees became the ones we worked with most, but during this transition time we kept in contact with both Soviet and Russian officials since no one was sure who had access to government funding.

The proposed MBA project had a number of unique aspects. First, its principal goal involved the creation of a new business and economics curriculum, created by coalition faculty in partnership with Soviet experts. Unlike several other initiatives by major American and Canadian universities, in which they simply transported their curriculum to the Soviet Union, this program grew out of work by Russian and American faculty cooperating as full and equal partners. Its second distinctive related to the explicit grounding of this MBA curriculum in moral and ethical values. For the coalition faculty, this meant biblical values, a factor fully known, understood, and requested by Soviet leaders. They welcomed this integration of moral values into the course material, observing that this aspect of education had been lost and needed to be recovered in their society. The third distinctive rested in the fact that this program involved a group of American colleges and universities in cooperation with a group of Soviet higher-education institutions. Being not a program of a single institution but a major cooperative program between several education networks offered the hope of much greater distribution and use in the Russian Republic.[12]

[11]Bernbaum, "MBA Consultations in Moscow in August–September, 1991," 1.
[12]Bernbaum, "MBA Consultations in Moscow in August–September, 1991," 2-3.

During negotiations with Soviet leaders by faxed messages in spring 1991, and following a brief trip to Moscow and Leningrad in July by a small delegation from Eastern College, which Marge and I joined, the final details for the MBA program emerged. While in Moscow in July, we witnessed the celebration of the election of Boris Yeltsin as president of Russia. When we returned to the States, invitations went out to the academic deans of coalition member schools soliciting applications from business and economics faculty who might be interested in participating in the MBA project. We received an impressive number of applications, and the decision to select the final team was a difficult one for Geiger and me, the codirectors of this initiative.[13]

Meanwhile, as the selection process continued, plans for a three-week consultation between coalition and Russian partners in August and September 1991 were finalized. Geiger and I learned that the Russian State Committee would fund this three-week consultation out of their resources (250,000 rubles or approximately $10,000) because inflationary pressures caused budget crises at Soviet universities. Another surprise came: the Russian State Committee decided that if they paid for the Soviet's half of this project, they wanted the twenty-seven Russian universities qualified to offer graduate credits in business to use these curriculum materials, not just the original nine Russian universities.

While this exciting news clearly encouraged us, the expansion of the program presented new challenges. The original plan for 13 coalition professors to work in teams with 40 Soviet faculty required reconsideration. We were told that 150 professors would be invited to participate in this consultation, and in addition Soviet leaders insisted that two days of the consultation be canceled so coalition faculty could meet with industrial-plant managers and new company executives. After careful deliberation, the following faculty members were chosen for the American team and assigned their part of the curriculum project:

- Kenneth Armstrong, Anderson College (Indiana), strategic planning

- James Coe, Taylor University (Indiana), entrepreneurship

- James Engel, Eastern College (Pennsylvania), marketing management

---

[13]John A. Bernbaum, memorandum for the record, "Trip Report on Visit to the USSR (July 1991)," July 18, 1991, RA. The delegation from Eastern College included Professor Lin Geiger and Glenn Geiger, Professor Jim Engel and Sharon Engel, and Vice President David Cassidy and Corrine Cassidy.

- Linwood Geiger, Eastern College, macroeconomic analysis

- James Halteman, Wheaton College (Illinois), microeconomic analysis

- Alec Hill, Seattle Pacific University (Washington), business law

- Dennis Proffitt, Grand Canyon University (Arkansas), financial management

- Kurt Schaefer, Calvin College (Michigan), managerial economics

- Ray Vander Weele, Calvin College, managerial accounting

- John Visser, Dordt College (Iowa), international business

- Ronald Webb, Messiah College (Pennsylvania), organizational behavior

- Van Weigel, Eastern College, ethical decision making

THE CHALLENGES AHEAD

As the coalition team worked on the plans for the first major seminar on the MBA project, scheduled for August 1991, we knew the obstacles were serious. Western economists were predicting a 20 percent drop in gross national product and hyperinflation, and one observer said that 1991 would be the "year of economic collapse in the USSR."[14] We also knew that most Russian universities we visited lacked the material basics, such as computers, copiers, technology, and adequate libraries, for graduate education. In addition, Russian undergraduate economics and business training was weak. Many course syllabuses we had seen listed books and articles by Marx and Lenin but few standard texts in economics, management, and organizational behavior, for example. We also knew that we had to be creative, especially in areas such as business law and ethics.

Yet we also had a sense that this was a unique opportunity, especially for Christian educators from liberal arts colleges and universities. Never in the history of Christian higher education in America had an opportunity like this emerged. All of the experience that we gained in the MBA project proved to be helpful when the decision was later made to establish the Russian-American Christian University in Moscow. These first steps proved challenging, like every other opportunity in the USSR. The context constantly changing, often in dramatic new directions, taught us Americans that we had much to learn and that we needed to be slow to offer advice to our Russian colleagues when

---

[14]Dimitri Simes, "Gorbachev's Time of Troubles," *Foreign Policy* (Spring 1991): 97-99.

we had never experienced anything like what they were going through. Humility was needed.

James Billington, a respected scholar of Russian culture and the librarian of Congress from 1987 to 2015, wrote in the *Washington Post* as we were struggling with how to handle these opportunities: "The United States has a special role to play [in the institutionalization of democracy in the USSR]. . . . What is needed is not another government program, but an all-American engagement of private and local organizations in helping all of the peoples of the Soviet Union build the infrastructure and absorb the ethos of modern, pluralistic democracy."[15] This joint Russian-American MBA project was one of those private initiatives that had the potential to be of great benefit during Russia's revolutionary period.

---

[15]James H. Billington, "U.S.S.R.: The Birth of a Nation," *The Washington Post*, September 8, 1991.

5

SURVIVING THE COUP

ON AUGUST 17, 1991, OUR FOURTEEN-MEMBER delegation of coalition faculty nervously flew from John F. Kennedy International Airport to Moscow for a three-week seminar that would launch the Russian-American MBA project.

My initial impression of the faculty delegation was positive. They all seemed to be excited about this opportunity, to be open to being taught by our Soviet counterparts, and to have no sense of arrogance that we had all the answers. Most of us were appropriately frightened by the challenge before us, and good-natured teasing helped to elevate the emotional atmosphere.

After we landed in Moscow, our first meal took place at a high-end restaurant downtown. Following a leisurely luncheon, we were escorted to Red Square and walked around the famous landmarks near the Kremlin, an impressive experience for those in Moscow for the first time. Most of us never expected we would ever be in the capital city of our Cold War rival and be warmly received as friends and academic colleagues.

By midafternoon we arrived at a conference center outside the city, where we would be housed. By US standards, the main conference building and grounds reminded me of a run-down church camp, although the building that housed us had obviously been recently upgraded.

THE COUP

After the overnight flight to Moscow, a full day of tourist activities, and a surplus of food, most of us slept very well. The next morning, while dressing after my shower and shave, I was shocked to hear a reference to Gorbachev in the past tense during a BBC news report on my shortwave radio. I immediately turned up the volume and heard Soviet news agencies announcing that Mikhail Gorbachev had been removed for "health reasons." What a shock! When I went down the hallway to the rooms of my colleagues to report this frightening news, no one believed me. When I finally convinced them that it was true, they were as stunned as I was. The news cast a cloud over our breakfast conversation. We had traveled over five thousand miles to hold a conference with our Russian colleagues to find ourselves caught in the middle of a coup—a first for all of us.

The planned departure for the conference center was delayed by several hours because of the coup, and as we traveled by bus into the city, we saw rows of army tanks and troop carriers headed toward the Russian White House. No one seemed to be in a panic. We saw no evidence of any disturbances; rather, there were a lot of soldiers and military hardware. When we arrived in the conference room and the meeting began, many empty seats surrounded us, and none of the top leaders from our host institutions showed up. Members of the Russian delegation made some preliminary remarks and described the three-week schedule but indicated that some changes might be necessary. We decided to make the best of the situation, so we tried to continue with our planned schedule, despite the fear of violence that pervaded the conference center and all of Moscow.

When asked to introduce the American delegation, I drew a map of the United States on the blackboard and asked the delegates to stand, introduce themselves, and draw in their state and the location of their college. My wife, Marge, gave me this idea, and it worked very well. We had many laughs, which helped to lighten the stress. After some opening sessions in the afternoon, the American delegation left earlier than originally planned and headed to the US Embassy to register, as we were advised over the radio. As expected, traffic was heavy because of the large number of army tanks and personnel carriers scattered throughout the city. A large crowd had gathered outside the embassy entrance, and we had to push our way through it with help from our Russian hosts. Each of us registered but quickly learned that there was no new news about the coup and that no telephone service at the embassy was accessible to make calls home. We also learned that phone service at the institute had been cut off, so we climbed back on our bus to return to the conference center outside center-city Moscow.

BBC became our constant companion for the next few days. I brought my shortwave radio to dinner, and all of us heard the news. Boris Yeltsin had called a general strike and directly challenged the leadership of the coup. He stood on a tank by the Russian White House, where leading Soviet officials had offices as well as the Soviet parliament (the Supreme Soviet), and bravely declared the coup an illegal action, one that would be resisted by his government. He also made it clear that Gorbachev's reforms would be continued. We also learned that the coup leaders had closed down many newspapers and radio and TV stations and that only nine newspapers continued to be published, papers that all supported this right-wing coup. One note of encouragement we heard described the strong reactions from the West against this coup attempt, especially from Great Britain, France, Germany, and the United States.

We met after dinner for an evening debriefing session, which we started that night and continued during the coup. Some members of our delegation were very nervous and wanted to discuss optional strategies for getting out of the country. We asked our hosts to check with the airlines about flights out of Moscow, but few available flights could be found. Gradually we understood that, in the middle of this coup and any potential violence that it generated, the safest place to be was outside the city at the conference center rather than being located in downtown Moscow. I must admit I was very excited to be in the middle of the coup. A historian lives to witness history in the making! But I also knew I had responsibility for this delegation and had to take their concerns seriously.

The second day of the coup, Tuesday, August 20, began with no news from the BBC about any violence in Moscow, and the meetings for the day, scheduled at the retreat center, proceeded as planned. The sessions went well, and the first meeting of small groups took place when Russian faculty members were connected with American professors who shared their special business discipline. No Russians were in attendance with expertise or interest in business law, so Alec Hill was free and felt strongly about heading downtown, with one of our hosts, to attempt to make a call to the States and pass along messages to our schools and family.

In the afternoon Lin Geiger and I met alone to discuss the events going on around us and agreed that we were in the project for the long haul and needed to tell our Russian hosts that we would stay until they felt it was no longer safe. When we shared this decision with the Russian faculty, one female professor stood up and said, "Don't worry, we will protect you from harm with our bodies!"

Others joined in and said they were so happy with our decision, even though they knew we could leave or at least try to do so.

After several good sessions with our Russian colleagues and an interactive session on the use of case studies by James Halteman, my American colleagues finally began to engage their Russian counterparts and enjoyed the exchanges. The case-study session provided an excellent example of the challenge of working crossculturally. When Halteman laid out the facts of the case, the Russian professors immediately interrupted him, asking, "How can we trust these facts? How do we know they are true? How can we work on this problem unless we can figure this out?" The noise level in the room escalated, and faculty shouted out their thoughts, but not maliciously, nor to subvert the discussion. We Americans quickly realized that we had to learn how to operate in a different cultural context.

Several times during the day I checked my shortwave radio in attempts to get news from the BBC. The growing general strike in Moscow and the potential for street violence that might result from it or from encounters with the soldiers worried us. While we felt safe at our quiet retreat center, we knew that violence could easily spread to Moscow's outlying areas. That night we gathered around my radio and learned that President George H. W. Bush had contacted Yeltsin and pledged him US support; his efforts to contact Gorbachev were unsuccessful. A number of European countries withdrew financial support from the USSR, and Japan also threatened to do so. We learned that a crowd gathering around the Russian White House in defense of Yeltsin was growing and that fifty thousand people were demonstrating in Leningrad. Two hours later, at 9 p.m., the BBC reported frightening news: a hundred more tanks were on their way toward Moscow, and Yeltsin was trying desperately to mobilize resistance in case of an attack. Both inside and outside the White House, preparations accelerated for a pending clash with the troops. Our American delegation, deeply troubled by what appeared to be a major battle in the city, anxiously discussed what practical steps we could take. We asked our hosts to return our passports by noon the next day (our documents were being held for "registration purposes," a normal procedure in the USSR). We also asked that a bus be made available to get some faculty to the airport, if needed. Our final request concerned finding an available phone so we could call our families and give them an update on our status. The American delegates' emotions escalated when we did not come to agreement on the kinds of events that meant we should try to leave. We finally decided that anyone could try to leave when they wanted to but that most of us would wait until the US Embassy told us to leave.

The possibility of an attack on the Russian White House and the gathered crowds there was frightening, and fear of growing violence made sleep difficult that night. As soon as I woke up the next morning, I turned on the BBC and learned that several clashes had occurred and that three young people had died after being crushed by tanks, but there had been no assault on the White House. Soldiers stationed at every major intersection helped to contain the potential for violence, but so far no force had been used against civilians who did not challenge the soldiers. The BBC continually repeated Yeltsin's speech on Soviet TV the previous night. He said the "days of the conspirators are numbered" and that "clouds of terror are gathering, but light will come." He also said, "You can create a throne of violence, but you can't sit on it very long."

Rumors began to spread on Wednesday morning that a crisis had occurred among the conspirators, while several leading Russian officials, who had remained silent until now, had joined Yeltsin in the White House and pledged him their support. To the surprise of everyone, Mstislav Rostropovich, the famous musician and cellist, showed up at the Russian White House, greeted Yeltsin, and asked for an assault rifle to help in the defense, if needed.[1] Encouraging signs began to appear. The Wednesday noon report from BBC announced that leading KGB officials openly supported Yeltsin as well as members in KGB units and in army ranks. The BBC evening news reported that barricades were going up around the parliament building in Leningrad to defend Mayor Anatoly Sobchak, a friend and ally of Yeltsin.

The third day of our conference, the sessions began late as usual. The meetings for the day proceeded, and when the small groups began their discussions, I gained access to the phone in the office of the director of the retreat center. I contacted Miles Stump, a student from Seattle Pacific University who was studying in Moscow and had met Alec Hill. I asked him to call Hill's wife and ask her to contact the coalition staff in Washington, DC, and then ask them to call our families to assure them of our status. He said he had tried to make the calls but had not yet secured permission to use an international line.

---

[1]Yeltsin shares this story of Rostropovich's visit in his book *The Struggle for Russia* (New York: Random House, 1994), 85–86.

When I called the US Embassy to ask for their advice, they told me to call every day or so. I was told if the situation worsened, they would not be able to call all the US citizens in Moscow, so we needed to take on this responsibility. When I returned to the conference center, the local staff told me that our passports would not be available until late in the afternoon and that buses could be arranged quickly if we decided to leave the country. The staff made it clear that they considered us very brave people for staying in Russia with all the chaos, disorder, and possible danger.

At 4:30 p.m. on Wednesday, the BBC reported that the coup appeared to be collapsing. Members of the so-called Emergency Committee had tried fleeing the country, and Yeltsin had ordered their arrest. Tanks also began pulling back from the city, and the Soviet Defense Ministry ordered the immediate withdrawal of all its troops. We learned that these events now empowered the leaders in various Soviet republics to take advantage of the situation and demand independence from Moscow's control. Within the next hour, the BBC reported that all eight coup leaders had either fled or been arrested and that a plane was on its way to the Crimea to bring Gorbachev back to Moscow. This news went far beyond the hopes and prayers we had expressed. The delegates at our conference center hugged each other, yelled out in joy, and cried, and we joined in their celebration. We formed a big circle in the parking lot in front of the conference center, held hands, and sang "We Shall Overcome," a song led by our Russian colleagues. One of the vice rectors of MASI had been a part of the crowd that gathered to defend the Russian White House and had stayed there overnight on Tuesday when the attack by elite military forces was expected. When he arrived at the conference center on Wednesday night, he was greeted as a hero by both Russians and Americans.

The evening dinner turned out to be a lighthearted affair, as everyone was in high spirits. After dinner we had a volleyball game with eight US faculty and six Russian professors, with lots of laughter interspersed between the volleys. When we returned to our rooms for the evening, my room was jammed full of Americans who listened intently to the BBC news broadcast, while the Russians watched TV in the lobby. We learned Gorbachev had returned to Moscow and all of the decrees of the Emergency Committee had been rescinded.

News reports made it clear that Yeltsin emerged as the man of the hour, not Gorbachev, and that the reform process would be accelerated. But one high-ranking Russian politician who was familiar with Yeltsin made this observation about Russia's new leader: "The Russian president is committed to democracy, but does not know exactly what it is." A Western commentator added, "There is little in Yeltsin's background—first as a successful party functionary and later as a revolutionary tribune—that prepared him for the role of a democratic leader in the midst of profound political and economic crises."[2] It did seem clear from things that Yeltsin had said during the past three days that he was focusing primarily on developments in the Russian Republic and that he believed the other Soviet republics needed to take care of themselves.

Before we headed to bed that night, we decided to revise our schedule and plan a celebration dinner downtown the next night with our Russian colleagues. The third day of meetings had gone well, but the Americans were frustrated because of the lack of business textbooks, computers, and copiers.

The next morning, when the small groups began, I met with Alec and learned that Miles Stump had connected on a call through to his grandparents in Mercer Island, and they agreed to contact Alec's wife and my wife, Marge, with news about us. After several good sessions with faculty, together with news from the BBC about big celebrations in downtown Moscow, we told our hosts that we wanted to take them out for dinner at Pizza Hut. We took a bus to the train station and then a commuter train to the metro, where we got out on Red Square. We decided to walk to the Russian White House, where fireworks took place, and climbed on the barricades. We saw the Russian imperial insignia, a crucifix being carried by a priest, and a small group of Russian nationalists sitting around a bonfire in front of the White House.

With buses and trolleys not operating in center-city Moscow, we decided to walk the one or two miles to the Pizza Hut for our dinner. We did not get there until 9:40 p.m. The restaurant was supposed to close at 10 p.m., but they graciously let us order a total of eight pizzas for our group of eighteen. We enjoyed a wonderful time of celebration, and the pizza never tasted better! We did not return home until 2 a.m., exhausted but so excited for our Russian friends and for our own safety.

---

[2]Dimitri Simes, "Russia Reborn," *Foreign Policy* (Winter 1991–1992): 50-51.

GETTING BACK TO WORK

At the conference center in the outskirts of Moscow, the mood among the Russian and American faculty and staff became upbeat and hopeful. No one needed to fear for our safety, and the collapse of the Communist Party seemed evident. Communism had failed, but no one yet knew whether democracy would replace it. Meanwhile, our job required us to get back to work and develop strategies for preparing the new Russian-American MBA curriculum that would integrate moral values and lay out a framework for teaching graduate students about the free-market system.

The next two and a half weeks of the conference involved sessions with lectures, offered by both Russians and Americans on topics related to business and economics, and small group meetings, where the content of each curriculum module was hammered into an acceptable format.

The failed coup, along with all of the radical changes taking place in Russia following the arrest of the coup leaders and Yeltsin's emergence as Russia's leader, affected our conference. Changes in Russian leadership occurred at different levels. No one knew for sure who was in charge and who had access to funds for our three-week conference. Based on our experience organizing academic meetings in the States, we were not prepared for how our Russian hosts operated by often making radical changes in the schedule without considering how these changes would affect the Russian delegates. If the conference organizers wanted to organize certain events for the Americans, they did so. We felt sorry for the Russian faculty, who had to travel out to the conference center by commuter train or bus and frequently arrived to discover that we had been taken elsewhere.

We also were troubled by the lack of competent translators. Those assigned to us were very cooperative and friendly people but had little or no familiarity with business and economic concepts and terms. When we asked for more seasoned translators at the halfway point in the three-week conference, we learned that they were not available. The number and quality of Russian faculty was also disappointingly low. While some were quite capable, most were not; they simply were not competent graduate-level educators. We had been told to expect seventy-five to one hundred Russian faculty, but most of time there were twenty-five in our sessions.

The coup also affected the location of our conference, which was moved from a cultural center in Moscow to the retreat center outside the city, not easily accessible. While a reasonable meeting facility, the distance from the city created difficulty for the Russian faculty, since only a few of them could afford to stay overnight and their schools were not willing or able to subsidize their participation. The third week of the conference also turned out to be a disappointment since Russian universities began their classes, and a significant number of the faculty, without any indication to us about their decisions, no longer attended the meetings.

Periodically during the last two weeks of the conference, the Americans met with representatives of each of the various universities and institutes, who told us about their schools and invited us to sign exchange agreements with them. This deepened our friendship—as did the volleyball games at night. We also discovered that our Russian colleagues enjoyed singing, and they often asked us to sing American songs, some of which they knew. All of us enjoyed singing and laughing.

During the farewell banquet the night before we left Moscow, one of the Russian leaders stood and offered a toast in which he thanked us sincerely for respecting them. He said their situation was very difficult because of the attempted coup, and they were embarrassed by all the problems that came as a result, yet he and his colleagues appreciated that we treated them as peers. As we departed Moscow, I had intense feelings of ambivalence. I wanted badly to see my wife and children, but I did not want to leave Russia. I felt drawn to the country, and returning to the States had little appeal to me in comparison to experiencing a nation's momentous changes. World history stood center stage, and we were leaving! I also knew I would miss the BBC—my shortwave radio had become a good friend.

Surviving the coup and celebrating its failure with our new Russian friends helped to solidify our relationships with key leaders. If the coup had been successful, we would not have had the opportunity to work with Russian educators, and the invitation to start a Christian college in Moscow would surely have been rescinded. Living through the attempted coup gave us an understanding of life in Soviet Russia, an intensive experience of working with Soviet faculty, and friendships with educational leaders that proved to be of enormous value over time.

We arrived the day before the coup and left three weeks later from a country that would never be the same. The kind of country it would become, however, no one knew. As Martin Malia noted in September 1991, "The former Soviet Union this summer has, at last, made the exit from communism that most of Eastern Europe accomplished in the autumn of 1989."[3] We were there to witness it!

---

[3]Martin Malia, "The August Revolution," *New York Review of Books*, September 26, 1991, 22.

MEETING WITH GORBACHEV AND THE KGB

WHEN WE RETURNED TO THE STATES after the failed coup and the conclusion of our three-week seminar with Russian faculty, I sent a letter to Vladimir Kinelev, the top higher-education official in the Yeltsin government, reporting on what had occurred in the first year of the Christian College Coalition's partnership with his State Committee on Science and Higher Education. The letter, dated October 3, 1991, reported that much progress had been made in the first twelve months since we had signed the Protocol of Intentions in Washington, DC, the previous October. Nine student-exchange programs had been established with Russian institutes and universities, plus two with Ukrainian universities and one in Kazakhstan. Nine faculty exchanges were arranged, and professors from each country traveled overseas to participate onsite in the programs. In addition to the Russian-American MBA project, four exchanges took place for English- and Russian-language teachers.[1] The USSR Initiative appeared to be off to an amazing start. The only initiative not supported during the first year was the invitation from Kinelev to establish a Christian college in Moscow. Without the support of the coalition's board of directors, this request remained unanswered, but it continued to be a priority for me and the leadership team of the coalition, especially its president, Myron Augsburger.

Upon our return home, as a high priority I closely tracked developments in the USSR in order to understand the dramatic changes occurring in the country and to gain a better grasp of the context in which we were being invited to work.

---

[1]John A. Bernbaum to Vladimir G. Kinelev, October 3, 1991, RA.

Our entire delegation knew that we were being asked to draft an MBA curriculum for use in Soviet universities and institutes and that our Russian faculty colleagues wanted to deepen their understanding of democratic and free-market values and institutions. Both sides knew they had to increase mutual understanding.

Gorbachev's resignation as general secretary of the Communist Party of the USSR on August 24, 1991, made a dramatic statement about the collapse of the Marxist-Leninist system, but he continued in his position as president of the Soviet Union, the union of fifteen republics. As we continued with the student and faculty exchanges, no one knew who was in charge. Yeltsin, the hero of the resistance to the coup, bolstered his position when in June 1991 he became the first popularly elected president of the Russian Republic, the largest and most powerful of the fifteen republics in the USSR. In the months following the coup, Yeltsin and Gorbachev battled over control of the government in Moscow. Immediately after the coup collapsed and its leaders were arrested, Yeltsin signed a decree during a session of the Russian parliament dissolving the Communist Party of the Soviet Union. In the middle of the turmoil following the failed coup, no one seemed to object to the president of Russia dissolving the Communist Party for the entire Soviet Union. The following day Yeltsin recognized the independence of three Baltic republics—Lithuania, Latvia, and Estonia—and Ukraine's Supreme Soviet adopted a declaration of independence. With the USSR unraveling, the ruling elites began taking sides with either Gorbachev or Yeltsin.[2]

In the succeeding months, Yeltsin and Gorbachev both tried to exert leadership, but Yeltsin had the clear advantage. In his memoirs Yeltsin highlights that he and Gorbachev met only eight times between August and December 1991, thereby isolating Gorbachev from critical Kremlin issues that needed to be addressed.[3]

ANOTHER UNEXPECTED INVITATION

On the same day that I sent my report to Kinelev reporting on the first year of our partnership, I received a letter from Mikhail Morgulis, director of Project

---

[2]Lilia Shevtsova, *Yeltsin's Russia: Myths and Reality* (Washington, DC: Carnegie Endowment for International Peace, 1999), 11-12.
[3]Boris Yeltsin, *The Struggle for Russia* (New York: Random House, 1994), 106.

Christian Bridge. Morgulis was a Russian émigré with experience in the publishing industry and numerous ties with Russian authors and some Kremlin officials. He had become friends with Peter and Anita Deyneka and through them had learned about the Christian College Coalition and the evangelical network in the States. The letter stated that the Gorbachev, Yeltsin, and leaders of the Supreme Soviet of the USSR were inviting me to join a delegation of "influential Christian leaders" to meet with high-level Soviet government leaders, including the two presidents. Most of the nineteen-member American delegation—evangelical pastors and missionaries or heads of Christian nonprofit organizations—had prominent leadership roles in Christian circles and had organizations that were active in the USSR. My role as a Christian educator with the Christian College Coalition apparently qualified me for this honor. The Deynekas and Morgulis determined who would be invited, and they were asked to select American religious leaders by Konstantin Lubenchenko, the chairman of the Supreme Soviet of the USSR. I was overwhelmed. I had no idea why I was chosen but learned later that Peter and Anita Deyneka recommended me to Morgulis.[4]

The invitation included a letter to the American delegation from five members of the Supreme Soviet, led by Lubenchenko. The text, translated into English, read as follows:

> In the difficult, often agonizing transitional period that our country is experiencing in moving from that of a totalitarian system to parliamentarianism, a market economy, and an open society, spiritual and moral values acquire a great, if not paramount, significance in their ability to guarantee us against confrontation, civil conflicts, the erosion of moral foundations, and the lowering of standards.
>
> We know the role which your Christian organizations are playing as you follow the great words of Christ: "Faith without works is dead." You are able to assist in the social development of a country and you are able to establish friendly relations with other countries, including the Soviet Union.

The letter noted that the leaders of the Soviet Union were asking for assistance and that their people "are devoted to the moral values of Christianity."[5]

---

[4]The majority of this chapter is based on my forty-one-page trip journal, the thirty-two pages of trip notes compiled by the staff of Christian Bridge, and Philip Yancey's *Praying with the KGB: A Startling Report for a Shattered Empire* (Portland, OR: Multnomah, 1992). Appendix A of Yancey's book includes a list of the nineteen members of the American delegation.

[5]Konstantin Lubenchenko and four colleagues to the "Leaders of Christian Movements in the USA," September 19, 1991, RA.

In response, our delegation returned a message to the members of the Supreme Soviet, through Lubenchenko. Our letter clearly stated:

> We are not coming to promote Americanism or capitalism, though we appreciate our country and are aware of the benefits free markets have provided. In fact, we are profoundly aware of our national shortcomings and are fearful that our national religious heritage is being undermined. [It then summarized our purpose for coming to Russia]: first, to encourage understanding and facilitate cooperation between American Christians and the governments of the USSR, Russia, and Ukraine; second, to promote Christian ideas and values as a means of positively influencing family life, social problems, business ethics, education, democratic structures, humanitarian ventures, and charitable activities; third, to support understanding and cooperation between Protestants, Orthodox and Catholics; and fourth, to promote religious freedom and equality of rights for all religious groups.[6]

When our delegation arrived at the airport in Moscow on October 29, 1991, after an hour spent going through customs and finding our luggage, we discovered that a Soviet television crew was waiting for us and wanted to interview our leaders. We recognized immediately that this visit was going to be a high-profile event. Our delegation organizer, Morgulis, noted in his remarks to the reporters that this was the first delegation of Christian leaders ever to be invited to Moscow by the Soviet government. As guests of the president, our delegation received VIP treatment: frequent television coverage, private tours of the Kremlin museums, daily feature coverage in the national print media, and an itinerary that included meetings with Gorbachev and Yeltsin, members of the Supreme Soviet, and officials of the KGB.[7]

MEETING WITH THE KGB

On the evening of our first day, our delegation was escorted to the front door of Lubyanka, the feared headquarters of the KGB. Our night meeting was being held on October 30, known as the Day for Remembering Victims of Repression. During the failed coup attempt in August 1991, protestors had managed to secure a large crane, which they used to topple the statue of Feliks Dzerzhinsky, the founder of the Communist Party's secret police, located in the plaza in front of

---

[6]The text of this message can be found in appendix A of Yancey's *Praying with the KGB*, 91-93.
[7]Yancey, *Praying with the KGB*, 12.

the KGB building. For several days the protestors let the statue dangle above its pedestal, a decision that symbolized the triumph of freedom over fear. As we discussed the removal of Dzerzhinsky's statue, several delegates reminded us of the apostle Paul's visit to Athens, where he commented on the statue to the unknown god. We hoped that the Russian people would replace this deified Soviet figure with the God of their Christian faith and not leave the pedestal empty.

I will never forget the feeling I had when we entered the infamous building. I had read a great deal about the KGB during my graduate school days and knew of its role in the repression of Christianity for seventy years, but my knowledge was academic, and I had little personal exposure to the dreaded secret police. My excitement gave way to other emotions as I watched members of our delegation get out of the bus and approach the building with hesitation and in some cases tears in their eyes. Many of the older leaders in our group who came from Russia and Ukraine trembled as they entered through the massive wood doors because they personally knew many Christians who had been brought into this building, interrogated, tortured, imprisoned, and frequently never heard from again. For the seasoned missionaries in our delegation such as Peter Deyneka who had been prohibited from entering the Soviet Union for decades and who were intimately tied to the struggles of persecuted churches, our visit with the KGB represented a momentous event.

The host of our visit, General Nikolai Sergeyevich Stolyarov, had become famous in the Soviet Union because of his heroic flight to the Crimea to rescue Gorbachev during the failed coup of August 1991. He defied military orders, commandeered an aircraft, and flew Gorbachev back to Moscow. For this act of bravery, Colonel Stolyarov was promoted to general and assigned to one of the top positions in the KGB.

At the start of the meeting, Morgulis referred to General Stolyarov as a hero and asked him what thoughts went through his mind during the attempted coup. The general downplayed his own role and said the real heroes were the ones who guarded the Russian White House and protected Yeltsin from attacks by the forces under the control of the coup leaders. He noted that the coup leaders tried to do to Gorbachev what had been done to Khrushchev in 1964—quietly remove him from power—and they did not expect the people to resist.

The entire ninety-minute discussion with Stolyarov, televised by the Soviet media, took place in a room filled with reporters and with three large pictures of Lenin,

Dzerzinsky (founder of the KGB), and Gorbachev on the wall behind the head table. Questions from our delegation were very direct, and General Stolyarov did not hesitate in responding to any of them, in many cases in a very somber tone. Will there be restitution for the victims of the KGB? What about the gulags (prison camps)? Will they be closed? Is there a sense of repentance for the crimes that were committed? Who is responsible for the murder of priest Alexander Men in September 1991?

The most surprising comments made by General Stolyarov concerned the spiritual needs of the Russian people. He said, "In our past the Communist Party told us that religion divides people, but we now know this is wrong and that belief in God can unite our people." He went on to describe the work of missionaries in the Soviet Union as "absolutely important now" and emphasized the need for "good words and good deeds." He made it clear that "something very symbolic is happening here because of your presence and what you represent." He continued: "Your humanitarian help is needed now."

When Joel Nederhood asked him about the gulags and what he intended to do about this repressive prison network, tension increased in the room. Stolyarov paused briefly and then said: "I have spoken of repentance. . . . There can be no *perestroika* apart from repentance. The time has come to repent of the past. We have broken the Ten Commandments, and for this we pay today."[8]

At the end of the meeting, Morgulis gave Stolyarov an illustrated Bible for his children and offered a moving prayer for the future of the Soviet Union and for the health and well-being of its leaders, especially for the general. When we returned to our hotel and watched the 11 p.m. television news, we saw extensive coverage of the meeting; all of the American delegates appeared in the news story, and the film clips included Morgulis's gift of the Bible and his closing prayer. We learned later that the viewing audience of the evening news totaled over 130 million Soviet citizens.[9]

MEETING SOVIET PARLIAMENTARIANS

The next night we had another remarkable experience. We were brought to the Grand Kremlin Palace, a huge building built in the nineteenth century as a

[8]Yancey, *Praying with the KGB*, 33.

[9]John A. Bernbaum, "American Christian Leaders Visit with KGB Leaders," *Chronicles from Russia*, October 31, 1991, RA.

residence for the czars. The palace, an impressive structure with beautiful chandeliers and hallways covered in frescoes, illustrated the wealth of the czarist heritage. When we entered the conference room, our hosts ushered us to seats behind a long wooden table with twenty members of the Supreme Soviet directly across from us. We were warmly greeted by the members of the Soviet parliament, which was such a stark contrast to how the Soviet government had treated Christians for seventy years. Until fall 1990, atheism had been the official doctrine of the Soviet government, and now, a year later, nineteen evangelicals were sitting across the table from twenty parliamentary leaders.

Konstantin Lubenchenko, the newly elected chairman of the Supreme Soviet, served as the host for this meeting, and we learned after the trip about his key role in arranging the invitation for us to come to Moscow. Nine months earlier, Lubenchenko had visited the United States to see democracy in action. While staying at the Washington Sheraton Hotel, where the National Religious Broadcasters' Convention took place, he met several missionaries who had heard him speaking Russian and invited him to attend the National Prayer Breakfast, being held the next day. Following the breakfast, they managed to introduce him to President George H. W. Bush and other government leaders. As a result of this experience, a friendship developed with a number of American evangelical leaders, including Peter and Anita Deyneka, and through them Morgulis and his organization (Project Christian Bridge) made his acquaintance. As the chairman of the Supreme Soviet, Lubenchenko had the connections to extend the invitation for Christian leaders to visit the USSR as guests of the country's leadership and to secure the support of both Gorbachev and Yeltsin.[10]

Lubenchenko had also played a critical role during the attempted August coup. When the coup began, he could not communicate with other members of his reform-minded caucus in the Supreme Soviet, and he faced pressure from the nominal head of the parliament, Anatoly Lukyanov, to provide a document that would legally justify the coup. He quickly mobilized members of his caucus and wrote a stinging refutation of any legal basis for the coup. His heroism and political courage resulted in his subsequent election as chair of the Supreme Soviet once the coup collapsed.[11]

---

[10]Yancey, *Praying with the KGB*, 24.
[11]James H. Billington, "The True Heroes of the Soviet Union," *Washington Post*, August 30, 1991.

When our delegation discussed the trip, we urged each other to avoid any tone of triumphalism and to approach the Soviets with respect. We also decided to be honest about the weaknesses of our country and the American church in particular. But when several of our delegates criticized American society and its churches, these Soviet leaders quickly dismissed the criticisms. For these deputies, the American church seemed to be the only hope for their demoralized citizens. Later in the discussion, one member of parliament asked about the possibility of opening Christian colleges in the USSR, which surprised all of us. To me, this comment supported my strong desire to move forward with the invitation to establish a Christian liberal arts college in Moscow, although the invitation was still not supported by the coalition's board of directors.

The leaders of the parliament seated with us feared anarchy in their society and the total collapse of its institutions. They had heard that Christians made good citizens, supported their leaders, and had a strong work ethic. They wanted this for their country and thought that religion might be the key missing factor.[12]

MEETING WITH GORBACHEV

During the busy schedule arranged for us by our Soviet hosts, our delegation had only a vague awareness of the power struggle going on in the background between Gorbachev, president of the USSR, and Yeltsin, president of the Russian Republic. Our schedule changed almost every day, and we knew that we might never get to meet with these two leaders as we had been promised. We never did have the opportunity to meet President Yeltsin, but the meeting with Gorbachev was finally set for November 4, 1991, the last day of our visit.[13]

The conversation with Gorbachev took place in the Kremlin and lasted for thirty-five minutes. The discussion centered on the future of the USSR and the role that religion and democracy could play in its development. "Changes in Russian history have usually been accomplished by bloodshed," Gorbachev noted, "but we want change through democratic means. If we succeed, it will be good for the entire country." President Gorbachev also expressed appreciation for the

---

[12]Yancey, *Praying with the KGB*, 25-26.

[13]From the beginning, I knew there was a possibility that I might miss this opportunity to meet the two presidents. My son Mark was getting married in Washington, DC, and there was no way I could miss this wedding on November 3. When the date to meet President Gorbachev was arranged for November 4, I was disappointed but had made my choice. Needless to say, Mark has been repeatedly reminded of the sacrifices I made to attend his wedding.

delegation's statement that "faith without works is dead." He emphasized that while encouraging words were appreciated, concrete assistance was needed during this time of transition for his country. Vladimir Zots, an assistant to the president, repeated this same theme and urged our delegation to "give concrete answers about how the Soviet Union can be helped."

Gorbachev seemed vigorous, healthy, and fully in command of the meeting. Early in his opening remarks, he said, "Let me be honest with you; I am an atheist. I believe that man is at the center and must solve his own problems. That is my faith. Even so, I have profound respect for your beliefs. This time, more than ever before, we need support from our partners, and I value solidarity with religion." At this time in the meeting Lubenchenko, who stood next to Gorbachev, broke in, saying, "But if the president finds betrayal repugnant, shows compassion for his fellow man, encourages freedom, respects the decency and rights of individuals, and has the goal of moving toward the good, then perhaps words don't matter so much. Perhaps by deeds he is a believer, if not by words." Gorbachev laughed and responded: "I do not object. I must say for a long time I have drawn comfort from the Bible. Ignoring religious experience has meant great losses for society."

Our delegation agreed that Gorbachev appeared to be in good humor and obviously enjoyed the meeting. He shook our hands at the beginning and afterward took time to do so again. When Morgulis closed the session with prayer, Gorbachev bowed his head and closed his eyes. As he left the room, he said, "It has been a long time since I met with a delegation that came offering to help and not to criticize."[14]

REFLECTIONS ON OUR UNIQUE OPPORTUNITY

Before we left Moscow, we also had a meeting at the US Embassy with the deputy mission chief, James Collins, who told us that this was his third term of service in the USSR. He noted that the nation seemed to be in search of its identity, trying to understand who they were and what they believed. He said that a few years ago a delegation like ours would not have been invited officially or even welcomed. But now there was a desperate search for what could hold the country

---

[14]This report is based on Philip Yancey's description of the meeting with Gorbachev (*Praying with the KGB*, 61-68) and the Christian Bridge trip notes, 29-31, RA.

together. They wanted to know what holds America together in order to decide whether our model could help their country. Collins also remarked that private organizations were becoming the dominant factor in Soviet-American relations, more important than official government-to-government relations. He stressed the importance of friendships in Russian culture and encouraged us to build partnerships boldly with the leaders we met. He concluded by emphasizing that people had largely rejected the Communist Party and were totally disillusioned with the leaders who spent seventy-four years leading them on the road to no-where. But he also warned that reactionaries still had their hands on the levers of power, so the challenge of reforming the system would prove to be a long battle.

Most of the delegates on our trip knew that our visit could possibly be used by the Soviet government for purposes other than what we intended. I think Joel Nederhood spoke for all of us when he said, "We all felt very strongly that once they tried to use a group of people who represent Christ as openly and as strongly as our group was able to do, they were going to get more than they bargained for."[15]

THE END OF THE USSR

Shortly before our delegation left Moscow in early November, we visited numerous dumping grounds around the city where statues of Stalin, Lenin, and Dzerzhinsky lay in piles with children climbing over them. Walking through these graveyards of statues proved to be sobering as we thought about the price the Russian people paid for their experiment with Marxism-Leninism. The Museum of the Revolution surprised many people when it put up a display that highlighted the resistance to the coup, while the Lenin Museum was simply closed down "pending reconstruction."

Before we arrived in Moscow, in early September, Gorbachev had assembled the Congress of Peoples' Deputies, but leaders from only ten republics showed up; five republics no longer had any interest in this body and its efforts to control their future. As the meetings came to an end, the delegates and Gorbachev agreed to dissolve the congress. This harsh reality made it clear that Gorbachev no longer had a job and that Yeltsin had complete political control in the Russian Republic. On December 26, 1991, a farewell party took place for Gorbachev in

---

[15] "Broadcaster Nederhood: Soviets Welcome Help in Perestroika," *World Magazine*, November 16, 1991.

the Oktyabrskaya Hotel, the luxurious hotel in which we were housed. Gorbachev promised Yeltsin that he would stay out of politics, and in return he received a modest retirement package.

Within seven weeks of our departure, the country dramatically changed. "Now Russia faced a great historical moment," wrote David Remnick, "an elected president occupying the Kremlin for the first time in the thousand-year history of Russia, the hammer and sickle gone from the flagpole, the regime and empire dissolved."[16] All of these developments allowed us to build bridges to Russia in ways that did not exist previously. The intense desire to understand how religion could strengthen the country, bring social cohesion, and build up a hardworking citizenry seemed to be on the minds of the leaders we met. Communism had failed them, and now they searched for answers in religion, particularly Christianity. Could we help? We left Moscow struggling with this question and wondering how to respond.

---

[16]David Remnick, *Lenin's Tomb: The Last Days of the Soviet Empire* (New York: Random House, 1993), 500.

7

READING RUSSIA RIGHT

JUST BEFORE I LEFT THE UNITED STATES for a four-month teaching sabbatical at Nizhni Novgorod State University in spring 1992, the coalition leadership team agreed that the opportunities developing in Russia were extraordinary. For the first two years following the visit of the Soviet educators' delegation in September 1990, the coalition served as a catalyst, with a minimal commitment of no more than one-third of my time directing this effort. A major push to create interest about the work already done and the exciting possibilities for the future with the wide-open window of opportunity seemed essential.

THE RUSSIAN INITIATIVE

The coalition's board of directors agreed with the staff's proposal that a Russian Initiative be created, with four principal goals: (1) coordinate and facilitate faculty and administrators on sabbatical leave to work with Russian universities and institutes on educational reform, as they requested; (2) assist Russian faculty in the preparation of curriculum materials for use in Russian schools and in teacher training; (3) encourage and assist the establishment of student exchange programs between coalition colleges and Russian universities, including the possible development of a coalition exchange program modeled on the coalition's Latin American studies program; and (4) conduct a feasibility study regarding the establishment of a Christian college or university in the Russian Republic, in response to the invitation of the Yeltsin government. The fourth goal was a breakthrough for the staff and indicated that the board was at least open to considering the possibility of launching a Christian liberal arts college in Moscow.

The board approved of the staff proposal on the condition that a minimum of twelve coalition colleges agree to join the Russian Initiative and contribute $5,000 per year for three years to fund a program director and support staff. Each participating school would designate a campus representative, who would serve on a strategy council. The invitation to coalition member schools was sent out on February 14, 1992, and if positively received by member schools, the Russian Initiative would be launched on July 1, 1992. Fifteen coalition member colleges quickly agreed to join, and I was asked to serve as the Russian Initiative program director.[1] The excitement among coalition member schools was palpable as numerous student and faculty exchanges developed, and Russian-language programs blossomed on ten coalition campuses.

When Marge and I were teaching at Nizhni Novgorod State University on sabbatical, we traveled to Moscow to assist in a ServiceMaster Corporation Business Lecture Series held at the Russian Peoples' Friendship University, Moscow State University, and Plekhanov Institute of National Economics. A team of speakers, invited by Russian colleagues at these schools, gave lectures on building Christian values into business-education programs as Russia's market economy emerged. The American delegation included Augsburger, the coalition's president; Richard Halberg, professor of business and economics at Houghton College in New York; Shirley Roels, chair of the business and economics department at Calvin College in Michigan; and Andrew Steer, senior economic adviser at the World Bank.

Roels summarized their work as follows: "We really needed each team member. Myron stressed the link between ethical values and Christian discipleship, Andrew explored the global trend toward market economics and defined their necessary underpinnings, and Dick and I shared the responsibility for articulating various aspects of business integrity, structure, and curriculum." Russian students and faculty were eager participants, and some of the lectures were followed by intense question-and-answer sessions.

---

[1]The fifteen coalition schools that joined the Russian Initiative were Belhaven College (Mississippi), Biola University (California), Calvin College (Michigan), Dordt College (Iowa), Eastern College (Pennsylvania), Eastern Mennonite College (Virginia), Eastern Nazarene College (Massachusetts), Geneva College (Pennsylvania), Gordon College (Massachusetts), Huntington College (Indiana), Lee College (Tennessee), LeTourneau University (Texas), Olivet Nazarene University (Illinois), Point Loma Nazarene College (California), and Southern Nazarene University (Oklahoma).

As an indication of the openness on the part of our Russian hosts, the coalition subsequently agreed to a request from Russia's International Center for Human Values to publish one hundred thousand copies of the coalition's supplemental textbook, *Business Through the Eyes of Faith*, coauthored by Roels, John Eby of Goshen College in Indiana, and Richard Chewning of Baylor University.[2]

The first meeting of the strategy council for the Russian Initiative took place in Washington, DC, in September 1992. Augsburger shared his desire with the delegates from the fifteen participating schools that we seize this opportunity to share the treasure of Christian education with colleagues in Russia. The delegates also met with the cultural attaché from the Russian Embassy, who offered his assistance in identifying Russian institutions for sister relationships with coalition schools. The highlight of this first meeting was the discussion with James Billington, librarian of the US Congress and a leading authority on Russian history and culture. When we told him about the coalition's programs in Russia, he said,

> What you are doing is tremendously, seminally important. Thoughtful people in the Russian system know there is a better way to run a society . . . without it being a self-indulgent society. This is why they have come to you. We need to reach out to [the Russian people] in ways that accent their renewed interest in the spiritual dimension. This is something you are uniquely equipped to do.

Before the meeting ended, ten of the fifteen members agreed to develop a proposal for a new coalition-run student exchange program in Russia, similar in structure to the coalition's American studies program and Latin American studies program.

All of us involved in the strategy council knew that we needed to deepen our understanding of developments in Russia and pay close attention to the dynamics in this rapidly changing nation. In my role as director of the Russian Initiative, I began reading daily news reports from Russia and attending seminars at various think tanks in Washington, DC.[3] Access to these resources and my experiences in Russia, both during the failed coup in August 1991 and while teaching in Nizhni Novgorod, gave me insights that convinced me that Western

---

[2]Christian College Coalition, *The News* (June 1992): 1, RA.

[3]A number of news services available at that time, such as *Johnson's Russia List*, provided summaries of articles from English-language newspapers worldwide as well as translations from Russian-language newspapers.

journalists and scholars did not see the full picture of what was going on in the former Soviet Union. They did not read Russia right because of their secular bias.

A FAULTY DIAGNOSIS

The radical changes that took place in Russia were unique phenomena in modern history, completely unanticipated by Western scholars. The massive Soviet Empire unraveled, and the Union of Soviet Socialist Republics imploded—not as the result of a war or even of revolution in the streets. Conventional wisdom did not prepare us for these events. In 1983 the Center for Strategic and International Studies, one of Washington's leading think tanks, published a book titled *After Brezhnev*. The volume contained the results of an intense eighteen-month research effort by thirty-five scholars. Their task was to sum up all the available knowledge on the Soviet Union and the central issues that Soviet society faced, and these scholars came to this conclusion: "All of us agree that there is no likelihood whatsoever that the Soviet Union will become a political democracy or that it will collapse in the foreseeable future."[4]

Hedrick Smith's popular book *The Russians* also got it wrong. When he followed this book, issued in 1976, with its companion, *The New Russians*, in 1990, he admitted his mistake: "I left Russia sixteen years ago thinking that fundamental change was impossible. And I wrote that in my book *The Russians*. The decline and stagnation that sank into place for the next decade, into the mid-eighties, seemed to confirm this judgment. Soviet politics appeared as frozen as the Siberian tundra. As it turned out, of course, I was wrong."[5]

No fault should be ascribed to Western scholars for not seeing these dramatic events coming, since almost no one did. But once they occurred, they were consistently misdiagnosed, which is troubling. Why did communism fail, and what caused the complete collapse of the former Soviet Union? Western scholars have answered the question in several different ways. One group basically believes that Mikhail Gorbachev should get most of the credit. Robert Kaiser, the *Washington Post* correspondent stationed in Moscow during these critical years of *perestroika*, puts it this way: "In just over five years, Mikhail Gorbachev transformed the

---

[4]Robert F. Byrnes, *After Brezhnev: Sources of Soviet Conduct in the 1980s* (Washington, DC: CSIS, 1983), xvi.
[5]Hedrick Smith, *The New Russians* (New York: Random House, 1990), xvi. Smith's earlier book was *The Russians* (New York: Ballantine Books, 1976).

world. He turned his own country upside down. He woke a sleeping giant, the people of the Soviet Union, and gave them freedoms they had never dreamed of. He tossed away the Soviet Empire; he ended the Cold War. These are the most astounding historical developments that any of us are likely to experience."[6]

Other Western scholars, mostly conservatives, give President Ronald Reagan the credit. Although Reagan was not the catalyst for the revolutions of 1989, they argued that he created conditions that proved indispensable for these events to occur. Advocates of this perspective point out that his powerful rhetoric about "the evil empire" laid bare the cruelty of the Soviet regime. Reagan's policies of exporting democracy, supporting anticommunist resistance movements around the world, and the Strategic Defense Initiative (SDI) undermined the Marxist regime in Moscow.[7]

A third group of Western scholars argues that the reasons for communism's failure related primarily to economic factors. The technological and managerial sluggishness of the Soviet economy brought the entire system to a grinding halt by the mid-1980s, and Gorbachev could read the handwriting on the wall. The pressing need to overhaul the Soviet economy and to dismantle the centralized planning functions controlled by the Communist Party is credited by many observers as the source of the revolution. No one, not even Gorbachev, expected the whole system to unravel; he wanted to reform socialism, not dismantle it.[8]

The vast majority of Western analysts focused their attention on these political and economic causes for the collapse of communism. In the aftermath of communism, what Vaclav Havel calls "the post-Communism nightmare," this same preoccupation with the political and economic spheres dominates the writings of foreign policy elites in the West. Unfortunately, analysis that ignores the moral and spiritual dimensions of communism's failure results in a faulty diagnosis. Political and economic factors are important in understanding communism's collapse, but they do not tell the whole story.

---

[6]Robert G. Kaiser, "Gorbachev: Triumph and Failure," *Foreign Affairs* (Spring 1991): 160.

[7]Many of the books written about the collapse of communism by Western journalists stationed in Russia focus largely on the importance of American political leadership in undermining the Soviet regime; for example, see Fred Coleman's book *The Decline and Fall of the Soviet Empire* (New York: St. Martin's, 1996).

[8]An example of this analysis would be Anders Aslund's *How Russia Became a Market Economy* (Washington, DC: Brookings Institution, 1995).

To illustrate this point, essays by two of the best-known scholars of modern Russia are worth exploring: national security council adviser to President Jimmy Carter (1977–1981), Zbigniew Brzezinski, and Harvard professor and Russian history specialist, Richard Pipes. Brzezinski's book *The Grand Failure: The Birth and Death of Communism in the Twentieth Century* is one of the few studies published before 1989 that discussed the explicit overthrow of the communist regime as one of four possible options. Few scholars were brave enough to imagine this radicality. In Brzezinski's entire book, there are only four references to religion and a few passing references to the "moral roots" of Soviet society. His list of the ten dynamics of disunion highlights economic factors, political pressures, ethnic forces, and foreign policy concerns.[9] Clearly these all are significant, but there is much more to the story. In Richard Pipes's essay "The Soviet Union Adrift," which appeared in *Foreign Affairs* in early 1991, the same limited perspective becomes evident to the reader. The distinguished Harvard professor describes the Soviet Union as a "thoroughly decrepit structure" and then analyzes the Soviet crisis. Although he notes that the most visible manifestation of this crisis was economic, in his judgment the "root problem" was political. After that articulation, he then discusses the "vertical conflicts" between conservatives and democrats, and the "horizontal conflicts" between the center in Moscow and the republics.[10] While his essay offers many helpful insights, his analysis is essentially confined to the political and economic spheres, including ethnic conflicts.

The failure of Marxism-Leninism actually resulted in five revolutions that unfolded simultaneously. First, a political revolution occurred, which resulted in the people's rejection of the Communist Party as the sole ruler of their state and in the related emergence of new political factions. This led to a dismantling of the one-party political regime and the creation of free elections for the presidency and the parliament (Duma). Second, an economic revolution took place resulting from Gorbachev's decision to restructure the economy and remove the restrictive controls of the centralized planning bureaucracy. Socialism gave way to free-market initiatives, and radical changes followed quickly. Third, an imperial-military revolution developed in which Russia voluntarily gave up its empire in Eastern

---

[9]Zbigniew Brzezinski, *The Grand Failure: The Birth and Death of Communism in the Twentieth Century* (New York: Charles Scribner's Sons, 1989).

[10]Richard Pipes, "The Soviet Union Adrift," *Foreign Affairs—America and the World* (1990–1991): 70-87.

Europe and dissolved into fifteen independent republics. These decisions to release satellite states and move back Russia's borders to their eighteenth-century position without being forced to do so by military defeat were remarkable. In addition, Gorbachev agreed to reduce the size of Russia's impressive nuclear arsenal and to dramatically reduce the size of its standing army.

Foreign policy analysts have focused all of their attention on these three spheres of dramatic change in Russian society, but they missed two other revolutionary dimensions. A social revolution, a dramatic domestic upheaval, exploded, in which all of the supporting mechanisms for families and communities collapsed, such as Young Pioneers and their summer camps. Houses of culture, often owned and operated by industrial plants, were abandoned when these plants lost their state-supported subsidies. Many families who relied on these camps and cultural centers that provided places for their children to play and learn sports and dancing, for example, were left with no external support for domestic assistance. The fifth and final revolution, intimately related to the other four revolutions, involved a moral and spiritual vacuum created by decades of communist atheism. The revolutionary changes related to societal and spiritual angst are those that foreign policy elites have largely missed.

Because analyses in the West are mostly done by secular-minded scholars and journalists for whom religion is unimportant and transcendent values are of little interest, it is not surprising that this moral and spiritual crisis is overlooked. Within the US government, especially among foreign service officers, where a genteel secularity is the default position, there is a deafness to the religious convictions of the overwhelming majority of humanity, convictions that provide the story line through which their life's meaning is read.

LISTENING TO THE RUSSIANS

What is surprising, however, is that these moral and spiritual factors were overlooked even when Russian leaders involved in the drama made repeated references to them. In Gorbachev's bestseller *Perestroika*, he discusses the reasons for his and his colleagues' "new thinking" related to the restructuring of the Soviet Union. He describes how Communist Party leaders in the late 1970s "began to realize that the country began to lose momentum"; a kind of "braking mechanism" had formed, affecting social and economic development. In addition to economic stagnation and deadlock, Gorbachev identifies the "gradual erosion of the ideological and moral values of our people." He notes how a "breach had formed between word and deed" that caused a "decay" in public morals.[11] To the author of *Perestroika*, the challenge was clear: to restructure Soviet society, including its moral life. In Gorbachev's words: "Today our main job is to lift the individual spiritually, respecting his inner world and giving him moral strength and help. . . . *Perestroika* means the elimination from society of the distortions of socialist ethics, the consistent implementation of the principles of social justice. It means the unity of words and deeds, rights and duties."[12] Gorbachev clearly describes aspects of a moral and spiritual revolution.

During his visit to the Vatican in 1989, Gorbachev again made his views explicit. He said,

> We need spiritual values, we need a revolution of the mind. This is the only way toward a new culture and new politics that can meet the challenge of our time. We have changed our attitude toward some matters—such as religion—that, admittedly, we used to treat in a simplistic manner. Now we not only proceed from the assumption that no one should interfere in matters of the individual's conscience; we also say that the moral values that religion generated and embodied for centuries can help us in the work of renewal in our country.[13]

Gorbachev obviously was not blind to the moral and ethical crisis of Marxism-Leninism. Neither were his colleagues. From the many examples that I could choose, I will pick only one. Fyodor Burlatsky, one of the leading democratic reformers in the Soviet Union, a man chosen by Gorbachev in 1987 to head the new Soviet Public Commission for International Cooperation on Humanitarian Problems and Human Rights, voiced it this way: "The Soviet Union has to be a free country where everyone can pray to his or her own god. In fact, religion has to play a role in our return to elementary moral values. There have been so many crimes and so much corruption in our history, nobody knows what the foundation of morality is anymore."[14]

---

[11] Mikhail Gorbachev, *Perestroika: New Thinking for Our Country and the World* (New York: Harper & Row, 1987), 18-22.

[12] Gorbachev, *Perestroika*, 30, 35.

[13] "East-West: Gorbachev, God and Socialism," *Time* magazine (December 11, 1989), 37.

[14] Stephen F. Cohen and Katrina Vanden Heuvel, eds., *Voices of Glasnost: Interviews with Gorbachev's Reformers* (New York: Norton, 1990), 191.

Most Western scholars failed to see that a moral and spiritual revolution preceded and in fact made possible the political and economic revolutions of 1989–1991. The prestigious *Foreign Affairs* journal published twenty-one articles concerning these events in the first two years after the fall of the Iron Curtain; only three articles even mention the role of the church or the moral and cultural revolutions that occurred, while focusing largely on political, economic, and ethnic factors. The same blindness is evident in other leading journals such as *Foreign Policy, World Politics*, and *The National Interest*.

Throughout Eastern Europe and the former Soviet Union, clerical and lay leaders prepared the way for the dramatic, nonviolent changes that occurred. Pope John Paul II, a great inspiration for many people and countless Christians active in human-rights groups and humanitarian organizations, helped to build the groundswell of support that eventually led to democratic change.

Scholars should have seen the moral and spiritual dimensions of the anti-communist revolutions not only because of explicit comments and writings of Eastern European and Russian leaders active in these movements, but also because the evidence was readily available in published literature and the popular media. A moral and spiritual revolution had been underway for years, stimulating the consciences of many and giving them a basis for hope that their repressive regimes would be overthrown. Despite one of the most systematic persecutions that religious communities have experienced in modern times, religious faith in the USSR was not destroyed but showed signs of vibrancy and renewal during the 1970s and 1980s.[15]

In my many trips to Russia in the early 1990s, I often asked Russian university students about their favorite books. One book stood out with no challenger in sight: Mikhail Bulgakov's *The Master and Margarita*. I know a number of Russian students who read this book more than twenty times. This brilliant novel, written in 1940 but not published until 1967 because of the opposition of Soviet censors, creatively weaves together three stories. The first is a love story about an author, named the Master, and his girlfriend, Margarita. The second is a delightful satire of life in Moscow in the 1930s, in which a professor of black magic (who is Satan,

---

[15]For an overview of various religious communities during the Soviet regime, see Eugene B. Shirley Jr. and Michael Rowe, eds., *Candle in the Wind: Religion in the Soviet Union* (Washington, DC: Ethics and Public Policy Center, 1989), and Barbara Von Der Heydt, *Candles Behind the Wall: Heroes of the Peaceful Revolution That Shattered Communism* (Grand Rapids: Eerdmans, 1993).

portrayed as Professor Woland) causes havoc through his supernatural powers. The third story deals with the encounter between Jesus and Pilate leading up to and including Jesus' brutal crucifixion. This book was read by thousands of Russian students and the intelligentsia during the 1970s, 1980s, and 1990s. A brief summary of the principal message in *The Master and Margarita* would be this: only a fool believes there is no God. The brilliance of Bulgakov, writing under the repressive censorship of the Stalinist period, consists in his use of Satan's testimony to prove the existence of God. The book demonstrates the power of moral and spiritual ideas, often ignored by Western scholars, which prepared the ground for the political and economic changes that followed.

Many other examples in the creative arts and in mass media illustrate the basic crisis that Marxist-Leninist ideology was going through. Films were one of the major influences at work during the 1980s in this moral and spiritual revolution. For example, the film *Repentance* presents a powerful surrealist allegory of the Stalinist terror and the cult of Stalin. The film, written in the early 1980s and produced by Tengiz Abuladze in 1984 but only released in 1986, two years after Gorbachev came to power, caused a political earthquake. The essential moral lesson of the film, graphically depicted in its final scene, occurs when an old woman appears at the window of a cake maker's home and asks "Is this the road to the church? Does this road lead to the church?" The cake maker replies, "This is Varlam Street [the street named after the movie's dictator, who is clearly Stalin]. It will not take you to a church." As the old woman walks away, she says, "Then what's the use of it? What good is a road if it does not lead to a church?"

MISDIAGNOSIS LEADS TO THE WRONG CURE

A misdiagnosis leads to a faulty or insufficient cure. Western foreign policy elites clearly understood the dramatic changes in the USSR with the collapse of the one-party state and its centralized economic planning bureaucracy, but they failed to understand how these revolutionary changes had their roots in the corrosive deterioration in the moral and ethical values of Soviet society. Foreign aid programs from the West, especially from the United States, proved to be superficial responses that failed to address deeper cultural and moral weaknesses. Seminars on the mechanics of the free market or how to organize political parties did not help in these traumatic days of the late 1980s and early 1990s. Advising

Russians to replace Soviet-style economic and political institutions with Western-style structures proved to be shortsighted. Seventy years of communism did serious damage to the moral and cultural foundations of Russian society, and the depth of this damage was not fully understood in the West.

Michael Novak argues that the practice of democratic capitalism has been informed by presuppositions and values that are essential to the development of its political and economic structures. Core, requisite values form the foundation of a liberal, pluralistic culture on which democratic political and economic institutions can be built. Without these core values, such as trust, integrity, and accountability, democratic capitalism cannot be developed. The success of democratic capitalism is based on the inherently greater moral and spiritual foundation of its underlying social system, grounded in respect for the rights of individuals created in God's image.[16]

The euphoria that followed the collapse of the Soviet Union in December 1991 blinded many Western opinion makers, as well as Russian officials, to the difficult realities that lay ahead. The collapse of the Soviet economy and the support network for families that it subsidized left the vast majority of Russians in desperate straits. The ruble collapsed twice in the 1990s, and the entire savings of most families evaporated. The breakdown of political authority opened the door for widespread corruption and massive theft of the country's natural resources by unscrupulous oligarchs. To the average Russian, and for many Russian professors, the words *democracy* and *capitalism* correlated with anarchy, exploitation, and lack of concern for the vulnerable in society.

Rebuilding Russian society from the rubble of the Soviet regime was no easy task, and it was a task made even more complex by failure to understand the need to address the deep cultural and moral issues at stake. The experience of living in an atomized Soviet society, which prevented individuals from working together, required a massive change of mindset. People needed to be encouraged that the days of fear and terror had passed, and rebuilding society required their full participation. Trust needed to be restored in a society where it had been destroyed. Speaking the truth needed to be practiced in a society where double-talk was a way of life, a way to survive the grasp of the KGB.

---

[16]Michael Novak, *The Spirit of Democratic Capitalism* (New York: Simon & Schuster, 1982), 31-48.

Restoring integrity and developing truthfulness, critical moral values that underlie democratic capitalism, required cultural change in the postcommunist world, since these values were lost under Soviet leadership, as Gorbachev and his advisers realized. Western foreign policy elites failed to see how cultural institutions, including churches, could play a much more important role in this process, were they given the opportunity and the support needed.

These insights became increasingly clear to me in 1992 and 1993 as the coalition began to expand its work in Russia. People of faith had an important role to play in partnering with Russians who were asking for our help. This was a time to act, while the openness was so evident. To be effective, Christian educators needed to take a servant posture: listening to the concerns of our Russian friends and humbly offering assistance, especially as they struggled with the question of how to rebuild the moral foundation of Russian society; supporting them by studying their history and culture, learning about their experiences under the communist regime, which meant hearing their stories without offering advice about how they should become like the United States. Offering authentic help required that we try to interpret Russia correctly, read Russia right, and try to assist them as they searched for answers to the challenges that would lead to their future development. Having never experienced anything like what they were going through, we needed to partner with them in humility and ask how we could help.[17]

---

[17] I came to these conclusions in early 1993 and summarized what I had learned in an unpublished speech, "Doing Scholarship with Both Eyes Open: A Case Study of the Collapse of Communism," RA; the contents of this presentation were later published as a chapter titled "Getting Russia Right," in *God and the Global Order: The Power of Religion in American Foreign Policy*, ed. Jonathan Chaplin (Waco, TX: Baylor University Press, 2010).

8

SEIZING THE INITIATIVE

THE EXCITEMENT GENERATED IN THE FIRST few years of the Russian Initiative grew rapidly as many member colleges and universities engaged in student and faculty exchanges. The coalition's board of directors hesitantly agreed to support a feasibility study for a Christian college in Moscow, and their willingness to do this was largely due to repeated encouragement from Augsburger, the coalition's president, and its vice presidents.

With limited financial resources and a small coalition-based staff, for which I served as a part-time director, strategic networking became a key to moving the project along. Unless we could mobilize the larger Christian community, especially those with expertise related to Russia, prospects for success seemed limited. I initially became discouraged to find that there were few Christians with Russian expertise, at least in the networks with which I was familiar, but I knew that encountering and enlisting such people had to be a top priority.

THE FORMATION OF THE AMERICAN WORKING GROUP

While the coalition's strategy council, made up of campus representatives from the Russian Initiative's fifteen partner colleges, focused on student and faculty exchange programs with Russia and Ukraine and the possibility of establishing a Russian studies program, I needed another group of advisers with Russian expertise to articulate a strategy for a Christian college in Moscow. I knew a small number of colleagues with expertise in Russia, and they in turn led me to a few others. The first meeting of the initial group of advisers who showed interest in building a Christian college in Russia took place by phone on September 28, 1992, and included six participants: Peter and Anita Deyneka (Deyneka Russian Ministries), Mark Elliott (Institute for East-West Studies at Wheaton College), Kent Hill (Institute on Religion and Democracy in Washington, DC), Daryl McCarthy (International Institute for Christian Studies, headquartered in Overland Park, Kansas), and me. The members of this informal advisory team agreed to call themselves the American Working Group (AWG).

Several members of the group had been thinking and praying about the possibility of establishing a Christian college in Russia for a number of years, and they quickly agreed to work together on this project, taking advantage of the unexpected request of the Russian government. The earliest draft of a concept paper for a Russian Christian college had been prepared years earlier by Ivan Fahs, a professor of sociology at Wheaton College, who brainstormed together with the Deynekas about such an idea before the invitation I received in October 1990. They wanted to see a Christian school built but had no idea that American Christians would actually be asked by Boris Yeltsin's minister of education to do it.

After an extended conversation, we reached consensus on a working title for the college: the American Protestant University of Russia. The group sensed that the word *American* would be removed from the title at a later date, but in the meantime it served as a helpful descriptive word in the founding phase. The group believed intensely that this would be an evangelical project, but we also wanted to work cooperatively with other religious communities such as the Roman Catholic Church, the Russian Orthodox Church, and mainline Protestant denominations. A second approach, offered by Daryl McCarthy, proposed the establishment of a Christian college on the campus of an existing Russian university; we referred to this as the "Cambridge model."

The working group asked Kent Hill and me to draft an initial proposal for the college and a startup budget, while others in the group worked on recruitment of additional Christian educators to join the project. The seed had been planted for growth, and the six of us decided to reconvene in two months as we excitedly began our work, knowing that the task was overwhelming especially for a group with limited financial resources.[1]

---

[1]John A. Bernbaum, memorandum for the record, "Feasibility of a Christian College/University in Russia," September 28, 1992, RA; Daryl McCarthy, "Conference Notes," September 28, 1992, RA.

DEVELOPING A VISION STATEMENT

In fall 1992 and spring 1993, the working group focused its attention on preparing a strategy for building the college and had long governance and funding debates. One of the key first steps involved the drafting of a prospectus for a liberal arts college in Moscow, one that subsequently went through numerous revisions. By April 1993 the working group reached agreement on a prospectus, including a new name—Russian-American Christian University (RACU). The vision statement for RACU read as follows:

> The Russian-American Christian University is a comprehensive liberal arts university grounded in the tradition and doctrines of historic Protestant Christianity, offering to Russian students an educational program which will train them to be agents of renewal and reconciliation in the academy, church, society and the marketplace. The goal of the university is to train students to do God's work in God's world.

Rather than attempt to create a new vision statement, we chose to take advantage of 150 years of experience in Christian liberal arts education found at Calvin College and simply borrow its mission statement. We knew that over time it would need to be revised to more appropriately fit the Russian context.

The prospectus also included an implementation timeline that set the goal of offering the first classes in September 1994. The immediate first steps included the organization of a board of trustees with American leaders, the draft of corporate bylaws, and the creation of a 501(c)(3) not-for-profit, tax-exempt corporation in order to process charitable contributions to RACU. Once the structure and governing principles were completed, recruitment of leaders for RACU was the top priority, as well as identifying Russian partners to serve as potential board members and faculty.[2]

Shortly after approving the prospectus, the working group hosted a conference at the Billy Graham Center at Wheaton College in April 1993. The participants at the meeting, titled "Christian Higher Education in the Former Soviet Union," shared reports from their organizations already active in higher education or in ministry to university students in Russia.

After presentations by four members of the working group, a two-hour animated discussion took place. The participants supported the idea of a Christian

---

[2]John A. Bernbaum, draft prospectus, Russian-American Christian University, April 5, 1993, RA.

college in Moscow, but not an evangelical institute (the "Cambridge model") af-filiated with a public university. The majority of those present favored a uni-versity that would primarily serve the Russian Christian community, since its members had been denied access to higher education for decades, but it should also be open to others interested in a values-centered curriculum. The clearest message, already shared by the working group, focused on the need to identify and include Russian Christian educators from the beginning, and the attendees agreed to help identify them.[3]

Following the Wheaton conference I returned to Russia, in May 1993, and during my visits with Christian leaders in St. Petersburg, Moscow, and Nizhni Novgorod, I found widespread support for the establishment of a Christian college, with Christian leaders in all three cities making the case that the new school should be located in their city.[4]

After hearing this encouraging news, the working group held a meeting at Wheaton College on May 28 and decided that the new college should be located in Moscow because of the size of the Christian community in that city and our extensive network of contacts with Moscow leaders. The working group also agreed that the working title of the new school should be "Russian-American University," without the word *Christian* in the title, as suggested by several Russian educators. With the support of a generous grant from the Mustard Seed Foundation, work began on two major meetings in Moscow to be convened in October to assess the interest of key leaders, both Christian and non-Christian, in this initiative.[5]

LAYING OUT THE VISION FOR A CHRISTIAN UNIVERSITY IN MOSCOW

With a draft prospectus for the Russian-American University in hand and trans-lated into Russian, members of the working group headed to Moscow to share the vision with key Russian leaders. The first meeting, on October 28, 1993, in-volved a full-day consultation held at the Central House of Tourists. Peter Deyneka welcomed the thirteen Russian Christian leaders and shared his view

---

[3]Margery Bernbaum, "Conference Report," April 22, 1993, RA.
[4]John A. Bernbaum, "Trip Report: Visit to Russia (May 1993)," 11, RA.
[5]John A. Bernbaum, American Working Group meeting report, "Christian Higher Education in the For-mer Soviet Union (May 28, 1993)," RA. Two new members joined the American Working Group: Lynn Buzzard (Campbell University School of Law) and Rev. Ronald Lush (Global Initiatives).

that spiritual reformation was the key to the success of all other reform efforts in Russia and that at the heart of spiritual reformation must be education. In his judgment, "where the university goes today, the country goes tomorrow."

Myron Augsburger and I, representing the Christian College Coalition, articulated a vision for a Christian liberal arts university and distributed a Russian translation of excerpts from Arthur Holmes's book *The Idea of a Christian College* and the draft prospectus. When asked whether this concept of a Russian-American University appealed to them, the leaders unanimously expressed their enthusiasm. Having been denied access to higher education because of their faith, these Russian Protestant leaders knew the importance of higher education for their people and showed gratitude for our initiative. As the meeting came to an end, the entire group stood to offer closing prayers, and tears began to flow as these Russian Christians leaders asked God for guidance in creating this school, something they never imagined could happen in their lifetime. The passion of these prayers and the tears deepened my commitment to this initiative. More than ever, I knew we had to make this happen.

Out of this meeting came a decision to move forward, and two Russians agreed to accept leadership responsibilities in the formation of a Russian board: Alexander Zaichenko, an economist at the prestigious Academy of National Economy and president of the Association of Christian Businessmen, and Boris Gontarev, academic dean of the Academy of World Civilizations and a close associate of Campus Crusade's work in Russia. We asked both men to attend the dinner meeting scheduled for the next night with Russian educational leaders, which they agreed to do.

The next day, October 29, a second dinner meeting took place at the Radisson Hotel for Russian educators who had expressed interest in the possibility of a new private Christian university in Moscow. Despite the political turmoil in Russia, these leaders, all of whom were very busy people, accepted our invitation. Once again, Augsburger and I sketched a vision for a Christian liberal arts university and shared excerpts from Holmes's book and the draft prospectus; following our presentation, Zaichenko and Gontarev made supportive statements from their perspective as Russians. The response from the guests was encouraging, with many offers of assistance from these secular educators and a willingness to serve on a Russian working group.

Both meetings encouraged the American Working Group and confirmed its commitment to move the initiative forward quickly. The only discouraging time came the next day, October 30, when the working group met with expat American evangelicals at a retreat center outside Moscow. After reporting to them on the previous two days of meetings, this group showed no support for the vision and threw up all kinds of potential obstacles. Peter Deyneka later explained that these missionaries, busy with their own programs, clearly hesitated to show enthusiasm for new projects for fear they might be asked to get involved and add more work to their already heavy loads. Because Peter is a gracious man, I trusted his judgment, although the attitude of the missionaries frustrated me. Before we left Moscow, the working group asked Zaichenko to serve as the Russian project director while I served as his American counterpart. Our immediate principal responsibility to propose names of key leaders to serve as members of the board of trustees or the board of advisers now became urgent.[6]

When the working group reassembled in the States following the consultations in Moscow, one of the primary discussion topics concerned who would provide the needed leadership for the American partners. The group came to a consensus that the Christian College Coalition should be the lead institution in founding a Christian liberal arts college in Moscow and, as a result, decided to ask the coalition whether I could be assigned full time to the Russian Initiative, which meant releasing me from my other responsibilities as the coalition's executive vice president. They decided to send a formal request to the coalition asking for its support of a new expanded leadership role for me as interim president of the college in Moscow.

In light of the meetings in Moscow, the working group changed its recommendation about the title of the proposed school and agreed that the earlier title, Russian-American Christian University (RACU), be used and that the university clearly be identified as an evangelical institution with references in its charter to the historic creeds of Protestant Christianity. Reports of Christian organizations entering Russia and using names for their programs that concealed their true intent troubled the group, and we decided not to hide the Christian character of

---

[6]The reports on these meetings are recorded in the following sources: John A. Bernbaum, "Trip Report: Visit to Moscow (October–November 1993)," November 11, 1993, 4-5; John and Marge Bernbaum, "Record of Meetings (October 28, 1993, and October 29, 1993)," November 16-17, 1993, RA.

the school. The working group also reviewed a timeline I distributed that proposed a launch date of September 1995 and agreed that offering summer English-language courses, following the example of Lithuania Christian College, would be a helpful recruiting tool and a way of establishing RACU's credibility as a quality educational institution.[7]

THE COALITION'S LEADERSHIP ROLE

In January 1994 I prepared a document titled "Update on the Feasibility Study for the Russian-American Christian University (RACU)" and shared a letter with the coalition president and staff from the American Working Group requesting that my coalition responsibilities be changed from three-quarters' time to full-time leadership of the Russian Initiative. My report also made the case that a major component of my full-time role would be the establishment of the first Christian liberal arts university in the Republic of Russia. With the approval of the coalition's leadership, this proposal was brought to the board of directors for their review. Previously the board had not supported the coalition taking on this responsibility, but when the American Working Group's letter proposed that the coalition not be asked to fund this initiative, the board gave a thumbs-up. Now that the Russian Initiative had added new participating schools, the contributions of $5,000 per year per school covered the preliminary administrative costs of the project. Any additional funding, if needed, would now be the responsibility of the working group. At the coalition's board meeting on January 31, 1994, this proposal passed. My full-time work with the Russian Initiative began on July 1, 1994.[8]

BUILDING ON EARLIER SUCCESSES

While the birthing process of the Russian-American Christian University seemed painfully slow because of the initial lack of support from the coalition's board of directors, other parts of the Russian Initiative advanced rapidly. Twelve member colleges initially joined the USSR Initiative between 1990 and 1992; fifteen schools supported the Russian Initiative in 1992, and three additional members

---

[7]John A. Bernbaum, "Meeting Report—American Working Group (December 4, 1993)," December 8, 1993, RA.
[8]John A. Bernbaum, "Update on the Feasibility Study for the Russian-American Christian University (RACU)," January 12, 1994; Christian College Coalition board of directors' minutes, January 30-31, 1994, 4, RA.

voted to join by January 1994.[9] During the first two years, eleven coalition member schools launched student exchange programs in Russia and Ukraine, facilitated eleven faculty exchanges, and started ten new Russian-language departments. By spring 1994, 40 percent of the coalition's member colleges and universities were actively engaged in exchanges in Russia and Ukraine.[10]

In addition, the strategy council, made up of representatives from the member colleges of the Russian Initiative, determined that many coalition colleges were too small to be able to establish their own student exchange programs; they wanted to participate in a joint program in Russia, modeled after the Latin American studies program. The proposed Russian studies program would enable American students to spend a semester in Russia studying the language, culture, economics, politics, and religious life of the country, while interacting with Russian students and faculty and receiving a full semester of academic credit. A proposal, initially drafted by my wife, Marge, and later developed by the staff and members of the strategy council, involved basing the program in Nizhni Novgorod, with trips to Moscow and St. Petersburg to see the historic sites and meet with Russian church and government leaders. The program proposal was approved by the coalition's Student Academic Program Committee in December 1992, and student recruitment began. One year later, in January 1994, the first thirteen students arrived in Nizhni Novgorod, under the leadership of the program's newly appointed director, Harley Wagler, who was hired after a nationwide search. His extensive experience living in central Europe and his knowledge of Russian language and literature make him the clear choice as director.[11]

The Russian-American MBA project, another arm of the Russian Initiative, was not directly related to RACU, but the relationships that we developed while working on this program proved to be of great value in creating the new school in Moscow. The MBA project made progress during this period, but it faced increasing complications because of the economic difficulties in Russia. The staff referred to "the ten factor" reality of working in Russia—anything tended to be ten times more difficult, complex, and time consuming in Russia than in the States. Communication difficulties plagued team members, who attempted to

---

[9]Christian College Coalition/The Russian Initiative, *Russia Link* (Fall 1992): 1; Christian College Coalition/ The Russian Initiative, *Russia Link* (Spring 1994): 6, RA.

[10]Christian College Coalition/The Russian Initiative, *Russia Link* (Spring 1994): 3, RA.

[11]Christian College Coalition/The Russian Initiative, *Russia Link* (Fall 1993): 1, RA.

coordinate the drafting of their curriculum modules with their Russian colleagues. In addition, a substantial number of Russian business and economics faculty were hired by newly established Russian businesses for salaries many times that of a professor, a temptation most could not resist. This meant orienting new faculty members on various teams, slowing down the progress of their cooperative work.

Although only one new textbook reached publication by fall 1993, three Russian universities used the new MBA curriculum, and two of these used the course materials for two entire years. Efforts to secure US federal funding for the publication of these materials were rejected because of the inclusion of "Christian moral values."[12] The other program of the Russian Initiative involved the translation of textbooks for use in Russian universities. Russian educators arranged for the translation and publication of *Business Through the Eyes of Faith*, although they reduced their publication plans from one hundred thousand to twenty thousand copies because of economic constraints. They also agreed to publish four thousand copies of *Biology Through the Eyes of Faith*, another part of the Through the Eyes of Faith series, written by coalition faculty and published by Harper & Row.[13]

INCREASING INSTABILITY IN RUSSIA

The initial enthusiasm of coalition member colleges and universities for participation in student and faculty exchanges, including the new Russian studies program, continued to grow in the early 1990s, as did support for plans to establish a Christian college in Moscow. However, the political and economic struggles in postcommunist Russia intensified, complicating efforts to work cooperatively with our Russian partners.

Once Yeltsin became the dominant power in Moscow, as president of the Russian Republic, he decided he wanted to be totally independent, not tied to any political faction, including the democrats who had enthusiastically supported him during his rivalry with Gorbachev.[14] Corruption began to spread

---

[12]Christian College Coalition/The Russian Initiative, *Russia Link* (Fall 1993): 3, RA.

[13]John A. Bernbaum, "Trip Report (June 18–July 1, 1994)," 7-8, RA.

[14]Lilia Shevtsova, *Yeltsin's Russia: Myths and Reality* (Washington, DC: Carnegie Endowment for International Peace, 1999), 32. In addition to Shevtsova's detailed analysis of Yeltsin's leadership in the 1990s, see also David Remnick's *Resurrection: The Struggle for a New Russia* (New York: Random House, 1997) and Leon Aron's *Yeltsin: A Revolutionary Life* (New York: St. Martin's, 2000).

rapidly in early 1992, and Yeltsin's government stood accused of a series of scandals. His primary financial adviser, Yegor Gaidar, admitted that the greatest obstacle he faced in instituting reforms involved corruption among government officials. It soon became clear that many of the old elites from the days of Communist Party rule still held key positions in the government's huge bureaucracy, and most firmly opposed Yeltsin's reform efforts. This resistance, together with the growing power of right-wing nationalist groups, began to crowd out the democrats in the parliament. By fall 1992, less than a year after the failed coup, the Supreme Soviet and the Congress of Peoples' Deputies became Yeltsin's primary political enemies, and open warfare emerged between executive and legislative branches of the Russian government. After several efforts by the congress to impeach Yeltsin, he ordered an attack on the Russian White House, which housed the offices of members of the parliament.

This attack, which resulted in the deaths of a large but unknown number of victims and thousands of arrests, badly tarnished Yeltsin's image. Many Russians subsequently believed that his leadership followed the example of previous Communist Party leaders who murdered Russian citizens to secure their own positions. His moral legitimacy had been lost. At the end of 1993 and early 1994, the conflicts and contradictions in Russian life continued. A new parliament, elected with a majority of Communist Party delegates and ultranationalists who opposed Yeltsin's reform program, came to power. At the same time, a new constitution, approved by a popular referendum, significantly expanded the powers of the president. These conflicting results indicated the difficulties the Russian people were going through.[15]

Like many Westerners who followed developments in Russia in the Western press, members of the American Working Group viewed Yeltsin as a democratic leader, and we failed to understand that he was using democracy slogans as a battering ram to destroy the USSR's political institutions while building his own political structures, centered on himself. By the mid-1990s, it became increasingly clear that Yeltsin did not support an independent judiciary; he emasculated the power of the legislature and reduced the authority of local self-government. A handful of Western scholars now described Yeltsin and his colleagues as

---

[15]Fred Coleman, *The Decline and Fall of the Soviet Empire: Forty Years That Shook the World, from Stalin to Yeltsin* (New York: St. Martin's, 1996), 377-83.

"market bolsheviks," by which they meant that they viewed themselves as an elite ruling group entitled to impose progress and development on their country as they wanted it.[16]

Our Russian educational partners worked hard to reform their institutions, but the fact that the gross domestic product of the country had been reduced by 50 percent since 1989 created difficulties. In the three years since the failed coup of August 1991, it had become increasingly clear that the postcommunist transition was going to be painful. Educational reform was of interest to only a handful of government officials, and they had limited financial resources at their disposal.

This was the challenging environment we faced as we attempted to build Russia's first faith-based liberal arts college. We could sense the increasing tensions in Russian political life and personally witnessed the pain of economic upheavals and the stress this caused ordinary Russian citizens, but we knew we had to move forward as quickly as possible, since our Russian partners desperately wanted this new school to be established and promised to help us build it. By mid-1994, the momentum to build RACU finally began to grow, first in the States and then in Russia.

---

[16]Peter Reddaway and Dmitri Glinski, *The Tragedy of Russia's Reforms: Market Bolshevism Against Democracy* (Washington, DC: United States Institute of Peace Press, 2001), 624-29.

9

LAYING THE FOUNDATION IN RUSSIA

BEGINNING WITH THE FIRST MEETING of the American Working Group and reaffirmed by the conference at Wheaton College in April 1993, the American team knew the critical importance of getting Russians involved in the educational project from the beginning if RACU was to be an authentic bi-national institution. The meetings in Moscow in October 1993 with Russian Christian leaders and Russian educators accentuated the same point—secure Russian ownership.

PUTTING TOGETHER THE BOARD OF TRUSTEES

When I arrived in Moscow in March 1994, my initial impressions left me confused. Everywhere I traveled, people spoke about the increasing darkness, an image used repeatedly by both Russians and Americans living in Moscow. "It is getting darker and darker here"—these words often described the political paralysis, the continuing economic decline, and the dramatic increase in criminality.

Yet, in the midst of all of this darkness, I also saw some signs of hope that seemed to me to be candles of light. Courageous Russian Christians starting small businesses, opening publishing companies, establishing home churches, rewriting textbooks, and helping the poor and marginalized indicated to me that the negative signs were not the whole story. While on the macro level there was much to be concerned about, Russians—especially people of faith—quietly went about their work in their local communities.[1]

---

[1]John A. Bernbaum, "Trip Report: Visit to Russia (March 1994)," March 31, 1994, RA.

Peter Deyneka and I discovered that Alexander Zaichenko, whom we had met in October 1993 and whom we asked to serve as leader of a Russian working group, had taken his assignment seriously. He pulled together a small group of Russians, and they had already met six times before I returned to Moscow in March 1994 to discuss the first steps needed to launch the school. Their group became convinced that we should register RACU as a Russian legal entity rather than as a joint Russian-American corporation. This seemed to be wise counsel for a number of reasons. First, registering as a Russian entity as opposed to a joint corporation cost less and took much less time. In addition, the rising anti-Western sentiment in Russia, especially the growing efforts to restrict the activity of Western Christians in Russia, bolstered their position. The law on freedom of religion and conscience, approved by the parliament in 1990, drew repeated attacks from the conservative wing of the Russian Orthodox Church and nationalist groups, and this warning sign indicated that the initial warm receptivity we had experienced as Americans might diminish rapidly.

The Russian working group had strong convictions about offering an initial academic program in September 1994, and they proposed that we begin with two classes of first-year students, thirty students in a Department of Literature and Language and thirty students in a Department of Economics and Business. The Americans in the working group agreed with our Russian partners that courses be offered in both Russian and English and that an equal number of Russian and American faculty members be hired, but we had no strategy for how to recruit students.[2]

Following this exchange with our new Russian partners, we assembled the founding board of directors, and the first five board meetings held in 1994 and early 1995 laid the foundation for RACU. The founders, who have special legal responsibility according to Russian law, were Yuri Apatov (executive secretary of the Euro-Asiatic Federation of the Unions of Evangelical Christians-Baptists), Peter Deyneka (Deyneka Russian Ministries), Mark Elliott (Wheaton College), Evgeni Goncharenko (Moscow Christian Cultural Center), Vladimir Obrovets (research scientist), Alexander Zaichenko, board vice chair (Association of Christian Businessmen), and me. I was asked to serve as board chair.[3] Peter

---

[2]Bernbaum, "Trip Report: Visit to Russia (March 1994)."
[3]Evgeny Goncharenko and Vladimir Obrovets were added to the board of trustees in June 1994 and attended the first formal meeting of the board on July 25, 1994. Yuri Apatov was elected to the board in February 1995.

Deyneka played a key role in identifying Russian candidates to serve as trustees, since he knew the Protestant leadership in Russia better than anyone else.

In the early board meetings, the trustees wrestled through a number of key issues. The first involved the decision to register RACU as an educational institution rather than a religious organization. After much discussion, the board reached consensus on this issue because of the concern that the large number of Western missionaries entering Russia might cause a harsh backlash, and we had already seen signs of this; in addition, we wanted to build positive relations with secular Russian educators and Ministry of Education officials and to not be dismissed by them because they viewed RACU as a Bible college or seminary. A faith-based liberal arts college would be an unknown entity in Russia, and the board wanted to win acceptance for RACU as a quality educational program. As I have reflected on this decision over the years, I am convinced this proved to be a wise move that helped the school secure accreditation and gain stature in Russia.

Another key decision made during the first series of board meetings concerned the structure and academic program of RACU. The school's early prospectus described a new educational institution that would combine the strengths of Russian and American higher education and thereby become a new bicultural university. But when we discussed what this might mean, the board did not know how to proceed. After much discussion, the group worked through the idea of using the model of Christian liberal arts colleges from North America, which had been in operation since the late nineteenth century, with the expectation that this structure would be adapted over time to fit the Russian context. This was an exciting undertaking for all of us, because we knew that Russian students and faculty would be drawn to this new educational approach.

The trustees also recognized that it had to add new members to the board who could help the institution during the critical launch phase. Seven trustees, four Russians and three Americans, seemed to be a good start, but we knew that little financial power existed among the seven of us. Alexander Zaichenko told the board that he had problems finding qualified Russians to serve on the board without compensation; the idea of voluntary board participation, not known in Russia at the time, highlighted this issue, and the need for earning income in an unstable economic environment clearly ranked as a priority for Christian leaders.

We also needed to build a board of advisers to enhance the credibility of our new school, and we had more success with this effort. The first appointments to the board of advisers in 1994–1995 included Alexander Abramov (president of the Institute for the Development of Educational Systems), Arthur DeFehr (president of Palliser Furniture Company and founder of Lithuania Christian College), Boris Gershunsky (founder of the Russian Academy of Education), Mikhail Matskovsky (general director of the International Center for Human Values), William Pollard (former CEO of ServiceMaster), Andrew Steer (chief economist for the World Bank), and Nicolai Trofimov (vice rector of Russian Peoples' Friendship University).[4]

RACU'S FIRST STAFF MEMBERS

With a formally constituted board of trustees and new Russian and American advisers, the trustees turned their attention in 1994 and early 1995 to hiring staff, opening an office, registering RACU, planning the curriculum, and raising startup funds. The board also discussed the need to hire an administrator for RACU, who would organize the first set of courses, begin student recruitment, and locate an office for the university. The first American staff member, identified by Peter Deyneka, was Jay Shanor, a New Testament scholar and linguist from Biola University (Los Angeles), who planned to be in Moscow for the 1994–1995 academic year teaching Greek half-time at Moscow Baptist Seminary. He expressed a willingness to work with RACU on a half-time basis, and the board quickly agreed to this arrangement in July 1994. The board sensed that Shanor, with his fluency in Russian, could build relationships with key Russian Christian church and parachurch leaders.

When the board reassembled in Moscow in October 1994, it approved the signing of a lease for an office apartment in southwest Moscow, known as the evangelical corridor since so many Western missionaries lived in this area of the city. Shanor found a three-room apartment in the same complex where Zaichenko and some American expats lived. This place, often referred to as Brezhnev's Village because Leonid Brezhnev had these apartments built for his top advisers and KGB leaders, proved to be a good choice. We often saw limousines,

---

[4]For a complete list of the people who served on RACU's board of advisers, which totaled up to thirty members during the fifteen years of RACU, see appendix C.

accompanied by armed guards, pulling up to our buildings at all hours, apparently dropping off or picking up security or political officials who needed protection. With increasing criminal activity in Moscow, this seemed to be a safe place to locate our first office; it also served as an apartment for Marge and me when we traveled to Moscow three to four times each year.

FINDING A CAMPUS HOME

The economic difficulties of 1994–1995 greatly complicated our efforts to find a rental facility in which to house our new school. When I traveled to Moscow in March 1994, the concern about the increasing darkness and difficulty in the city characterized the views of both Russians and American expats that I knew; three months later, the mood in Moscow seemed more subdued and less volatile. Appearances indicated that the politics of confrontation had given way to the politics of grudging compromise. Everyone seemed convinced that President Yeltsin's power, both real political power and moral authority, had been significantly reduced. Despite the fears of some analysts, the radical nationalist groups in the parliament had not yet been able to take control of the legislature.

The reality of increased crime became headline news in Moscow. Everyone talked about it. An article in *Time* magazine, titled "Moscow: City on Edge," reported that more than three thousand murders took place in Moscow in 1993, an increase of 1,740 percent since 1987. A number of Western missionaries in Moscow had been victimized by young criminals, and their stories had a chilling effect on me during my visits.[5]

Marge and I returned to Moscow in October 1994, and two days after our arrival we witnessed Black Tuesday (October 11)—the day when the "Russian ruble fell through the floor . . . losing one-fourth of its value against the dollar in the worst one-day plunge since trading began in 1992," according to the *Moscow Times*. On Monday the exchange rate in Moscow was 3,081 rubles per dollar; the next day it dropped 850 points, to 3,926 rubles per dollar. I remember walking past a bank on Tuesday and seeing the exchange rate posted at 3,800 rubles per dollar and thinking someone had made a big mistake. I did not know that we had been caught in the middle of a frightening currency crisis.[6]

---

[5]John A. Bernbaum, "Trip to Russia (June 18–July 1, 1884)," 1, RA.
[6]John A. Bernbaum, "Trip to Russia (October 8-23, 1994)," 1, RA.

Finding a rental facility in this context proved extremely difficult. Alexander Komysev, RACU's part-time assistant responsible for finding a location for our school, had visited nineteen facilities by mid-June 1994; he utilized the services of eleven real estate companies and carefully documented eighty-four meetings with property owners and agents. On each of my trips to Moscow in the fall and following spring, I visited numerous university campuses that desperately sought renters. Leaders on these campuses wanted rental income because of reduced federal subsidies, and they assumed that because we had American support, we would build new facilities on their campus that we would share with them. We also looked at a number of industrial plants and office facilities whose managers wanted to rent their unused space, but the prices for renting facilities in Moscow at that time matched or exceeded rental costs in Manhattan and Washington, DC. In addition, in a number of meetings with potential landlords, they demanded that we give them part ownership of our school if we leased space from them.

The Russian working group had strong convictions about RACU offering its first courses in September 1994, but it became increasingly clear to them and the American trustees that this was not a possibility because of the difficulties in finding a campus location and the delays in preparing incorporation documents and then registering them with the government. But then a surprising opportunity emerged. Through our friendship with Nikolai Trofimov, I received an invitation to meet the new rector of Russian Peoples' Friendship University, Vladimir Filippov. He told Trofimov that he had great interest in cooperation with RACU, especially since his school had benefited from its participation in the joint Russian-American MBA program and its subsequent sister relationship with Calvin College. Trofimov arranged a meeting with Filippov for Marge and me, along with Jay Shanor and Alexander Zaichenko; Trofimov had become a good friend to Marge and me by this time, and we usually had dinner at his apartment whenever we came to Moscow.

After Trofimov's introduction, he asked me to share RACU's Christ-centered educational program, and when I finished my brief summary, Filippov said he had an interest in working with us and that his university welcomed a Christian perspective, as well as other perspectives, to be shared on his campus. It seemed so ironic to me that the leaders of this university, founded in 1960 and previously named Patrice Lumumba University after the Congolese independence leader, wanted to work cooperatively with our school. When the university was established at the height of the Cold War, its mission focused on training students from the developing world in Marxist ideology. The willingness of its new rector to offer the possible rental of campus facilities gave the board an unexpected boost because the university was highly ranked and its reputation as the third-best university in the country gave credibility to our program.[7]

As we left the campus, Zaichenko mentioned our plans to hold an English-language institute the following summer, and Trofimov immediately pointed out that the campus would be empty all summer, so why not use it for the institute. The two of us quickly drafted a protocol about leasing space at the university, and RACU's board of trustees enthusiastically endorsed this option. When I asked RACU's trustees whether they had any concerns about cooperating with Russian Peoples' Friendship University in light of its previous role as a principal propagator of Marxism-Leninism to students from the developing world, the response was, "No. This is a new day in Russia."[8]

Although the RACU board agreed that the opening of RACU had to be delayed until September 1995, they decided that our school would offer a series of classes in the spring of 1995 that would give RACU credibility and create interest in its program. In addition, they approved plans for a four-week English-language institute in July 1995, designed to enhance RACU's image and help recruit its first class of students, following the example of Lithuania Christian College. By the spring of 1995, we had signed a protocol with Russian Peoples' Friendship University that provided classroom space for these free, noncredit courses at its downtown campus, near the Shabolovskaya Metro station, as well as classroom and dormitory space on its main campus, on Miklukho-Maklaya Street, for the English-language institute in July.

Like most universities in Russia at that time, Russian Peoples' Friendship University was struggling to survive in a difficult economic environment. More than 130 commercial companies leased space on its campuses, many of which were small startup businesses that needed office space at a reasonable price; a number of them were operated by enterprising students from their school who decided to try starting a business, such as a small bookstore or café. Without this source

---

[7]The friendship with Vladimir Filippov, with whom I met periodically, not only helped RACU during this early stage of its development. Later, when he was appointed minister of education, RACU had this friend in a key position.

[8]RACU Board of Trustees meeting, "Record of Meeting in Moscow (October 18, 1994)," 3, RA.

of income, the university would probably have collapsed, since it was receiving less than 40 percent of its previous financial subsidy from the Ministry of Education. The university benefited from the lease income, and young entrepreneurs got a start in the new capitalist economy that the Russian reformers were attempting to build. This proved to be a win-win situation in a place where people were not familiar with this term.

RACU'S FIRST CLASSES

The decision by the board to delay the official opening of RACU until September 1995 especially discouraged the Russian trustees, but it seemed clear that the board had no choice. Everything we tried to do in the early stages of RACU's development took much more time than expected, and it became clear to the Americans that nothing could be done easily in Russia. Even simple procedures became complicated, and the board's refusal to pay bribes to get documents approved by government officials meant the work was often delayed.

By fall 1994, the hiring of Jay Shanor as acting vice rector for academic programs at least enabled the board to move forward with plans for offering introductory classes beginning in March and April 1995. RACU announced four five-week classes to be offered in the evenings at Russian Peoples' Friendship University's downtown campus. The courses, free and open to the general public, provided the board an opportunity to see what the interest would be. These first classes included the following: "The Protestant Reformation: An Introduction," taught by Tom Kay from Wheaton College; "An Introduction to Christian Apologetics," taught by Eugene Grossman from Deyneka Russian Ministries; "An Introduction to the New Testament," taught by Shanor; and "Christianity's Relationship to Other World Religions," taught by Daniel Clendenin from the International Institute for Christian Studies.

Each class attracted between twenty-five and thirty-five students, mostly university age, with some older adults as well. The interest level in the classes was extremely high, and students eagerly engaged the faculty in dialogue at the end of each two-and-a-half-hour session. When I visited these classes in April 1995, I noticed how attentive and respectful the students were. They took copious notes and, although hesitant to ask questions in front of their classmates, they flocked to the front of the class during the break and afterwards to engage the professor.

I told Kay, a professor of history, that he made history himself by teaching RACU's first course. School was now in session.

WEATHERING THE STORMS

During the early years of RACU's development, staying positive about the school's prospects was extremely difficult, in large part because of the tumultuous political and economic context. Starting a new college from scratch presented enormous challenges, and when the environment kept shifting, increasingly in a hostile direction, this made the task significantly more intimidating. The movement to revise the freedom of conscience law passed in 1990 represented one factor that we tracked carefully. Powerful forces in Russia did not believe that all religions deserved to be equally respected, and these elites insisted that the Russian Orthodox Church's position needed to be protected, especially from missionaries from the West and foreign cults. With the encouragement of Patriarch Alexei II, the Russian parliament, dominated by right-wing factions, drafted revisions to the 1990 law that made it illegal for foreign religious organizations to "engage in religious-missionary publishing or advertising-propaganda activity." Twice President Yeltsin returned the legislation to parliament unsigned, pointing out that some of its provisions violated international human-rights agreements that Russia had signed. When the struggle between Yeltsin and the parliament ended in the attack on the White House on October 4, 1993, and the President dissolved the parliament and ordered new elections, this pending legislation was invalidated. The mood that had generated this draft legislation, however, served as a warning sign.[9]

Meanwhile, among Russian educators who opposed the reform efforts of Gorbachev and Yeltsin, a growing fear of all the new private schools emerged. In the Federation Council, the upper house of the Russian parliament, a draft bill that "declares war on private schools in Russia" was proposed, according to the *Moscow Times*.[10] Two weeks later the same newspaper argued in an editorial that many of these private schools had "no business educating our children."[11]

Yeltsin's unfortunate decision to declare war against Chechnya on December 11, 1994, increased his unpopular standing with Russians. When I arrived in

---

[9]Anita Deyneka, "Russia's Restrictive Law of Religion: Dead or Delayed?," *East-West Church & Ministry Report* (Fall 1993).

[10]*Moscow Times*, September 2-8, 1994.

[11]*Moscow Times*, September 16-22, 1994.

Moscow in early 1995, the war in Chechnya had changed life in the country. The casualties of the war, both young Russian soldiers and the beleaguered citizens of Grozny, Chechnya's capital city, were graphically portrayed on television and newspapers every day and made it impossible for people in Russia to escape the grim realities of the war. As a result, President Yeltsin's popularity dropped to an all-time low. A poll taken just before my arrival indicated only 6 percent of the population had confidence in his leadership, as opposed to 85 percent in 1991. Commentators noted that the struggle for political power was no longer between Yeltsin and the parliament, which had lost considerable power to the executive branch of government, but between the center (Moscow) and the regions.

MEANWHILE BACK IN THE STATES

I spent a considerable amount of time in Russia between early 1994 and the summer of 1995, traveling to Moscow seven times, and the eighteen participating coalition-member campuses of the Russian Initiative continued to increase their involvement in student and faculty exchange programs. By the spring of 1995, while RACU finally made progress with its new board of trustees and plans for the future, 51 percent of the ninety coalition members were engaged in exchanges. Another positive sign: nineteen member schools offered Russian-language courses, up from ten schools in the previous year.[12] Russia had become the educational hot spot on the globe.

Beginning July 1, 1994, I started working full time on the Russian Initiative, with the majority of my time spent on developing RACU while also managing the new Russian studies program, which provided full-credit semesters for American students to study in Russia. This entailed recruitment of students, raising funds, and ensuring the quality of its academic program. In addition, I continued my involvement with the Russian-American MBA program, partnering with Lynn Geiger from Eastern College on this work.

Meanwhile, RACU's board continued its search for a Russian Christian educator who understood Christian liberal arts, someone who could be the first president of the school; it identified no viable candidates. Because Christians had been denied access to higher education in the USSR, very few Russian Protestants had graduate degrees. While some Russian leaders knew about Bible colleges, few

---

[12]Coalition for Christian Colleges & Universities/The Russian Initiative, *Russia Link* (Spring 1995): 1-6, RA.

had any familiarity with RACU's mission to equip emerging young Christians for leadership roles in their society with a quality, faith-based liberal arts education.

RACU'S SURPRISING INDEPENDENCE

Following the decision by Myron Augsburger to step down as president of the Christian College Coalition on June 30, 1994, the board and its new president subsequently made the decision that RACU no longer fit the mission of the coalition and that its support would end when the three-year term of the Russian Initiative concluded on June 30, 1995. I was surprised by this decision, since it seemed to me that the Russian Initiative, and particularly its plans to establish RACU, brought increased credibility to the coalition.

When RACU's American trustees learned of the coalition board's decision to no longer support RACU, they scheduled an emergency meeting in Wheaton, Illinois, on May 10, 1995, and asked whether I would be willing to stay with this project long term. I knew the time had come for me to make such a decision because of my growing passion for this opportunity. Since joining the Christian Colleges Coalition in 1976 as founding director of the American Studies Program, our staff had challenged students to be agents of justice and reconciliation in our world, and we grounded our academic program in extensive study of biblical teachings on justice and *shalom*. I felt it was time for me to stop just teaching about this, leave the comfort of the classroom, and put my convictions to work. After four years of involvement in Russia, it seemed to be the right time and place for me to test the viability of my faith in the challenging context of Russia's struggle to emerge from seven decades of communist rule. I remember talking about this decision with my wife, Marge, and my children. My daughter Susan, who was often ready to share her opinion, said, "Dad, you have had opportunities to accept college presidencies in the States. Why would you become the president of a college with no students, no faculty, no campus, and no funding?" A good question.

The American trustees proposed that I be appointed interim president (rector) and chairman of the board. Since they shared responsibility with me for raising funds for RACU, they decided to make decisions about my salary and benefits and communicate them to the Russian trustees, who supported their recommendations and my two job titles.[13] To leave a salaried position with the coalition after

---

[13]John A. Bernbaum, "Meeting of RACU American Board Members (May 10, 1995)," 1-4, RA.

nineteen years and accept a new role with no guaranteed salary and the challenge of raising my own support was a major risk, especially with the costs of raising my large family, but I knew I had to do it. In the four years since the invitation to start RACU in October 1990, I had become convinced that this school had to be created and felt a clear calling to be a part of this project.[14]

The American trustees immediately proceeded with the establishment of a US nonprofit corporation for the purpose of handling donations to the school. A new US corporate board was established with six trustees: the three American trustees from RACU and three additional colleagues (Richard Gathro, a vice president of the coalition; James Priest, a lawyer from Oklahoma who handled the incorporation process; and Andrew Steer, an economist from the World Bank).[15] Unlike the battle that we were soon to face in Russia getting RACU registered and licensed with the Moscow city government, a process that took three years, the US organization became incorporated as RACU/U.S., Inc., in Oklahoma and received nonprofit status from the Internal Revenue Service within one year.[16]

By summer 1995, basic governance of RACU had been established, a small staff hired, and the first classes offered. Russian ownership of the school still presented a challenge because of the troubling political, economic, and social context in the country; no one was sure what lay ahead, and Yeltsin's radical drop in approval ratings worried many potential supporters. Growing anti-Western attitudes also caused some Russians to distance themselves from our bicultural school. Because of these concerns, the trustees knew that RACU was a high-risk operation, especially since no Christian liberal arts college had ever existed previously in Russia. Trust between Americans and Russians had to be earned after the rivalry of the Cold War years, and we wanted the school to be a means to build long-term relationships with Russian partners and future faculty and students. The year 1995 marked the beginning of RACU's independence. With the foundation laid, the time to start building the school had come.

---

[14]During this critical time, I sought the advice of three coalition presidents whose schools were participants in the Russian Initiative, and they made it clear their schools would continue their partnerships with RACU. In addition, key advisers and friends enthusiastically encouraged me to take on this challenge, including Bill Pollard, John Dellenback, Dennis Bakke, and Ralph Veerman; many of them felt that separating RACU from the coalition was a positive development, and this proved to be true.

[15]The first meeting of RACU/U.S., Inc., took place on May 19, 1995. RACU/U.S., Inc., "Minutes of the Incorporators," 1-2, RA.

[16]James Priest handled the incorporation of RACU/U.S., Inc., in Oklahoma, where he served as an attorney, and the IRS granted 501(c)(3) status to the corporation on June 14, 1996.

10

LEARNING TOGETHER AND TELLING THE TRUTH

By spring 1995, RACU was no longer just an idea; it was up and running. With a small staff and office in place, an engaged binational board of trustees, and free evening classes generating interest in the school, RACU created exciting momentum. One of the most important factors at this stage of RACU's development was the relationship with the leadership of Russian Peoples' Friendship University. While the staff's efforts were unsuccessful in finding a campus facility, largely because of the economic instability in Russia, the Christian College Coalition's Russian-American MBA Project initiated key partnerships with Russian Peoples' Friendship University's business faculty and its top leadership. Partnering with this respected university gave RACU credibility, and our friendship with its well-known rector, Vladimir Filippov, and vice rector, Nicolai Trofimov, added strength to our initial reputation. Both of these leaders played important roles in RACU's launch.

In this opening phase of the school's development, we sought counsel from many sources about how to handle a startup operation in the Russian context. We talked with Western business leaders whom we met through the US-Russia Business Council and at various churches in Moscow that I attended. We also sought advice from Christian leaders in a wide range of Protestant churches and parachurch organizations who learned about the school. In addition, Western missionaries, who earlier showed little support for the establishment of RACU, slowly became more cooperative as they saw that RACU could help educate their staff and train them in English. In addition, several of my students from the

American studies program joined the foreign service and were assigned to the embassy in Moscow; their briefings about developments in Russia were very helpful. They shared lessons they learned from the experiences of the seventeen thousand Americans living in Moscow in the early 1990s.[1]

These insights were valuable since working crossculturally is always difficult, and deepening our understanding of the Russian culture was an important key during the first few years of work in Moscow.[2] The advice we received included:

- This is one market where the cliché of "putting a toe in the water" makes great sense. Start small.

- Stay focused on your core mission and avoid pursuing additional programs that take you away from your basic mission.

- Produce a quality product.

- Find Russian partners in whom you have confidence and then let them take the lead in the Russian marketplace.

- Keep a low profile and avoid newspaper and television coverage; you do not want to attract unwanted attention, especially in the early stages of development.

- Be a good citizen of the community and demonstrate your concern for your neighbors.

- Don't expect anything to happen quickly.

- Nothing is as it seems in Russia—so be wise and discerning and learn to read between the lines.

- "TIR" ("This is Russia") was often heard from Westerners, and it is a re-minder that things work differently in this culture, so flexibility is the key.

- "The ten factor" means that everything takes ten times longer to accom-plish in Russia than in the States. Get used to it and relax!

Russia is a low-trust society, so people cannot simply fly in, meet Russians, and sign deals. They must know the people they are dealing with, and this takes time

---

[1]John A. Bernbaum, "Trip Report to Moscow (June 18–July 1, 1994)," 8, RA.

[2]The counsel we received on how to work in Russia is described in numerous trip reports to Moscow that I compiled during 1994 and 1995; these trip reports can be found in "Moscow Trip Reports (1994–1998)," notebook #2, RA.

as each party learns to trust the other and determine whether their counterparts are reliable. It became clear that networking was of critical importance and, as a Russian-American school, we were encouraged to use all the contacts we had with the US Embassy and international businesses headquartered in Moscow.[3]

GETTING LEGAL

The first step for RACU required getting registered in Moscow as a legal entity. While this might sound like it would be a simple process, one of our first lessons in the reality of our task taught us that nothing in Russia is simple. Because Russia had no history of private educational institutions, no laws were in place to govern this process in the early 1990s. In June 1994, the board of trustees decided to ask the staff to draft a charter and bylaws and then seek support from Vladimir Kinelev, the chairman of the State Committee on Higher Education, who had initially invited us to start a Christian college in Moscow in October 1990. This followed advice offered by Trofimov: "Learn to do things the Russian way—if you know the top leader in the agency from which you need approval, go right to him and skip all the bureaucrats!"[4]

A number of important academic issues began to emerge, and we needed the counsel of Christian educators. Through my work at the Christian College Coalition, I had become friends with Stanley and Susan Clark. Susan had developed a passion for learning Russian and had spent hours studying Russian while doing household chores. At the time she had no connection with Russia and no explanation for this passion. Susan's interest in Russia rubbed off on Stanley, who served as vice president for academic affairs at Tabor College in Hillsboro, Kansas. They had shared with me their growing interest in Russia, so they immediately became an obvious choice when we needed assistance. Stanley agreed to travel to Moscow with me in June 1994, and I thought his fourteen years as a dean would be helpful as we began to develop RACU's academic program. I asked for his assistance in drafting an academic catalog, in creating a class schedule, and in establishing hiring criteria for faculty, both American and Russian.

Stanley and I also went to work on drafting a new charter that fit the vision for RACU. He did the bulk of the work, and together we submitted it to the

---

[3]These insights are recorded in my trip reports from 1993–1995, RA.
[4]Bernbaum, "Trip Report to Moscow (June 18–July 1, 1994)," 4.

American Working Group for its input before presenting it to the board of trustees in October 1994. After careful review of the new draft charter, which had been translated into Russian and sent out to all board members in advance of the meeting, the binational board unanimously approved it with one amendment stating that the board be composed of an equal number of Russians and Americans, a fifty-fifty balance. Without a legal address, however, the charter could not be submitted to the government for approval.[5]

After extensive negotiations with the leadership of Russian Peoples' Friendship University, we were able to negotiate the use of their school as RACU's legal address. It took another two years to complete the registration process for RACU as a nongovernmental (private) educational institution. This sobering process cost many hours of work and thousands of dollars in legal fees. We repeatedly refused to pay bribes to government officials who insisted they could not help us register the school unless we paid for the extra work required of them. As noted earlier, setting up a new corporation in the States and securing IRS approval for it to operate as a tax-exempt organization took one year. The same process in Russia took RACU three years.

RUSSIA'S POLITICAL STALEMATE

During spring and summer 1995, as RACU's evening classes and the summer English-language institute attracted its first students, the political climate in Russia, especially in Moscow, became increasingly turbulent. Dissatisfaction with the young reformers and fallout from the currency collapse of October 1994, as well as the unpopular war against Chechnya, continued to complicate life for the average Russian citizen. Some commentators argued that events indicated a growing weariness in Russian society as individuals began to think only of themselves and their survival.[6]

Yeltsin's failing health was another concern. In July 1995 he suffered a heart attack, and newspapers produced numerous stories about his pending resignation. One Russian journalist said, "In five years [since 1991], he has aged twenty years."[7]

---

[5]RACU board of trustees, "Record of Meeting (October 18, 1994)," 3-4, RA.
[6]Lilia Shevtsova, *Yeltsin's Russia: Myths and Reality* (Washington, DC: Carnegie Endowment for International Peace, 1999), 117-19.
[7]Jean MacKenzie, "Heart Trouble Puts Yeltsin in Hospital," *Moscow Times*, July 12, 1995, 1-2.

BUILDING RACU'S STAFF

Jay Shanor's one-year term of service as RACU's administrator ended in summer 1995, and we needed to find a replacement. The initial work that Stanley Clark did for RACU in the fall of 1994 with the charter captured his imagination, and the board learned that both Stanley and Susan Clark were willing to accept leadership positions at RACU beginning in July 1995. The board enthusiastically approved their appointment as the school's first full-time American staff members in Moscow. Stanley agreed to serve as RACU's vice president for academic affairs, while Susan accepted the position as director of personnel and community relations, a position she had previously held at Tabor College.[8]

LET'S TEACH ENGLISH!

During this early phase of RACU, while monitoring the political situation in Moscow, we studied the establishment of other international private schools, especially Christian institutions, and found there was much to learn from Lithuania Christian College, located in the city of Klaipeda. Mary Dueck, who developed and directed the Intensive English Language Program at Fresno Pacific College (Fresno, California) for ten years and also directed and taught the first English-language institute at Lithuania Christian College, heard about RACU, and we began a dialogue with her and her husband, Henry. We were thrilled to receive a proposal from the Duecks in July 1994 recommending that RACU organize a four-week English-language institute, preceded by a one-week orientation for teachers and placement testing. Lithuania Christian College had sponsored institutes like this, and they immediately generated student interest in the school and brought credibility to their academic program because of the quality of the instruction offered. They proposed an institute for up to 130 students with twelve faculty members who would teach five hours a day in one of four or five proficiency levels. The original proposal outlined morning sessions that included reading and writing, listening and speaking, and grammar. Afternoon elective courses would cover a diversity of topics, including "Literature of the Bible," "Family and Society," and "An Introduction to Business," as well as sessions on the Test of English as a Foreign Language (TOEFL) examination and American idioms, both of which were very popular with the students. These classes for university-level students were priced at $100 for one hundred

---

[8]RACU board of trustees, "Record of Meeting (February 16, 1995)," 1, RA.

Figure 10.1. English Language Institute faculty and staff on Russian People's Friendship University's campus (June 1995).

hours of instruction.[9] The board quickly endorsed this proposal and asked the Duecks to give leadership to the institute; they agreed.

When I contacted RACU's partner colleges and universities in the States to recruit faculty who would be willing to teach in the institute as volunteers, with RACU providing lodging and basic meal costs, encouraging responses poured in. With excitement, I reported to the board in February 1995 that fifteen highly qualified faculty members had been chosen for the volunteer teaching positions.[10] With an excellent teaching team, under the expert leadership of the Duecks, we knew that the faculty would present a positive impression of what RACU would be like. Arranging for visas and housing, organizing taxi pickups at the airport, and finalizing the details of the institute, including plans for lunches and special assemblies, created a heavy load for RACU's small staff, but all of us were delighted to be welcoming American faculty to Moscow and partnering with them to offer a quality language program.[11]

---

[9]Christian College Coalition, "ESL Faculty Needed!," *Russia Link* (Fall 1994): 4, RA.
[10]For the list of English-language institute faculty for July–August 1995, see appendix E.
[11]"English Language Institute Daily Journal and Trip Report (June–August 1995)," 38, RA.

After a three-day orientation program for our faculty to introduce them to life in Russia and cultural patterns that they needed to understand, the registration process for students wanting to attend the English-language institute took place on July 8. After filling out registration forms, students took written and oral tests to determine the level of instruction that fit their ability. A total of eighty students enrolled in RACU's first English-language institute—fewer than we expected but plenty to fill our classes.

The opening session of the English-language institute proved to be exciting. After Zaichenko and I, as heads of the Russian and American trustees, had the chance to greet our students, Mary Dueck took the microphone and told the students two things: "We want to be your friends, and we will learn more from you than you will learn from us as your instructors!" What revolutionary talk. I do not think any Russian faculty members ever opened their class with such a statement. Dueck spoke correctly. The faculty befriended their students and learned much from them about their life in Russia. This was exactly the kind of campus climate that RACU wanted to build. In the introductory meeting, Dueck introduced each faculty member and asked each to come to the blackboard and show the audience where they lived in the States by drawing their home state in the outline map of the United States we had drawn on the beat-up blackboard, a tactic we used earlier in the Russian-American MBA Project when we first met our Russian colleagues. Then, with the faculty on the stage, the Americans sang "God Bless America," followed by "God Bless Russia." The students responded enthusiastically.

After ten days of classes, our first institute assembly took place, hosted by James Wilkens. The program included a song sung in English by the beginners class, a reading of Psalm 103 by several faculty members, another song in English by the intermediate class ("John Brown's Car Has a Hole in the Tire") with all of the hand signals, a hilarious skit by the faculty titled "Amerikanskis on the Metro" (which poked fun at American tourists), and finally several songs by our male faculty quartet. I had the privilege of making some remarks and closing with prayer. Close friends of the Duecks attended the assembly and said to me, "We can't believe the rapport you've developed with these people in eight days! They probably never had teachers who cared for them as friends like this."[12]

---

[12]"English Language Institute Daily Journal," 67-68. Many similar insights from Deyneka were confirmed by Russian pastors, who also stressed the poor quality and training of Protestant leaders and the disunity that characterized Protestant denominations. "English Language Institute Daily Journal," 125.

The weekly assemblies for the students were one of the highlights of the four-week institute. Programs were organized by guest faculty with the assistance of the Russian students and usually involved serious devotional topics, along with lighthearted skits and songs. They were usually followed by receptions with drinks, cookies, cakes, and lots of balloons; they also served as a productive time for the students to practice their conversational English skills. The same positive atmosphere appeared evident with the Russian English-language teachers, who grew close to their American teachers as well. The spirit of RACU's guest faculty was remarkable and encouraged us as we discussed the future plans for the school. The graduation ceremony and the granting of formal certificates was an experience treasured by the students, since most of them had never participated in a formal academic ceremony.

RACU'S EARLY LEADERSHIP DECISIONS

The six meetings of the board of trustees in 1994–1995 laid the foundation for RACU, and many fundamental decisions about RACU's mission and role were largely settled.[13] The trustees made clear that they wanted me to serve as interim president until a qualified Russian educator could be found. While I agreed to accept this responsibility, I knew I had some difficult decisions to make about how I would divide my time between the United States and Russia. Because Peter Deyneka faced the same issue as president of Deyneka Russian Ministries, he helped me figure out how to handle this dilemma. We talked for hours about how to manage my presidency, since I needed to raise funds and recruit American faculty in the States while also overseeing the program in Moscow, which included building relationships with Russian leaders in government, business, and Protestant, Orthodox, and Catholic churches.

The first major decision we made was that I would follow Deyneka's example and make trips between Washington, DC, and Moscow, often three to five times per year. This decision to commute to Moscow meant I needed to find an apartment in Moscow rather than to continue asking Moscow friends to house me or renting expensive Moscow hotel rooms. I needed a home in Moscow if I was going to spend substantial time in the city.

---

[13]For a record of these discussions by the board of trustees, see the reports on their meetings in 1994–2004 in the "RACU Board Minutes (1992–2004)" notebook, RA.

Figure 10.2. RACU's first board of trustees and staff (April 1996). Pictured in back row: Vladimir Obrovets, Anita Deyneka, Peter Deyneka, Yuri Apatov, and John Bernbaum. Pictured in front row: Stanley Clark, Susan Clark, and Alexander Zaichenko. Absent: Mark Elliott and Evgeny Goncharenko.

A second fundamental issue concerned whether I should take two years to learn Russian and how this decision might affect my ability to serve as the institute's president. Peter Deyneka recommended that I not take the time needed to learn Russian because my leadership was needed now and we did not know how long this opportunity to establish RACU would last. He believed strongly that a wiser choice would be to use the services of translators. My graduate languages were German and French, and German especially came in handy several times in Russia. On numerous occasions I questioned this decision, but with time I gradually began to pick up common Russian phrases and had little problem moving around Moscow. I found that Russian government officials often enjoyed speaking English with me to demonstrate their language skills, and despite the quality of their English, it was better than my Russian!

A third decision was also clear to me. By late 1994 and early 1995, I knew I had to immerse myself in studying developments in Russia in order to give leadership to RACU. My lack of Russian-language competence was partially compensated by news sources, such as *Johnson's Russia List*, which became my required daily reading. Hardly a day went by when I did not read up on Russia. In an effort to educate RACU's trustees, which as a college teacher I felt compelled to do, I began writing two-page essays on Russian history, culture, literature, music, and religion. This practice required me to integrate the information I was reading and led me to draft popularized commentaries for distribution to RACU's board of trustees and advisers and increasingly to RACU's supporters. I carefully avoided any commentary on contemporary political issues, because I assumed anything I wrote would appear in my file maintained by Russia's enormous security services.[14]

A fourth key decision related to building a Christian liberal arts college in Moscow focused on choosing to train laity, rather than being a Bible college or seminary for training pastors and church workers, for which many people advocated during the formative years. As Peter Deyneka reported earlier, many Bible colleges and institutes existed in the former Soviet Union. An impressive number of them were built in the early 1990s. But no Christian educational institutions existed to train business leaders, economists, social workers, counselors, translators, or schoolteachers. These were the majors that our Russian trustees requested, so they became the first academic departments in our college. However, because RACU was a liberal arts institution, an academic entity largely unknown in Russia, with a substantial general education core, RACU students would also graduate with three minors in addition to their major field of study: a minor in the English language, which meant they would be bilingual; a minor in information technology with substantial computer skills and knowledge of various software programs; and a minor in theology with a strong emphasis on ethics and biblical morality. We were convinced that this program would make them very attractive to potential employers, and this proved to be true from the beginning of the school.

The fifth major decision focused on how to build a private educational institution, independent of federal funding from either the US government or the Russian government. Some Christians working in Russia advised us to register the school as a religious organization, since that would lead to less government regulation because theological schools were not of interest to the authorities. Our decision not to follow this advice proved to be a wise one, as pressure on foreign religious organizations in Russia continued to build in the mid-1990s. Being

---

[14]Beginning in February 1994 and continuing through June 2012, I wrote 140 "Reflections on Russia." These essays are accessible at BEAM-inc.org.

independent of either government also had critical importance because we sensed that our school would be identified by Russian xenophobic organizations as a CIA plant or tool of the American White House. Not accepting any federal funding from the Russian government was important because we knew with this funding would come interference and direction from government agencies. From my point of view, a private Christian college represented an example of the kind of democratic entities that Russia needed after its seventy years of hierarchical Communist Party control.

The sixth and final decision by the trustees in 1995 related to building a school that would not be affiliated with any specific Protestant denomination, even though all of our Russian trustees during this early period were Baptists. With increasing clarity the trustees learned that the active Christian community, measured by weekly church attendance in Russia in the mid-1990s, was less than 2 percent of the population, so they decided to accept students into RACU from a wide range of Protestant, Catholic, and Orthodox churches.[15] Once they were accepted, our goal was to encourage students to understand and respect each other because mutual respect between groups of people from different faiths was missing in Russia. At times when I wondered about this decision, especially after being approached by three Protestant denominations who promised to build us a campus if RACU became their denominational institution, but looking back I am convinced the board made the right choice.

AN EARLY ASSESSMENT OF RACU'S FUTURE

By the time the English-language institute ended and our guest faculty members returned home, the staff knew this initial stage of RACU had been a successful one. For a school with no facilities of its own, no full-time faculty, and a limited budget, we knew we faced enormous challenges in a difficult environment. However, we knew that RACU, once a vision, was slowly becoming a reality. For me, the desire to help educate Christian young people whose parents had been denied higher education because of their faith became my passion. I wanted to

---

[15]During the early 1990s, survey data reported that weekly church attendance was no more than 2 percent, even though interest in religion generally increased. Current research has documented that church attendance in Russia never grew to more than 9 percent (1998). "Russians Return to Religion, But Not to Church," Pew Research Center, February 10, 2014, 1-9, www.pewforum.org/2014/02/10/russians-return -to-religion-but-not-to-church/.

see young Russian Christians educated in business and economics, social work and counseling, literature and linguistics, equipped with the skills to become leaders in their country. Our staff had no interest in giving them a vision for making their country like the United States; in fact, we encouraged them to rediscover their own rich history, particularly the deep spirituality that still permeated their culture, despite efforts by Marxists to eliminate it.

Suzanne Massie wrote a startling essay in the *Washington Post* that expressed many of the concerns I had for Russia by 1994–1995. She made this observation:

> During twenty years of regular visits to the old Soviet Union, I read daily vilifications of the United States. The propaganda failed; I never heard a hostile word about America from ordinary Russian folk. . . . What the Communists failed to do in seventy-four years, we accomplished in three. Today Russians identify us with the "money disease" that has swept their country, bringing greed and crime in its wake. They call it "*bucksi.*"

Massie described how Americans had espoused the market economy as a panacea for all of Russia's woes and had dismissed the Russians' passionate search for identity and their striving to gather the strength of religion. Meanwhile, Russians were deluged with the worst of America: B-rated movies, old soap operas, images of violence, sex, and materialism.[16]

I shared Massie's insights and hoped that RACU would be an educational program that built up young Russian people with a constructive vision for the future of their country—young people of strong moral character who had a desire to live out their Christian faith in their homes, churches, and the marketplace, as RACU's mission statement put it. The spring classes and the summer English-language institute in mid-1995 encouraged us in this direction.

---

[16]Suzanne Massie, "To the Russian People, We're Ugly Americans," *Washington Post*, December 31, 1993, A21.

11

A NEW WAY TO EDUCATE

ANOTHER SURPRISING OPPORTUNITY

ON AUGUST 18, 1995, PETER DEYNEKA CALLED to tell me that five evangelical organizations were in the process of signing a contract to build a two-story office building attached to a large apartment building in southwest Moscow. His organization, Deyneka Russian Ministries, was involved with four other groups in constructing the building. Located across the street from the large Gazprom complex, Russia's huge natural gas conglomerate, the building occupied a good, safe location also convenient to the Metro. Deyneka said one of the five partners was considering backing out of the contract because of financial constraints and asked whether RACU would be interested in becoming a minority partner by purchasing a 9 percent share of the new office building. Deyneka estimated the purchase price to be $100 per square meter, so a hundred square meters would cost around $100,000.[1] This price was a good one, although the Moscow real estate market was beginning to accelerate.

With the potential provided by this new construction project, Deyneka's offer brought an enormous boost to the life of RACU. This opportunity would create enough space for several offices and two classrooms as well as possible use of New Life Bible College's three classrooms in the evenings. Our staff and board expressed immediate excitement about the surprising offer, and when we learned that the fifth partner had confirmed the decision to withdraw, we knew we faced an immediate challenge. Where would we secure the funds to pay for this entry into the construction partnership? Additional complications also emerged.

---

[1]John A. Bernbaum, notes from conversation with Peter Deyneka, August 18, 1995, CMC.

Because RACU was not yet legally registered and its charter was still not approved by the Moscow city government, RACU could not be a signer on the construction contract. Deyneka subsequently said that his organization, one of the two major partners in this purchase, along with New Life Russia (Campus Crusade for Christ in Russia), was willing to sign on RACU's behalf and would draft a contract with us to settle the terms.[2]

This unexpected and generous opportunity provided many positive benefits. In addition to RACU having its own office space and classrooms, being a member of the partnership included shared use of the cafeteria, which could also be used as an auditorium; a shared library; and a main reception area with controlled access to the building. Another positive effect came with the cross-fertilization and support from staff members of the other four ministries, all of which had considerably more expertise and experience working in Russia. While purchasing a small share of the office building was not a long-term answer to RACU's space needs, the arrangement would provide a stable base from which to grow the school. Escalating prices in Moscow indicated we should be able to easily recover our investment when we outgrew the facility. The total price for RACU's 150 square meters (1,500 square feet) was anticipated to be $95,000, of which $35,000 was due immediately, with the remainder due by February 1, 1996.[3] Should we and could we do this?

Telephone calls to RACU's trustees and to potential donors, both individuals and foundations, offered encouraging responses. In the judgment of almost everyone, this was an opportunity that should be pursued. The three American trustees, Peter Deyneka, Mark Elliott, and I, agreed about moving forward with this opportunity. We knew that responsibility for raising the funds would rest with us, not our Russian trustees. We decided to start fundraising immediately and make preparations for a formal vote of the board of trustees at the fall meeting in October. In the meantime, Stanley Clark spoke with our Russian trustees about the offer and reported that both he and Susan Clark "were feeling very good" about the building purchase, and so were the Russian trustees. Alexander Zaichenko made clear in his comments that this investment in Russia was a clear sign of the board's commitment to an ongoing ministry and, unlike many

---

[2]John A. Bernbaum, notes from conversation with Peter Deyneka, August 29, 1995, CMC.
[3]John A. Bernbaum, memorandum, "An Exciting Opportunity for RACU," September 29, 1995, CMC.

other Christian groups who came to Russia but left shortly thereafter, RACU was here to stay.[4]

In the fall of 1995, the Mustard Seed Foundation, the Jubilee Fund of the Herman Miller Company, and Stewardship Foundation stepped up with grants that allowed us to meet the tight deadlines and exceeded our wildest expectations. Raising money this quickly was not like any of my earlier fundraising experiences. With construction of the two-story office building scheduled to begin in October 1995 and estimated to be finished by March 1996, RACU would have ample time to move in and prepare for the formal opening of the new 1996–1997 school year.[5]

Once the board decided to seize this offer, we were concerned about our status in the building because RACU was not a legal partner and therefore did not sign the construction contract. Assurances from the leadership of Deyneka Russian Ministries in Moscow, headed by George Law, made it clear, however, that we would be invited to attend the meetings of the partners and would be able to share our perspectives on building-related issues, which proved to be a big task during the next twelve months. Stanley Clark was a regular attendee of these partner meetings, and I attended enough of them to know I was grateful not to be in Moscow for most of them. The tension between the two American-based partners (Deyneka Russian Ministries and New Life Russia) and the two Russian-based ministries (Child Evangelism Fellowship and Russian Christian Radio) was often high, especially when the American organizations wanted to invest in upgrades to the facility, which were usually opposed by the Russians. However, the advantages of sharing this facility far outweighed the difficulties because it encouraged cooperation between ministries that otherwise would have never connected. Translators were shared, advice on how to deal with government officials was given by those with experience, and money was saved with the shared use of a receptionist and security guards. This two-story building, even though it was modest from an American perspective, was a source of pride for Protestants because it was the first building of its kind since the Bolshevik Revolution of 1917.

---

[4]Stanley Clark, "Weekly Report," September 22, 1995, RA.
[5]"Foundation and Corporation Donors: Summary Report (1995-2003)," October 21, 2002, RACU Foundation Grants, RA.

AGREEMENT ON RACU'S UNIQUE EDUCATIONAL PROGRAM

On October 23, 1995, the board of trustees met in Moscow and enthusiastically endorsed the purchase of the space in the newly named Christian Ministry Center. As the meeting progressed, it was clear that the board was increasingly taking ownership of the school.[6] The other major board discussion focused on the draft charter and foundation agreement, written primarily by Stanley Clark. After a careful review by the board, the draft charter and a number of editorial changes were agreed on by consensus. A short signing ceremony was held to commemorate the occasion.[7]

The two-hour discussion about the charter and foundation agreement provided an opportunity for the board to review the mission of RACU, its governance and structure, the similarities and differences with Russian state educational institutions, and the uniqueness of the new binational institution we were attempting to build. The American Working Group and its members that became RACU's first trustees were initially thinking that we would work with our Russian colleagues to start the school and then over time turn it over to them. But in the early board meetings, the Russian trustees made it clear that they wanted the school to remain a binational institution that would continue to serve as a bridge between Christians in both countries.

This healthy exchange solidified agreement among the trustees and, together with the news of a new campus home, increased everyone's excitement about the school's future.[8] The board was also united on the qualities and skills that RACU was committed to develop in its graduates:

- bilingual fluency in Russian and English;

- computer competency;

- an understanding of the free market and democratic values and institutions;

- a grounding in ethical and biblical values and developing lives of integrity; and

- preparation for the marketplace through serving as interns in their intended professional fields.

[6]RACU Board of Trustees minutes, October 20, 1995, RBM.
[7]RACU Board of Trustees minutes, "Record of Meeting (October 20, 1995)," 1-2, RBM.
[8]John A. Bernbaum, "Saturday Morning Report," October 21, 1995, 1, Chron File, RA.

The board was being pressured to offer special programs articulated by some Christian leaders, but it renewed its commitment to building a faith-based liberal arts undergraduate program, beginning with two academic departments: (1) business and economics and (2) social work and counseling, with a third department in English language and literature in the near future.[9]

Building on the experience of the spring semester, RACU offered four courses in fall 1995 at the downtown campus of Russian Peoples' Friendship University, and forty students enrolled.[10] Meanwhile, I focused my attention on fundraising for our new campus base in the Christian Ministry Center and faculty recruitment for the opening of the first full year of RACU's undergraduate program, in September 1996, while the Clarks searched for both Russian professors and American missionaries in Moscow to join our faculty. In addition, work continued to get the school registered and licensed. We also prioritized faculty recruitment for the second English-language institute, scheduled for July 1996, and were thrilled when Carolyn Dirksen agreed to serve as director. She had considerable experience in this field, having taught English in China, Vietnam, and Ukraine, and had worked together with Mary Dueck on the first institute, so she knew the challenges and opportunities we faced.

During the winter and early spring months of 1995–1996, while Russians were focused on the parliamentary elections in December and the upcoming presidential election in June, the RACU staff carefully monitored the progress of construction of the Christian Ministry Center. Numerous delays occurred, and the Russian contractors refused to take responsibility for them. In addition, costs escalated as the Moscow real estate market heated up. Some commentators described these developments as "capitalism in one city" as opposed to capitalism taking hold across the vast country of eleven time zones. A growing economic gap separated the prosperous center (Moscow) from the increasingly impoverished periphery.

By the time I landed in Moscow and visited the site of our new office building with RACU's vice president, Stanley Clark, I was encouraged to see the roof completed and workers starting on the inside. However, skyrocketing prices for concrete and building supplies were driving up the costs for the five partners, and

---

[9]John A. Bernbaum, "Discussion of RACU Issues with the Clarks," October 28, 1995, Chron File, RA.

[10]The fall 1995 courses offered by RACU were the following: Eugene Grossman, Christian Apologetics; Mark Elliott, Christianity in Russia Since 1985; Stanley Clark, Introduction to Sociology; and Ron Brunson, New Testament Survey.

this was hard to explain to RACU's donors. What started out as an investment of $95,000 for 150 square meters (1,500 square feet) increased to $167,000 by December 1995 and then to $181,000 by April 1996. By the time it was finished, all the utilities were installed, and an adjacent parking lot was purchased, RACU's cost had reached $220,500. These radical price increases were happening all over Moscow, and our experience was not unusual. When we considered the price increases and saw the disappointing quality of workmanship on the exterior, our only consolation was the contractor's word that the inside work would be up to "Western standards." That, of course, remained to be seen.[11]

MAKING NEW FRIENDS

Networking and developing friendships in Moscow was a high priority for me and the RACU staff. One new friendship that developed at this time was a complete surprise. Back in February 1996, Marge and I hosted five Russians who were in Washington, DC, to attend the National Prayer Breakfast. One of our guests was Vladimir Platonov, chairman of the Moscow City Council (Duma) and a member of the upper house of the parliament, the Federation Council. We had a marvelous time with our guests, and they thoroughly enjoyed shoveling snow off our driveway and sidewalk and then completely around the house. They had never shoveled snow before and wanted to keep going! After a week and many good discussions and shopping ventures, we became good friends.

When I arrived in Moscow the following month, I called Platonov, and he arranged for his driver to pick me up and bring me down to the Moscow Duma for a tour and lunch. He asked about RACU, and I told him about our struggles getting registered and licensed. He immediately picked up the phone, called friends who were leading lawyers in Moscow, and told them, "Let's get this taken care of." A meeting was scheduled with the lawyers for the next day. This appeared to be yet another marvelous example of the hospitality Russians extended to those who became their friends.[12]

During this same trip to Moscow, I made other new friends, but this time they were Americans. About a month before my trip, Frank Roberts from Calvin College called me and said that two Christian businessmen from Milwaukee were

---

[11]John A. Bernbaum, "Notes on the Chronology of Costs—CMC File," July 31, 1997, 1-2, CMC.
[12]John A. Bernbaum to staff and trustees, "Insights from Life in Moscow," March 29, 1996, 2-3, Chron Files, RA.

going to Moscow as guest lecturers from the college, a part of Calvin College's expanding relationship with Russian Peoples' Friendship University. This relationship grew out of the Russian-American MBA project, which was a part of the coalition's Russian Initiative, and both schools agreed to send lecturers to the other's campus. Roberts encouraged me to call them, volunteer to escort them when they were in Moscow, and set up a dinner with Russian Christian businessmen, which I subsequently did, with the help of Alexander Zaichenko and his Association of Christian Businessmen.

My first meeting with Dennis Kuester and Milt Kuyers was on March 31, and after hearing the stories of their guest rooms in the international dorm at Russian Peoples' Friendship University, where our English-language institute faculty stayed the previous summer, I knew they were delightful men. Dennis described his room, where the average temperature was fifty-five degrees, while Milt's room was eighty-five degrees, but they laughed it off. They also described their first attempt at jogging near the university and being chased by guard dogs. Kuester commented that he was not worried. "I just had to run faster than Kuyers!" he said. After a visit to the Moscow Bible Church and time spent shopping at Izmailova Park, often referred to as Europe's largest flea market, we headed back to our apartments, struggling with a heavy snowfall and blustery winds. The two still had no complaints, just lots of laughs.

After lectures in various classes at Russian Peoples' Friendship University and a good dinner meeting at the Radisson Hotel with Russian Christian businessmen, I remember visiting with them just before they left Moscow. Kuyers said to me, "Dennis and I will each be sending you a check for $1,000 to help with expenses at RACU." I was very grateful for the gift, but the memory makes me laugh because both men subsequently became wise counselors and major donors of RACU over the next ten years. On my first visit to Milwaukee to follow up on our time in Moscow, I entered Kuester's huge office at M&I Bank, where he served as president, and his first words were, "How much do I have to give you so I don't have to go back to Moscow!" He had no idea how many times he and Kuyers would be in Moscow during the next decade, attending RACU graduations and meetings of the board of trustees.[13]

---

[13]John A. Bernbaum to Marge Bernbaum, "Sunday Night Report" and "Monday Night Report," March 31, 1996, and April 2, 1996, 1, 3, Chron Files, RA. These initial experiences in Moscow were repeatedly discussed over the years between the three of us.

RUSSIA'S ECONOMIC VOLATILITY AND THE
PRESIDENTIAL ELECTION OF 1996

While construction continued at RACU's new campus site, the pending presidential election on June 16, 1996, heightened nervousness because this was the first presidential election in postcommunist Russia. As one Russian analyst noted,

> There is nothing in Russia's political culture or traditions that leads one to easily imagine a peaceful, voluntary transfer of power. In a thousand years of Russian history, power has changed hands through assassination, palace plot, death in office and popular uprising, but never by elections and never by compromise. No czar or Communist general secretary ever gave up power by his own volition.[14]

This was the sober reality of life in postcommunist Russia.

The June election, with another substantial voter turnout of just under 70 percent, resulted in Yeltsin's first-place vote, with over 35 percent, and Zyuganov in second, with 32 percent. The runoff between the two winners in the first round took place on July 3, which Yeltsin won with almost 54 percent of the vote to Zyuganov's 40 percent; 5 percent voted against both candidates. The defeat of the Communist Party candidate was encouraging, but the challenges facing the re-elected president, Boris Yeltsin, were not going away.

LET'S TEACH ENGLISH AGAIN!

During spring and early summer 1996, while Russians were focused on the presidential election, the RACU staff was preoccupied with plans for the second English-language institute, scheduled to begin on July 3 and, like the previous summer, to be held on the impressive main campus of Russian Peoples' Friendship University. The goal was to offer one hundred hours of intensive language instruction for approximately 120 students and 20 Russian English-language teachers. The request for volunteer faculty from Christian College Coalition schools again resulted in an impressive team of eight skilled language teachers and three additional recruits who agreed to support them.[15]

Susan Clark reported that during one of the first days of registration for the English-language institute she arrived at Russian Peoples' Friendship University and met a man standing outside, waiting to enter the building. When she asked

---

[14]Quoted by Lee Hockstader, "The Vote Yeltsin Won't Lose," *Washington Post*, May 26, 1996.
[15]For a list of the English-language institute faculty for July–August 1996, see appendix E.

how long he had been waiting, he said, "For a little while." She found out later that he had traveled ten hours by overnight train in order to register for the English-language institute and would return home that night by another overnight train. That was a remarkable commitment to education, and we heard similar stories from other students who were drawn to the institute. By the time registration closed, 120 students and 7 Russian English language teachers had signed up for the institute, a 50 percent increase from the previous year.

On July 6 the students arrived on campus and handled waiting in lines to register like typical Russians, who waited in lines for everything, while our team worked frantically to get set up. The students were diverse in terms of ethnicity, age, and ability. After paying the fees and completing the registration forms, they were given oral exams by the faculty to determine class placement. Faculty interaction with the students and the students' warm response energized the teachers and impressed the rest of us.

Shortly after the beginning of classes, terrorists struck in Moscow two days in a row as buses exploded from bombs planted on them. Dozens of people were injured, as the bombs were detonated during the morning rush hour. Kremlin authorities immediately blamed Chechen terrorists, but no proof was immediately found.[16] The terrorist attacks set a sober mood in Moscow, but our location away from center city helped to give us some sense of safety.

Despite the heat, Stanley Clark had a remarkable experience in his afternoon seminar titled "Sociology of the City," a class available to any interested students and designed to show them the kind of classes to be held in RACU beginning in September. After forty-five minutes of class in a very hot classroom, Clark asked the class whether they wanted a break before the second half of the class began. No one moved. Finally one student asked, "Is the teacher tired?"

Clark said, "No."

The student responded, "Then let's continue."[17]

Clark said, "In all my years as a faculty member, this never happened to me."

I told our guest faculty, "These students are going to spoil you; you will not want to go back home when this four-week institute is over!" This was indeed the case, and many of our guest faculty later came back to Moscow to teach at RACU.

---

[16]Jennifer Rossa, "Bomb Rips Apart Bus in the Heart of City," *Moscow Tribune*, July 12, 1996; Lee Hockstader, "Blast Injures Dozens in Moscow," *Washington Post*, July 13, 1996.

[17]John A. Bernbaum, "Weekly Report," July 13, 1996, 1, Trip Notes from July 1996, President's Trip files, RA.

After reflecting on his experience in Moscow, James Vanden Bosch wrote:

> After forty years of teaching, I have never had a more gratifying season of teaching than I did in those two summers in Russia. I have never worked with more highly motivated students, or harder working ones, or more grateful students. It was common for students to thank us for the day's work at the end of every class. . . . On the day that we taught our final class at the Institute, many students wept, and the next day, after the closing ceremony and the distribution of certificates indicating the successful completion, they wept even more.[18]

Both Vanden Bosch and Carolyn Dirksen emphasized the struggles that these students experienced and how this affected them as their teachers. Dirksen noted that

> students were remarkable and interesting. We taught students across all levels of English language from novice to advanced, and each student presented challenges and opportunities. We met a family whose father had been imprisoned for years in Siberia, and we interacted daily with people who made immense sacrifices to be in the program. Economic adjustments at the end of the Soviet era made life difficult for many of our students, but they were hopeful that mastery of English would be a key for them.[19]

Vanden Bosch highlighted that

> our students were, in almost all instances, poor. Many of them worked full time at an education or a job during the week and then worked a part-time job at night and sometimes another part-time job on the weekends. Many of our students had one or two presentable sets of clothing to wear to a serious place like a university classroom, and they wore those clothes every day. Some of our students had a morning commute to campus of an hour or more, and then another commute home at the end of the day, and they typically did not show up late for class or leave early.[20]

Before the faculty left Moscow, we invited them to tour the RACU office in the apartment building near the Christian Ministry Center and then the center that was still under construction. Presumably the center was going to be ready to occupy by the beginning of the new school year, but this looked dubious with a walk through

[18]James Vanden Bosch, "Teaching in Moscow, 1996 and 1996," August 14, 2016, 5 English Language Institute files—Faculty Reflections, RA.
[19]Carolyn Dirksen, "RACU English Language Intensive, 1995–96," August 14, 2016, 2, English Language Institute files—Faculty Reflections, RA.
[20]James Vanden Bosch, "Teaching in Moscow, 1996 and 1996," August 14, 2016, 6, English Language Institute files—Faculty Reflections, RA.

Figure 11.1. Professor Jim Vanden Bosch's popular ELI class.

it. The building always left me with torn emotions. On the one hand, having our own facility to share with four other Christian ministries was a blessing and gave RACU some stability, although it was not a long-term solution; on the other hand, what we were getting for what we paid was depressing. Russian craftsmanship was so poor, especially on the exterior of the building, and the costs kept escalating.

The RACU staff was thoroughly impressed with our guest faculty. They were enjoying their courses and loved building friendships with the Russian students, who never before had faculty who cared for them like our faculty did, and the faculty also had productive staff meetings and were supportive of each other. If we could build a school with a faculty like this, it would be unmatched anywhere in Russia as far as I knew. Stanley Clark summarized both of our sentiments when he wrote in his weekly report, "It was a splendid institute, from start to finish, and the teachers brought great honor to RACU. The word is out: RACU offers quality Christian education."[21]

GETTING READY FOR OPENING DAY

The two summer English-language institutes, together with the evening courses offered for free in fall 1995 and spring 1996, were effective ways of marketing the

---

[21]Stanley Clark, "Weekly Report," August 4, 1996, 1, RA.

launch of RACU. While the second institute was under way, RACU finally received notification that it had been legally registered in the city of Moscow as a
"non-state educational institution." Our staff worked on this registration process
for several years, thinking that this was a simple first step in getting established,
but government officials were not interested in helping a new private Russian-
American school get started, especially since they knew very little about private
schools, and the laws kept changing as the government tried to keep up with all
of the changes occurring around them. Finally, the efforts paid off. Registration
gave RACU a legal face, with the right to hire staff, sign agreements, offer an
educational program, and enter the business mainstream, which also meant
paying taxes. RACU's charter had been accepted by the government, and RACU
became fully authorized to offer undergraduate, graduate, and professional educational programs. Gaining an educational license became our next goal, and we
were already working on all the documentation required. With registration complete and the charter approved, RACU could now openly advertise the beginning
of the fall program. The notifications were well-timed.[22]

When the institute ended in early August, the overwhelming question we
faced was whether the center would be finished in time for the beginning of the
school year on September 1, the traditional opening day for all schools in Russia.
One example of the challenges we faced related to the parking situated near our
building. We were encouraged to buy this piece of land or else we would find
residents of the apartment building linked to our office building occupying all of
the parking spaces, with no room for the staff of our five organizations. The
partnership began the process of buying the land and soon learned that we would
need approval of officials in thirty different agencies in Moscow. We eventually
purchased the land, but the process dragged on for months.[23]

When it became clear that the new center would not be ready for occupancy
by September 1, despite all of the promises, the staff scrambled to find a location
for the entrance examinations for new students and classroom space for the first
month or two of the school year. We learned from the leadership of New Life
Bible College that it rented classroom and office space in Moscow State University's Center for International Education, which was only one metro stop from

---

[22]Stanley Clark, "Weekly Report," June 29, 1996, 1, RA.
[23]John A. Bernbaum, "Tuesday Night Report," April 2, 1996, 1, Chron File 1995–1996, RA.

the Christian Ministry Center, and we were able to secure a contract with them for six weeks, although it meant we had to postpone the beginning of our academic year until September 7. After this was negotiated, we also made arrangements with the Russian Baptist Union to rent several rooms in their office building for entrance tests and oral interviews with new students. The pieces were falling into place, Russian style. We knew from the start that working in Russia required flexibility, so our Russian staff and the Clarks had shrugged their shoulders and gone out to find alternative arrangements that worked. The staff's response was: "This is a kingdom program, and we will find a way!"

12

RUSSIA'S GENERATION *NYET*

WHEN WE BEGAN TO RECRUIT for RACU's first classes, we faced a generation of twenty-year-olds who were an in-between generation, a generation caught in the transition between Marxism-Leninism and an unknown future. Commentators labeled them Generation *Nyet*, because for these young people the future of their country was bleak, and they expressed no interest in helping to change this. While many had confidence in their own personal futures, with reforms under way, they adopted a fatalism about the future of Russia in general and a hostility toward an ideology of any type. Their response was "No!" to any effort to mobilize them in support of societal change. Russian youth wanted to be left alone to "cultivate domestic gardens"—own some land and make a living, hopefully a good living, much better than what their parents knew.[1] By the mid-1990s, Russian young people had had enough of Boris Yeltsin, did not want a return to communism, and could find no viable alternatives. For them, escape from societal engagement was the only answer.[2]

As I reflected on this in-between generation, I was hopeful that RACU was going to be a novel experience for them and that it would prove to be a strong attraction, even for those surrounded by friends who felt fatalistic and hopeless in terms of their life in post-Soviet Russia.

RECRUITING RACU'S FIRST STUDENTS

The initial market for student recruitment at RACU was a small slice of Generation *Nyet*. RACU's priority recruits grew up in Christian families with parents

---

[1] John A. Bernbaum, "Russia's 'Generation X': Who Are They?," *Reflections on Russia* (July 1996): 1-2, Reflections on Russia file, RA. See also James H. Billington, *Russia: In Search of Itself* (Baltimore: Johns Hopkins University Press, 2004), 99.

[2] Alexander Bratersky, "Searching for the Future of 'Generation Nyet,'" *Moscow Times*, December 2, 1998.

and grandparents who had been denied access to higher education for decades because of their faith. The board of trustees wanted to equip youth from families marginalized by the Communist Party and prepare them for leadership in the new Russia. Until RACU was legally registered as an educational institution by the Moscow government, it was against the law for staff to openly advertise, so the only way to market the school was through the two summer English-language institutes in 1995 and 1996 and through the free evening classes offered in fall 1995 and spring 1996.

Students interested in applying for the first semester of classes, scheduled to begin in September 1996, often heard about the new school through their churches or pastors tied into Protestant networks that emerged in the late 1980s. Easy-to-find subway platforms often doubled as interview "rooms" with potential students who had inquired about applying. No public announcements were possible until RACU was legally registered, so the staff had to be careful. However, near the end of the lengthy registration process, some government officials indicated to our staff that they could begin public advertisement, since the delays were partially due to a delay in drafting government regulations for private educational institutions. Official registration, approved in June 1996, finally allowed the staff to launch a public marketing campaign just a few short months before RACU's September opening.

RACU's first students, born in 1979 and 1980, were seven years old when Gorbachev's speech revealed the crimes of Stalin and his colleagues; eleven years old in 1991, when the August coup collapsed and resulted in Yeltsin replacing Gorbachev as Russia's top leader; and twelve years old when the coup leaders were tried in court for their treasonous activities. Like most Russian youth of their age, these events were of no interest to them. They reflected many of the same attitudes of Generation *Nyet* by focusing mostly on the educational opportunities that allowed them to improve their lives. Like their peers, they also had no interest in politics or any form of public protest. Many of them came from families that suffered at the hands of the communist regime, and some of their parents and grandparents had been imprisoned because of their faith. This, added to the revelations about their country's true history, made them wary of any political engagement.

During the spring and summer months of 1996, RACU's staff and faculty worked on developing admissions procedures that reflected both Russian and

American educational practices. Creating a new binational educational entity was exciting. Showing respect toward local traditions while designing new approaches that fit a faith-based liberal arts college made it challenging as well. The admissions process, designed after hours of discussion among Russian and American faculty, involved a three-hour Russian-style written examination on a wide range of topics, plus an essay on one of four topics: Pushkin as a classic Russian writer, an evaluation of spiritual themes in Tolstoy and Dostoevsky, views on education in the new Russia, or addressing who was a hero in the applicant's life and why. Students who passed these written requirements, graded for content and grammar by two Russian-language specialists, then endured a personal interview by the admissions committee, composed of two Russians and two Americans.

This entire procedure was an intimidating process for the students, often accompanied by their nervous parents, especially the personal interview by four faculty with doctorates. Most mothers and fathers had themselves never attended a college or university, so they had no experience with this enrollment process, typical of Russian universities. I participated in the interviews of the sixty applicants for RACU's first freshmen class. Making decisions about which students to accept was a problem of prosperity for us, but a painful one, since we knew that we could only accept forty of these sixty precious young people and those who did not get accepted would miss this opportunity to improve their lives and the lives of their families.[3]

Considering the lateness of our recruitment effort because of the lack of official registration for RACU until June, we were pleased with sixty applicants and wondered how competitive it would be once the school opened. During the interviews, we realized that the desire to enroll at RACU was intense. These students wanted to be admitted very badly, and they made that clear. They told us that they learned about RACU from their pastors, Christian radio broadcasts, and announcements at seminars, so the staff's work paid off handsomely.

Much to our surprise, the students represented a broad spectrum of denominations. The largest number were Evangelical Christians-Baptist, as we expected, but there were also traditional Pentecostals, new charismatics, Jewish Christians, and Orthodox believers, as well as a few "seekers." Of the forty-three students

---

[3]John A. Bernbaum, "Weekly Report for August 25-31, 1996," August 31, 1996, 1-3, Chron File 1995–1996, RA.

chosen, twenty-eight enrolled in RACU as business majors and fifteen in the social work program.[4]

From the start we wrestled with tough crosscultural issues. The Russian faculty on the admissions committee often used rude language when pressing students on some of the wrong answers on their tests, ridiculing mistakes and badgering them about why they did not know the right answer. After a few sessions like this, I confronted the faculty and told them not to treat students like this, but they responded that that was a normal practice. While we knew that this shaming process had to be stopped, it took time for the Russian professors to understand, and for them this shift signaled that this new liberal arts university would indeed be different.

Figure 12.1. RACU's first freshmen class (September 1996).

Opening day took place at the rented facilities of Moscow State University's Center for International Education, a necessary last-minute shift since the Christian Ministry Center was not yet ready. The academic year officially began with refreshments and a short program in a small auditorium. Student volunteers helped prepare food and flower arrangements, so the room was attractively laid out for the rest of the newly admitted students and some attending parents,

---

[4]John A. Bernbaum, "RACU Support Letter," September 27, 1996, 1-2, SL.

which was not unusual in Russia. I greeted everyone and shared our vision for RACU, noting the school's uniqueness as a binational faith-based liberal arts college. Vladimir Obrovets shared a ten-minute devotional on Moses, Daniel, and Paul and their educational preparation, followed by Stanley Clark's overview, "The Idea of a Christian University." The staff then discussed RACU policies about tuition, work-study opportunities, and the fall calendar, and ended with a question-and-answer session. After refreshments, students took an English placement examination and then met with staff to discuss their tuition and pick up their textbooks. Excitement and anticipation filled everyone—students, parents, faculty, and staff. One young male student grabbed my arm, hesitated a moment, and then gave me a big hug and kiss. He said, "I am so happy I could jump for joy!" That was exactly how I felt on opening day at RACU—what a miracle to see this school begin its first academic year despite so many obstacles.[5]

RACU'S ACADEMIC PROGRAM: THE FIRST EXPERIMENT

The excitement surrounding the beginning of RACU's academic program was extraordinary. Forty-three freshman students began their academic year with two three-week modules in business, economics, and social work held in rented facilities owned by Moscow State University, where the opening day festivities were held. The real pioneers in this first class were the social work majors, since social work was a totally new academic discipline in Russia. During the Soviet era, the government maintained a clear position that social work courses were not needed in their socialist state, where there were no social problems. Social work as an academic field in Russia did not exist, and RACU was committed to change that.

From Clark's perspective as RACU's provost, the two three-week modules "went beautifully. The teaching was high quality, the students bonded with each other, and high standards were established, with an anticipated strong academic reputation for the university."[6] The remaining nine weeks of the first semester were devoted to two English language courses and a course on the history of Western civilization, offered in the Christian Ministry Center, where

---

[5]John A. Bernbaum, "Friday Report," September 6, 1996, 1-2, Chron File 1995–1996, RA.
[6]Stanley Clark, "Weekly Report," October 19, 1997, 1, RACU Chron Files 1997, RA.

RACU finally relocated in its completed building. The faculty and staff worked diligently toward the goal of getting the students to an advanced comprehension level in English by the end of their second full year.

Spring semester 1997 began with an exhilarating week of startup activities, according to the staff. All students from the first semester returned to campus, and four new students were added. In March 1997 I attended each class and visited with students, which often included some competitive Ping-Pong games in an activity room of the center. The dynamics at work in RACU's classrooms gave me a thrill to observe. One experience stands out in my memory. I attended the Introduction to Philosophy class taught by Vladimir Solodovnikov, a class that I had heard was very popular with the students. I sat in for the first forty-five minutes of the class and watched his opening presentation, followed by a student report on Thomas Aquinas. This struck me as unusual, since most Russian professors did not use student presentations, preferring instead to give straight lectures themselves. With the help of a student translator, I could understand that the other students enjoyed gaining new insights about Aquinas and Roman Catholicism, probably for the first time in their lives.

When the class ended, I retreated to work in the office upstairs. Two hours later, I returned down the hall and found Professor Solodovnikov and five students standing in the hallway discussing issues from the class. They were asking him which denomination was "the best," and he responded that there were people who love Jesus in every religious tradition; he encouraged them to be open minded as they studied different religious groups. That conversation led to a discussion about baptism and the various ways different churches viewed this sacrament. One of the students said to me: "This is soooo interesting! We have never heard things like this before!"[7] My letter to RACU supporters in May 1997 noted that "our first year was a great success and our first forty students had a marvelous experience. They bonded together, despite diverse denominational backgrounds, and became a Christian community of young scholars." The report included comments by a number of our students that they wished "summer was over so they could start classes again."[8]

---

[7]John A. Bernbaum, "RACU Support Letter," March 29, 1997, 2, SL.

[8]John A. Bernbaum, "Report from Moscow," May 29, 1997, 2, RACU Chron Files 1997, RA.

ECONOMIC CRISIS AND RELIGIOUS OPPOSITION
CREATE UNANTICIPATED CHALLENGES

When the trustees laid plans for the founding of RACU, all fully expected that the student population would be local only, drawn from the city of Moscow, which numbered over seven million in 1996, and that the campus would be for commuters who used the impressive Moscow metro system to access the Christian Ministry Center. Plans therefore did not include providing housing for students. However, much to our surprise, a number of students from outside Moscow showed up for the entrance examinations, in some cases traveling long distances without any assurance that they would be accepted and thus perhaps having to return home the next day. Accepting these gifted students, often from small provincial cities far from Moscow, would require support we did not anticipate.

When we interviewed one of the first students from Chelyabinsk, a city 930 miles east of Moscow, I learned that her father was a worker who made $120 per month and her mother was unemployed. They were a poor but deeply committed Christian family, and when we reviewed her essay on Pushkin, it was judged to be at the highest level by our two Russian evaluators. How could we turn her down?[9] The admissions committee eventually accepted twelve students like Olga from cities outside the Moscow region, and with the assistance of Vladimir Obrovets, we were able to find housing for them in a Pentecostal dormitory and later with Christian families. Housing subsidies of $60 per month, not in our budget, had to be added.[10]

During the second semester of RACU's first academic year, Stanley and Susan Clark interviewed twenty-six of the forty-three enrolled students and studied their personal files in order to learn more about their background and financial needs. They were stunned to see the poverty and broken homes of these students. Eleven of the students had no father at home, and in most cases the mother had a menial job or was unemployed. Family salaries ranged from $50 to $135 per month, while some lived with grandparents on small pensions. While we knew that many Christian families who lived in Siberian cities were poor and uneducated, marginalized because of their faith, the extent of their poverty was overwhelming. This reality deepened our commitment to educate them because we

---

[9]John A. Bernbaum, "Monday Night Report," August 26, 1996, 1, Chron File 1995–1996, RA.
[10]John A. Bernbaum, "Tuesday Night Report," September 17, 1996, 1, Chron File 1995–1996, RA.

knew that a college degree from RACU would transform their lives and allow them to earn salaries far above what they or their parents ever received previously.

When I met with our first-year students, I learned that some students were taking classes from 9 a.m. until 9:30 p.m. and did not have money for food during their long days. When asked, they said, "Don't worry, we are used to it." They wanted a quality education and were willing to do what it took to get it.[11]

Meanwhile, in the midst of this economic crisis, a growing opposition by Orthodox and conservative political leaders to foreign religions gained momentum. In June 1997, a new law on religious freedom was passed that created a dark cloud over the Protestant community in Moscow. The Russian parliament overwhelmingly approved of new legislation restricting the freedom of any religious organization not on a protected list, a list that included Orthodoxy, Judaism, Islam, and Buddhism, the four official religions in Russia. The law generated concern among Protestants and Catholics that a new Soviet-era period of persecution was coming. When President Yeltsin had the bill on his desk, no one knew what to expect from him. In July, Yeltsin vetoed the bill; but, on September 4, at the beginning of RACU's second school year, he signed the amended legislation. No one was sure what this would mean for RACU.

RACU'S SECOND FRESHMAN CLASS: MORE NON-MUSCOVITES

RACU's second freshmen class, in September 1997, had even more students from outside Moscow than the first. Of the forty-four new freshmen, half came to the school from distant locations, due to news of RACU being spread through church networks. As RACU's staff worked on student recruitment, it became obvious that getting males to register was a problem, because Russian law clearly stated that university-age male students were not eligible for exemption from the draft unless they were enrolled at an accredited university. Getting RACU accredited was a major goal and a huge challenge. The laws for private schools were slowly being formulated, and current regulations stated that new institutions could not qualify for accreditation until three classes had graduated from the school and had passed state examinations. This meant that accreditation was years away and that we needed to expect a student body with a significant female majority. The good news, however, was the receipt of RACU's educational license in December

---

[11]John A. Bernbaum, "President's Report, March 16-29, 1997," March 29, 1997, PresR.

1997. The Russian Ministry of Education was finally issuing licenses to private schools after extended delays. The license authorized RACU to offer a full range of undergraduate and graduate programs.

The addition of forty-four more students meant the Christian Ministry Center was jam-packed, and between classes it was hard to find a place to sit. The faculty, equally divided between Russians and Americans, offered classes in the fall semester and were joined by four more faculty in the spring. Stanley Clark had recruited an impressive teaching team, but we could see that sustaining the quality of the faculty would be difficult, particularly if maintaining a balance between Americans and Russian continued to be a goal.[12]

Figure 12.2. President Bernbaum and Provost Clark celebrate RACU's educational license (December 1997).

Tracking down additional classroom space if we wanted to keep growing constituted another challenge. In December 1997 RACU rented classroom space from New Life Bible College in the center, providing short-term relief.[13]

Two additional complications made life difficult for our out-of-town students. The first was access to medical services. Because these students did not have a

---

[12]Stanley Clark, "Weekly Report," August 15, 1997, 1, RACU Chron Files 1997, RA.
[13]John A. Bernbaum, "Wednesday Afternoon Report," December 17, 1997, 1, RACU Chron Files 1997, RA.

Moscow residency permit, they were denied medical service at Moscow hospitals, where staff refused to serve them. One student with a severe ankle sprain was refused service while she sat in an ambulance for over an hour. We realized we had to take steps to provide for them. Susan Clark became a part-time nurse, routinely dispensing bandages and aspirin and periodically transporting students to a private medical clinic run by a Christian doctor, Bill Becknell, with whom a number of students worked as volunteers. Getting Moscow residency permits was also a challenge because few landlords were willing to sign required residency documents without a substantial cash payment, which the students did not have.[14]

RACU'S THIRD YEAR: GROWTH OR NO GROWTH AND A LEADERSHIP CHANGE

The situation became even more challenging by the third year, when another thirty-five freshmen enrolled at RACU in fall 1998. We decided to admit only thirty-five freshman students for RACU's third year because of the lack of certainty about a campus location, since RACU had outgrown the Christian Ministry Center. The leadership team in Moscow made a strong case for no growth until this issue was settled, but RACU trustees and advisers were convinced that a no-growth policy would severely set back the school and could lead to its closure. Agreement was made to continue the recruitment policy but limit the number of new applicants. Once a contract was signed with the Center for International Education of the Moscow State University, and the number of rooms and offices was substantially increased, a robust competition for acceptance was evident. The staff quickly set a goal of recruiting thirty more students. The thirty-five freshmen made the RACU student body exactly one hundred in three classes. The fall schedule included twenty-seven courses taught in two languages by seventeen faculty, twelve Russians and five Americans. The only disappointment was the imbalance of Russian and American teachers, far short of RACU's goal of fifty-fifty.[15]

During summer 1998 Stanley and Susan Clark completed their three-year commitment to RACU and returned to the States. Susan agreed to continue working for the school three days per week to assist me in fundraising and faculty recruitment. The ensuing job search for a new provost at RACU brought in Hannes Furter, a missionary from South Africa who had worked for four years

---

[14]Susan Clark, "RACU Newsbits, February 15 to March 7, 1998," March 8, 1998, 1-2, Chron Files 1997–1998, RA.
[15]John A. Bernbaum, "RACU Support Letter," September 28, 1998, 1-2, SL.

at St. Petersburg Christian University. Hannes and his wife, Annamarie, moved to Moscow in August, just in time to experience the full weight of one of Russia's most severe financial crises. At Furter's first meeting with RACU students, they expressed great concern about the continuing existence of the school as well as their own difficulties, which in some cases meant they did not have any money for food. He reported, "We had to act immediately as several did not have anything to eat."[16]

The economic crisis began in May 1998, when the world's oil prices dropped dramatically and financial panic struck Russia. Stock prices dropped 10 percent on May 20, then 22 percent in one week. By July 1998 the Russian stock market had lost more than 60 percent of its value from ten months earlier. One month later the ruble was in free fall, and the new victims of the economic crisis were Russia's middle class and those living on or near subsistence-level incomes. The ruble was trading for less than one-third of its value when the school year began in September.[17]

For a number of the new students, there was genuine uncertainty about whether they would be able to complete their studies because of the economic crisis. Many lost their part-time jobs, and so did their parents. Russian banks closed, and accessing the school's bank accounts was impossible. While Hannes was introduced to his new responsibilities with the academic program, Annamarie took charge of student affairs, which meant handling the increasing number of student requests for financial aid. She quickly formed a committee of staff and faculty to help decide how to handle the many pressing financial needs. The staff knew we had no choice but to help these students, even though we did not have the funds in hand; we had to ask our supporters to help us meet the needs or the school would be in jeopardy.

RACU'S FOURTH AND FIFTH YEARS: STEADY GROWTH

By the beginning of RACU's fourth year, there was an impressive increase in the quality of the freshman class. The thirty-two new students who attended the opening assembly in September 1999 after successfully competing for the limited number of available openings entered with strong academic records; more than half of the new group were immediately placed in advanced English-language

---

[16]Hannes Furter, "Weekly Report," September 18, 1998, 1, MC—September 1998.

[17]Lilia Shevtsova, *Yeltsin's Russia: Myths and Reality* (Washington, DC: Carnegie Endowment for International Peace, 1999), 246-60.

classes. They were also a diverse group: slightly more than half came from Moscow and the surrounding region, while the rest came from all over the Russian Federation as well as from Ukraine and Belarus. Orthodox, Catholic, and Adventist students joined those from various Protestant denominations, a truly ecumenical student body.

RACU's enrollment at the beginning of the fourth year was 112 full-time undergraduates, of which thirty-seven were placed in a total immersion English-language program at a second campus location. The goal of this new program was to help these students become bilingual prior to beginning regular university classes, a necessity with both American and Russian faculty and their reliance on predominantly English-language texts in economics and social work. These students received full-time instruction in English from a staff of six faculty members in grammar, academic reading, composition, and listening/speaking.

The increasing competition for entrance into RACU posed a complex problem for the staff and faculty. If students were largely evaluated on the basis of the quality of their high school education, those from outside Moscow and St. Petersburg were often unable to compete because of the inferior quality of their provincial schools. Yet many of these students were from Christian families who had been marginalized because of their faith and forced to move to distant locations in Siberia. The staff agreed, despite some resistance from Moscow-based Russian faculty, that we needed to give them opportunities as well.

By year five, with another entering freshman class of thirty-nine in September 2000, enrollment was at 130 full-time students, slightly over the number allowed by RACU's education license. The board's vision of educating a new generation of Christian youth to be salt and light in the Russia of the future was becoming a reality.

Table 12.1. RACU's first five freshmen classes (fall 1996–fall 2000)

Term	Total	Female	Male	Business & Economics	Social Work
Fall 1996	43			28	15
Fall 1997	44	26	18	22	22
Fall 1998	35	26	9	20	15
Fall 1999	30	23	7	15	15
Fall 2000	39	24	15	21	18

RACU STUDENT VOLUNTEERS

In many ways RACU students shared the characteristics found in Generation *Nyet*, especially their disinterest in politics. When RACU staff interviewed third-year students in spring 1999, they found them to be "very weak on their general knowledge of the market and current events. None of them really reads newspapers or magazines on business, finance or politics. Without exception, they are ill informed."[18]

However, one aspect of RACU students that stood in sharp contrast to the rest of Generation *Nyet* was their willingness to volunteer nights and on weekends in the local churches they attended and in numerous ministries that they learned about during their courses at the school, especially their social work classes. When Hannes Furter joined the staff, he seemed concerned that the spiritual life of RACU students was not deep enough, but his worries were countered by faculty members, who testified that most of their students were very active in their churches and often volunteered to go on medical mission trips. In February 2001 ten RACU students served as volunteers during their Christmas and New Year's vacation and accompanied twenty Russian and American medical doctors and nurses to the Komi Republic, a far northern region of European Russia, where prisons, orphanages, and remote villages are populated by minority tribes. The trip was organized by Agape Medical Center, and the trip organizers were Yana and Peter Smirnov, RACU students and later staff members, who worked for the center while attending school full time.[19]

Generation *Nyet* students at RACU were setting themselves apart from the rest of their in-between generation. Their faith and passion for their country prepared them for future service, and the faculty and staff at RACU had the privilege of helping them figure out their calling.

---

[18]Hannes Furter, "Weekly Report," April 10, 1999, 1, MC—March–April 1999.
[19]John A. Bernbaum, "RACU Support Letter," February 21, 2001, 1, SL.

13

ASSEMBLING RACU'S
BUILDING BLOCKS

THE YEAR 1996 MARKED AN IMPORTANT milestone in the history of Russia's postcommunist transition as well as the founding year of RACU. For Russians, Yeltsin's stunning reelection in July, after lagging behind in opinion polls through spring 1996, ensured that the Communist Party would not return to power, as many feared. Although Yeltsin's government survived the threat of defeat by the Communist Party candidate, Gennady Zyuganov, his victory represented "the exhaustion of promise," in the words of David Remnick, a staff writer for the *New Yorker*. Remnick wrote, "Power in Russia is now adrift, unpredictable and corrupt. . . . In the new Russia, freedom has led to disappointment. . . . Under Yeltsin, power at the Kremlin has become almost as remote from the people it is supposed to serve as it was under the last communist general secretaries."[1]

From the perspective of many observers in the West, Russia's hoped-for transition from communism to a democracy was not happening. After his reelection as president in 1996, Yeltsin, who began as a reformer, ended with a compromised regime that many Russians described as a "mafia state." He assumed the role of an elected monarch, while his colleagues ran the country.[2]

Within months of Yeltsin's reelection, the new school year began in Russia. The opening of schools on the first day of September always presents a major event in Russia, with pageantry and traditions unmatched in the West. I was often in

---

[1]David Remnick, "Can Russia Change?," *Foreign Affairs* (January–February 1997): 35.
[2]Lilia Shevtsova, *Yeltsin's Russia* (Washington, DC: Carnegie Endowment for International Peace, 1999), 269.

Moscow on September 1 for the opening of RACU's fall semester and have periodically visited local schools to witness their celebration. Streams of young children, accompanied by their parents, assemble in front of the school for the opening ceremony; each child carries a beautiful bouquet of flowers for the teachers. Parents and students alike are dressed in their finest clothes, with polished shoes and carefully manicured hair. Everyone looks good on September 1.

But in 1996, the beginning of the school year was a sober occasion. Russians across the country faced a crisis in education. Russian newspapers reported that there were over twenty-six hundred teaching vacancies in Moscow alone, and the education minister bemoaned the fact that only 50 percent of the one hundred million textbooks needed for basic courses in Russian schools had been produced. Financial subsidies were given to political elites rather than to support education, continuing a pattern in which education remained one of the country's lowest priorities. This difficult situation for educators was made especially aggravating in a context where the mayor of Moscow, Yuri Luzhkov, was initiating costly building projects in anticipation of the capital city's 850th anniversary celebration, in September 1997.[3]

RACU'S UNIQUE STUDENT LIFE PROGRAM

In sharp contrast to the climate on Russian university campuses, where federal funding was dramatically reduced and Generation *Nyet* students were frustrated by the reforms that were promised but not delivered, the RACU campus was full of excitement. Unlike their experiences in high school, and in some cases on Russian state university campuses, where a few of our students were previously enrolled, RACU students took part in a vibrant campus life that included weekly convocations, which were voluntary but very popular; a student council that discussed substantive campus issues and offered advice to the staff on certain topics; a student-generated school newspaper; and concerts by student musical groups that also performed in local churches.

The weekly convocations introduced students to a wide range of speakers, both Russian and American, and a diversity of Christian perspectives. In addition to presentations by RACU's president and deans, the students heard the

---

[3]John A. Bernbaum, "RACU Opens Undergraduate Program," September 16, 1996, 1, RACU Chron Files 1996, RA.

testimonies of various RACU faculty, including some remarkable stories of former atheists who had rejected hostility toward God and became people of faith. For many Protestants, it was the first time they listened to devotionals by Orthodox priests, including Father Gleb Yakunin, whose daughter Anna attended RACU. The weekly sessions covered a wide range of topics, from people who ran recovery programs for alcoholics to outreach programs for orphans. Over the first few years the students gradually became involved in the planning for these weekly convocations and provided the music.

Special social events were also offered free to RACU students, and many of them attended activities in the city for the first time, such as the circus, a ballet in the large Kremlin concert hall, a hockey match between Canadians and Russians, and end-of-the-semester parties, which they never wanted to end. Following the final examination week in May 1997, the staff hosted a party featuring special music, a meal, games, the presentation of small gifts, and some group prayer. The bonding that took place with the first class was impressive, and it was a joy for the staff to witness these friendships. The students were also thrilled to get RACU T-shirts and a class photograph.[4]

Several experiences at RACU stand out as unique for Russian university students. One of the disciplinary problems that the staff faced in the first few years was cheating during examinations. Students often copied answers from other students at nearby desks and did so with little hesitation. They also freely plagiarized papers written by classmates. When discussing the issue, students told the American faculty that cheating was not unusual and was done everywhere they had gone to school. They also justified their actions by stressing the importance of helping each other because this was a "communal society" that put less stress on individual achievement.

Stanley Clark came up with a wise response. He asked a number of student leaders to serve on a committee to write a policy on honesty for the school, and their recommendations were subsequently reviewed by the staff and faculty at RACU and became school policy. Having a policy drafted by students themselves was an indication that RACU viewed its students as active contributors to the institution, not just passive participants.[5]

---

[4]Stanley Clark, "Weekly Report," May 18, 1997, 1, RACU Chron Files 1997–1998, RA.
[5]Stanley Clark, "Weekly Report," November 9, 1996, 1, MC, November–December 1996.

Another remarkable experience developed because of the vision of a business professor and a gifted student. RACU's original offices and classrooms were located in the Christian Ministry Center, a building shared with four other evangelical organizations. On the lower level of the facility was space for a cafeteria, which was owned and managed by three of the building partners. Getting a food service started in this space was a challenge because of all the complicated city health regulations and government officials who sought "encouragement" by bribes before they would issue the necessary permits.

The staff asked one of our students, Alyona Kremorenko, who had some catering experience, to take charge of the cafeteria. This was an important issue because many of our students from poor families were not getting proper nourishment, and the staff wanted them to at least eat a substantive lunch every day. Alyona initially worked with Annamarie Furter, and together they recruited students on work study as workers and taught them good work habits.

Then Pete Wozniuk arrived in Moscow. A retired businessman from Iowa, he agreed to come to Moscow for a semester to teach business courses at RACU. When he learned about Alyona's role in the cafeteria, he used her participation in his Principles of Marketing class to teach her and other classmates how to start and grow a business, using the cafeteria as a case study. After doing market research, Wozniuk challenged them to use their imagination to grow this cafeteria, which he called "the Emporium," into a successful operation. Alyona employed twenty students and greatly expanded the cafeteria to serve the entire building.[6] Wozniuk continued to train RACU students as young business leaders for years to come.

A student council was also formed in the early years of the school, and it created a place where student concerns could be openly discussed. If needed, meetings with staff were arranged to hear these concerns. During the economic crisis of fall 1998, the student council organized a meeting for students in which they expressed their deep concerns that RACU might not survive. While student activism of any kind was not characteristic of Generation *Nyet*, the campus environment at RACU encouraged their initiatives.

Because of RACU's binational character and its quality English-language program, some Russian trustees worried that RACU students would join the

---

[6]John A. Bernbaum, "RACU Support Letter," April 7, 1999, 1-4, SL.

steady stream of Russians moving to the West after 1991. When two American trustees funded a full-year scholarship for a RACU student to attend Calvin College, the same concerns were raised. They were heightened when the first scholarship winner in 1998 never returned to Russia, and we subsequently learned that she never intended to, despite her promise to do so. While it became clear that there was no way to legally force students to return to their homeland, the decision was made by the staff to continue to support the Calvin scholarship program because we needed young Russians to experience a quality liberal arts education with the expectation that they would come back to RACU to help us build one, which a number of these scholarship winners did.

FACULTY RECRUITMENT: THE ONGOING CHALLENGE

Launching RACU created a range of challenges that seemed overwhelming at times. The scarcity and availability of quality Russian texts, especially in social work, and the necessity of translators for classes taught by American faculty presented unending challenges. Before the Clarks left Moscow, they clearly saw one of the biggest long-range challenges to be the recruitment of American faculty, even though finding suitable textbooks and quality translators was also difficult. After two excellent English-language institutes in summer 1995 and 1996, with high-quality faculty volunteers from the States, we did not anticipate having to struggle to recruit teachers. However, when it became evident that longer-term faculty from the States were less available than we had hoped, the staff turned to various formats that worked best, such as short-term courses. For American faculty, the issue of bringing a family to Russia during this time of turmoil was part of the problem; another complication came from the restrictions stateside home campuses put on the use of sabbatical leave. Teaching overseas was not an option at many Christian College Coalition schools, and almost no one felt called to give up their current position for a risky time in the postcommunist world.

The greatest success in faculty recruitment came when David Broersma and his family, which included four children, agreed to join our faculty. David and Cathy had been involved in overseas missions for several years before David completed his undergraduate and graduate programs. He had visited the Soviet Union in 1995 with his pastor, John Chisholm, and this experience created his interest in possibly working there. Lonna Dickerson, who had taught at RACU in the summer language institutes, encouraged David to contact me, and we met at Wheaton College in October 1996. I knew in the first five minutes of our meeting that I had to get him to Moscow, and he agreed to visit in December. Because of my Ménière's disease (radical vertigo), which limited my international travel for two years, I was unable to go with them as planned, but the Clarks graciously hosted them and quickly agreed that we needed the Broersma family. Fortunately David and Cathy "fell in love with the vision of RACU and the students," according to his reflections on this visit to RACU. David completed his doctoral dissertation in linguistics, raised support from friends at his church in Champaign-Urbana, Illinois, and arrived in Moscow in July 1998. He took leadership of the English-language program, which eventually became RACU's third principal academic major, and eventually served as RACU's provost. The recruitment of the Broersmas was a cause for much celebration, but few celebrations for faculty procurement followed because of the scarcity of volunteers. While RACU was able to recruit some Western missionaries and business people to teach at the school, the pool of American faculty was very small. Finding academics to chair RACU's two main departments, business and economics and social work and counseling, was difficult, and locating candidates for those positions required years.

Recruiting Russian faculty came easier. Russian faculty who joined RACU had impressive credentials, but many had become Christians later in life and had little understanding of how to integrate their faith with their academic disciplines. When this became apparent, the staff organized professional training seminars for the faculty, but many of the Russian professors were not open to new ways of teaching. This structural weakness in RACU's faculty development was never resolved. While some Russian faculty were mentored by their American colleagues, others were proud of their Russian training and chose not to pursue further study of how their faith integrated with their course materials.

Our longer-term plans for faculty development were modeled after the summer workshops sponsored by the Christian College Coalition, many of which I managed along with Karen Longman. We also had plans to connect our Russian faculty with the programs offered by the International Association for the Promotion of Christian Higher Education. Unfortunately, lack of funds made these plans difficult to implement, along with resistance from Russian professors who were not interested in summer training programs because that was when they were headed to their dachas in the countryside.

RUSSIA'S POLITICAL AND ECONOMIC INSTABILITY

The biggest challenge by year three was not an internal issue but the chaos in Russia's political and economic life. The Furters arrived in Moscow to take over leadership and had barely moved into their apartment when a major crisis hit Russia. I arrived in Moscow along with the Furters, and together we witnessed another shifting of the ground beneath us. The economy was in crisis, the political factions were at war, and the average Muscovite was desperately trying to survive. The ruble was in a free fall, beginning at six rubles per dollar, then trading on the streets for seven, soon eight and quickly nine rubles per dollar; within a week the exchange rate had plummeted to twenty rubles per dollar.

Rumors of economic collapse began to spread and some banks were mobbed by people trying to withdraw their savings. However, other than occasional mob scenes, the streets were calm and people seemed resigned to weather yet another storm. This particular devaluation of the ruble was only the most recent of numerous defaults experienced by the Russian people, who repeatedly suffered the total loss of their savings. The Russians experienced two depression-scale shocks in the 1990s, comparable to the Great Depression in the United States in the 1930s. For Americans working in this context, we began to understand why the Russian people no longer trusted anyone in authority and why so many assumed that efforts to build democracy in their country were the cause of these economic disasters. For them, *democracy* had become a dirty word.[7]

RACU'S ACADEMIC PROGRAM MATURES

The political struggles in Russia did not directly affect RACU and, in fact, the mood on campus remained positive. The economic crisis did hurt. With the currency suddenly in a free fall, students who paid their tuition one day were followed by students who paid the next day but at a rate 20 percent higher. We were surprised how well they took this in stride, just like their parents and others who

---

[7]John A. Bernbaum, "Update from Moscow: Reflections on a Crisis," September 5, 1988, 1-5, RACU Chron Files 1988, RA.

were accustomed to living in constant uncertainty. Living costs continued to rise, including housing, food, and transportation expenses. The poorer students who came from outside Moscow especially suffered during the fall of 1998, but gradually by the new year the economy stabilized.

RACU's academic program slowly developed into a more complex and attractive structure, although the difficulty of finding competent translators and textbooks accessible to students with limited English language capability continually hampered curriculum development. Finally the faculty recommended that students should have advanced English and computer skills before being admitted into the third year of RACU's undergraduate program. After lengthy discussion between the faculty and the board, an intensive English program was approved and initiated in fall semester 1999.[8] This immediately improved the quality of RACU's academic programs.

By the opening of RACU's fifth year, in September 2000, RACU had a full academic program that included a new English major under the leadership of David Broersma. The staff and faculty were convinced that its English program was one of the best in Moscow, and our students clearly excelled in their English-language ability in comparison to graduates from some of the best-known schools in the region. A number of internship supervisors noted that the language skills of RACU students were unmatched by other interns; we were told that some of the graduates from Moscow State University could not write a full paragraph in English when asked by their boss, while RACU graduates were completely comfortable operating in either Russian or English. This was not only good publicity for the school but also a wonderful Christian witness. Young people previously banned from higher education because of their faith commitment were proving to be hardworking, bright, dedicated, and leaders among their peers.

Meanwhile, a decision was made to move the English program back to Moscow State University's Center for International Education, where the first two months of classes at RACU were held, and this relieved the space pressure on the Christian Ministry Center. At the same time, Hannes Furter and David Broersma agreed to share leadership at RACU; Broersma assumed the role of academic dean, while Furter served as the chief operating officer and, among other things, spent time looking for larger campus facilities to house RACU long-term.

---

[8]David Broersma, "Need an Update," September 14, 1999, 1-2, RACU Chron Files 1999, RA.

Enhancing RACU's English language program and its computer labs became important building blocks in preparing our students for the marketplace. One of RACU's goals, as articulated in the school's mission statement, was to equip students to enter the job market with an education that emphasized practical workplace skills. With this in mind, our business faculty developed internships to link theory with practice. RACU's membership in the American Chamber of Commerce in Moscow and the Russian-American Business Council opened up many business internship opportunities. Soon it became apparent that our students, with English-language competency, computer skills, and basic management training, were attractive candidates for employment in the businesses where they served as interns.[9] In addition, the business faculty and staff worked together to create business forums, inviting distinguished American and Russian business leaders to formal dinners during which they shared insights they learned as professionals; each dinner also included a lively question-and-answer session. Meeting competent business leaders who were people of faith surprised and encouraged our students, who previously assumed, along with most Russian Christians, that businesspeople were all crooks.

The social work faculty, under the leadership of Ruslan Nadyuk, developed close relationships with American professors who taught as adjunct faculty at RACU. Together the Russian and American professors developed internships for their upper-level students. Many of these opportunities resulted from visits their classes made to various human-welfare agencies. Getting competent students with practical marketplace experience—and strong English-language skills— proved to be an attractive option for potential employers. Unlike business majors, however, the salary levels for social workers, a new profession in Russia, were very low and created difficulty for graduates who wanted to work in this field because they were unable to live on salaries that were below subsistence levels in Moscow. Many of these students found employment in other jobs, usually based on their English language and computer skills, and worked as volunteers in social-welfare agencies, often with orphans and disabled children.

With each new freshmen class, the academic program of RACU continued to grow; by the fourth and fifth years, thirty to forty classes were offered each semester, with an equal number of faculty. The ongoing difficulty of maintaining

---

[9]John A. Bernbaum, "RACU Support Letter," November 30, 1998, 1-2, SL.

Figure 13.1. Dr. Ruslan Nadyuk, dean of the Social Work and Counseling Department.

a balance between Russian and American professors, as originally intended, increased. This was partially balanced by summer modules, which primarily involved guest faculty from the States. The students continued to affirm the benefit of having both Americans and Russians teach their courses, often using very different teaching styles. Most Americans used a more interactive teaching approach with an emphasis on student participation, while the Russian professors gave lectures with less discussion.

RACU'S FIRST STRATEGIC PLAN

While day-to-day operations provided adventure, the board, faculty, and staff knew that RACU needed grounding in a well-thought-out strategic plan.

Discussions about the future direction of RACU were a regular agenda item for each meeting of the leadership beginning in 1997 and every year thereafter. The first draft strategic plan, prepared in RACU's Washington office, was shared with all of the governing bodies of the school during the second and third years after the school opened. Finding a permanent facility to house the school remained the most demanding matter.

The ten-year strategic plan, titled "Equipping Russia's Future Leaders," began with the following mission statement:

> The Russian-American Christian University, established in the Russian Federation, is a comprehensive liberal arts university grounded in historic biblical Christianity. RACU is the only Christian higher education in Russia specifically committed to preparing young Russian Christians for leadership in the marketplace, the arts, law and government, and the helping professions.

In addition to a list of the strengths and opportunities of RACU, the challenges and obstacles received emphasis, including the lack of a legal tradition in Russia governed by the rule of law, an educational bureaucracy that operated with Soviet-style control patterns, the absence of a history of private higher education, institutionalized corruption evident in every facet of Russian society, growing hostility toward the West, the relative poverty of the Christian community, the lack of charitable giving to nonstate institutions, and the challenges of working crossculturally for a binational organization.

The strategic plan was formally endorsed by the board of trustees at its meeting in Moscow on November 13-14, 1998, along with the decision to launch a capital campaign for "acquiring, renovating, furnishing, equipping and maintaining new facilities for RACU in one location within Moscow near public transportation." The board also approved a guideline "for acquiring a fully operational facility."[10] In addition, the board agreed to hire a longtime friend, Ralph Veerman, to serve as my development consultant and adviser; his company, Veerman & Associates, works with Christian ministries in management and major gift development, so his expertise was a good fit as RACU launched its capital campaign.

THE SEARCH FOR NEW FACILITIES AND THE A TEAM

From the beginning, the search for facilities was one of the major challenges facing RACU's leadership team. The purchase of 9 percent of the Center for Christian Ministry was a miraculous surprise, and it provided a campus for the first three years of the school. Moscow State University's facility was the second campus location, and it served as RACU's campus for the following three school years. During this time the board instructed the staff to begin a search

---

[10]RACU Board of Trustees meeting, "Minutes—November 13-14, 1998," 2-3, RACU Board of Trustees Meeting Files, RA.

for facilities that could be renovated if necessary. During the 1999–2000 school year, the staff toured forty-five to fifty different facilities but found nothing that was suitable and reasonably priced.

Hannes Furter, with occasional assistance from Vladimir Obrovets, RACU's Russian vice president, had responsibility to search for a new campus location. David Broersma was asked to take responsibility for the school's academic program as a result. In addition, a friend of mine from graduate school, Charles Mast, who retired from the foreign service after primarily serving overseas in the Middle East and Asia, agreed to help in this search process, and he traveled to Moscow eight times from 1998 to 2000. As an experienced diplomat and economics officer, he was well-equipped for this role, although working in Russia is a challenge for anyone. During his work for RACU, Mast visited more than thirty facilities but continued to find them overpriced and located in unsuitable areas, often wedged between heavy industrial plants. He became a regular member of the RACU staff for three years and attended numerous board meetings both in Moscow and Washington, DC, where he gave the trustees updates on recent facility visits.

Another miraculous provision occurred in our search for property when Ralph Veerman introduced me to a group of business leaders in Atlanta who had been challenged by an urban pastor in Atlanta, Bob Lupton, to use their business skills to build God's kingdom in their city. Real estate experts, architects, and contractors agreed to work together to convert an old, vacated prison into low-income housing, and soon they launched other projects in the city as well. When Ralph and I met with the group's leaders—Billy Mitchell, a leading real estate developer, and Tom Ventulett, one of Atlanta's top architects—they decided it was time to go international and agreed to travel to Moscow to examine several potential building sites as possible campus locations for RACU. They became known as the "A Team" (Atlanta Team), and we had no idea at the beginning what valuable advisers they would become in RACU's future. Although the buildings we examined during their trip to Moscow in April 2000 did not prove to be acceptable, they helped the staff determine the parameters for RACU's search and advised us on how to construct a plan for reviewing available options. Over time they became close friends and significant donors, as well as expert advisers, to RACU's capital campaign and facility development.[11]

---

[11] The members of the A Team were Billy and Gladys Mitchell, Tom and Beth Ventulett, Chris Humphreys, and Parker Hudson. Mitchell and Hudson were real estate executives, Ventulett was one of Atlanta's

YELTSIN AND PUTIN: THE SURPRISE SUCCESSION PROCESS

While RACU's fifth year opened in September 1999 with an upbeat attitude on campus and a predictable, stable fall schedule, the political environment in Russia proved to be full of surprises and totally unpredictable; by the end of the 1990s, it seemed that no one was really running the country. Yeltsin's decision to appoint Vladimir Putin head of the Federal Security Service (FSB) in July 1998, and then as prime minister in August 1999, was totally unexpected. For many political analysts, Putin was an unlikely choice. He was an unknown figure who previously served as a KGB officer in East Germany and later as a close associate of Mayor Anatoly Sobchak in St. Petersburg. Few expected that his appointment as prime minister was designed to prepare him to succeed Yeltsin. When compared to all the previous rulers of Russia, Putin was exceptional. "He was the first ruler of Russia to be a child of the latter half of the twentieth century [born in 1952]; the first since Lenin to be city-born, to be fluent in a foreign language, and to have lived abroad; the first to have cut his teeth in the special services; and the first to enter politics after Soviet rule capsized."[12] This appointment was approved by the parliament because no one took Putin seriously.[13]

The forty-six-year-old prime minister, in response to an invasion of Dagestan by forces from Chechnya and then explosions of apartment buildings in Moscow and other cities, resulting in more than three hundred deaths, immediately made it clear that he was going "to bang the hell out of those bandits." He later escalated his language and declared, "We will go after them wherever they are. If, pardon me, we find them in the toilet, we will waste them in the outhouse." For many leading political figures, Putin was committing political suicide by launching a new ground war in Chechnya, but his conduct of the war proved to be immensely popular.[14] Putin's approval ratings went from 33 percent in August 1999 to 65 percent by October. The Russian people saw him as a young, dynamic leader, who promised stability and security for Russia, and he was viewed as a promising

---

leading architects, and Humphreys was a major contractor in Atlanta. Ralph Veerman planned the two-week trip and helped me build strong relationships with these business executives.

[12]Timothy J. Colton, *Russia: What Everyone Needs to Know* (New York: Oxford University Press, 2016), 134.

[13]Lilia Shevtsova, *Putin's Russia* (Washington, DC: Carnegie Endowment for International Peace, 2003), 9-31.

[14]Steven Lee Myers, *The New Tsar: The Rise and Reign of Vladimir Putin* (New York: Alfred A. Knopf, 2015), 152-64.

prospect to replace a sick, exhausted Yeltsin, who reminded many older people of Brezhnev.[15]

When Yeltsin surprised everyone with his decision to retire early, an announcement he made on New Year's Eve, the path was now open for Putin's succession as Russia's next president. Putin's only real campaign platform was released the night of Yeltsin's resignation, and his five-thousand-word manifesto, called "Russia at the Turn of the Millennium," acknowledged Russia's diminished status in the world, revealing that its gross national product had dropped by half in the 1990s and was now a tenth of that of the United States and a fifth of China's. The platform stated that fifteen years of substantial economic growth would be required just to reach the level of Portugal. His stated goal was to restore national unity, patriotism, and a strong national government, but without "an official state ideology in Russia in any guise."[16]

Russians streamed into voting booths on March 26, 2000, to elect a new president of Russia. Sixty-nine percent of the population voted, despite the fact that the outcome did not appear to be in doubt. Many of the people we knew in Moscow had high expectations that Vladimir Putin would give Russia the leadership needed to overcome the many economic, political, social, and moral challenges facing their country. In an interview during the election campaign, acting president Putin talked about the need to strengthen the moral fiber of the Russian people and stated that any program "should start from the revival of people's morals." These words gave Christian leaders we knew great hope that this young president would help rebuild their country. His election with 53 percent of the vote, as compared to 29 percent for the second-place candidate, Communist Party leader Zyuganov, made him indisputably the people's choice. When I wrote RACU's supporters after Putin's election, I stated my conviction that "now is the time to aggressively pursue our ministry, while watching to see if the new president does what he has promised in terms of continuing democratic and free market reforms, as well as protecting freedom of conscience and religion."[17] The prospects for RACU seemed bright, but no one knew what to expect.

---

[15]Shevtsova, *Putin's Russia*, 35-43.
[16]Myers, *New Tsar*, 177-81.
[17]John A. Bernbaum, "RACU Support Letter," April 7, 2000, 1, SL.

14

BIRTHING IN CHAOS
The First Five Years

UNTIL 2000, RACU KEPT A LOW PROFILE in Moscow. This had been deliberate, but it was about to change. Following recommendations from key Americans who lived and worked in Moscow, the university's leadership had decided early on to build the academic program without attracting undue attention because we knew a Christian liberal arts university was an unusual educational institution in Russia. We thought it would be best to build a quality program and let the graduates of the program serve as evidence of its value. In year five (2000–2001), the low-profile days were over. The staff and faculty prepared for a transition to go public.

The key factors in this transition year were, first of all, plans for RACU's inaugural graduation on May 19, 2001, when our graduates would walk across the stage, receive their diplomas, and enter the Russian job market. Second, during 2000–2001, RACU students working in business and social work internships for the first time provided a variety of employers with an opportunity to evaluate their performance, and the initial reviews were positive. Third, RACU's board and staff had committed to locating and buying a campus facility during this year so we could move out of leased space into our own building, making RACU one of the first private universities in Russia to have its own property, something sure to attract attention. Fourth, pursuing accreditation with the Russian Ministry of Education required documenting in detail the mission and goals of our institution for their officials to review. Finally, the leadership continued to build networks aggressively in Moscow with corporate leaders and government officials in order to introduce them to the university, open up additional internship sites, and create potential employment opportunities for our graduates.[1]

THE GROWTH OF PRIVATE COLLEGES AND UNIVERSITIES IN RUSSIA

The establishment of RACU in 1996 was part of a nationwide movement in which private colleges and universities opened all across the country. The number of colleges and universities in Russia grew by 75 percent in the eight years from 1992 to 2000, and the number of students grew by 50 percent.[2] In Moscow alone, fifty-three new institutions were established, covering every academic discipline from business to the liberal arts and sciences, with the majority offering business and economics programs.[3]

In Moscow a number of elite private schools were established, and the tuition costs for these schools made them inaccessible to the average Russian. These institutions, the New Economic School and the International University in Moscow, had the benefits of government support and in some cases took over facilities previously owned by the Communist Party. They were also quickly granted accreditation, while all the other private schools had to go through a seven-year vetting process. While many Russian leaders sent their children to these prestigious schools, others sent their youth to top schools in England and the States.[4]

A number of private Christian colleges were also established by Orthodox and Catholic leaders, as well as Seventh-Day Adventists, and several Bible schools began to broaden their academic programs as well.[5] RACU's uniqueness was its faith-based liberal arts curriculum, and Ministry of Education officials seemed puzzled by the school's program. They generally took the position that the ministry would support our institute if we did what we said we would do in

---

[1]John A. Bernbaum, "RACU Support Letter," October 16, 2000, 1, SL.

[2]Leon Aron, *Russia's Revolution: Essays, 1989–2006* (Washington, DC: AEI, 2007), 119.

[3]S. Frederick Starr, "Weaning Russia's New Colleges from Western Aid," *The Chronicle of Higher Education*, October 26, 1996, A60.

[4]For a review of Russian higher education since the collapse of communism, see Jeroen Huisman, Anna Smolentseva, and Isak Froumin, eds., *Twenty-Five Years of Transformations of Higher Education Systems in Post-Soviet Countries: Reform and Continuity* (London: Palgrave MacMillan, 2018).

[5]Perry L. Glanzer and Konstantin Petrenko, "Private Christian Colleges in the Former Soviet Union (Parts 1 & 2)," *East-West Church & Ministry Report* (Winter–Spring 2006); see also "Resurrecting the Russian University's Soul: The Emergence of Eastern Orthodox Universities and Their Distinctive Approaches to Keeping Faith with Tradition," *Christian Scholar's Review* (Spring 2007).

our mission statement. Despite the economic difficulties facing most Russians, a commitment to education remained a high priority, and this commitment encouraged us in the early years of RACU. Our close ties to evangelical church leaders also served as a reliable source for student recruitment.

NETWORKING IN MOSCOW

In a relational culture such as Russia, where there was a low level of trust and substantial competition by other private schools, the leadership of RACU critically needed to build friendships with key officials, and this responsibility became a top priority for me when I was in Moscow on my frequent trips each year. The provosts and faculty of RACU were preoccupied with building the school's academic program, so relationship building in Moscow and in Washington, DC, was the president's task.

My friendship with President Yeltsin's minister of education, Vladimir Kinelev, continued to deepen. My periodic personal visits with him and copies to him of my annual written updates on RACU kept him updated on the school's progress. After serving on Yeltsin's cabinet until March 1998, Kinelev became the director of UNESCO's Institute for Information Technology in Education, which occupied a newly furnished twelve-million-dollar center about ten minutes from RACU. It was loaded with the latest informational technology equipment.

When I visited his new facility in August 1999, Kinelev invited RACU to partner with his Institute in sponsoring seminars and workshops in distance education because "he knew we did quality work." At the end of our discussion, I invited him to join RACU's advisory board, and he quickly accepted my invitation, indicating he "was honored to be invited!"[6] We will never be able to determine how important Kinelev's role as education minister was during these startup years of RACU, but it appears to have been significant. When challenged by education officials, our response was often the same: "We were invited to come here by the Yeltsin government and its education minister, Dr. Kinelev." This usually defused confrontations with obstinate bureaucrats and revealed how important personal relationships were in Russia.

---

[6]"Erratic Yeltsin Ousts Three Cabinet Ministers," *Los Angeles Times* (March 1, 1998); John A. Bernbaum, "Weekly Report from Moscow," August 30, 1999, 2, RACU Chron Files 1999, RA; John A. Bernbaum, "RACU Support Letter," December 6, 1999, 2, SL.

Two key leaders at Russian Peoples' Friendship University became important in RACU's development as well. Nicolai Trofimov, vice rector and well-known academic geologist, became a close friend dating back to his visit to the States in 1990 as a part of the initial Soviet delegation. He was the one who had taken the hands of his colleagues when I was asked to open the dinner meeting in Moscow with prayer in October 1990, which everyone else did as well. During the next few years our friendship blossomed, and he insisted that I have dinner with his family every time I was in Moscow. Marge was also a part of this family connection, and the two of us became close friends of Olga, Nicolai's wife, their daughter Maria, and their granddaughter Anna. These were occasions in which we got to know each other's families, and our family became their "American family." Trofimov helped to build our relationship with his university, of which he was one of the founders, and RACU's leasing of classrooms there in the early years proved to be an invaluable solution for our space problem. He counseled me about how to operate in Moscow and later agreed to serve on RACU's board of advisers. He also personally introduced me to Russian Peoples' Friendship University's rector, Vladimir Filippov. During my first meeting with Filippov, Trofimov described his visit to the States and our friendship and while doing so literally held my hand as a sign of his relationship with me. While it was uncomfortable for me at first, I realized he was indicating the nature of our partnership, and Filippov responded with great warmth.

In 1998 Filippov was appointed Russia's minister of education, so RACU had another key relationship among the country's top education officials. Filippov, a strong supporter of Russia's state-controlled system of education, also became an advocate for private education and the healthy competition he believed private schools created. In addition, he encouraged a shift away from memorized knowledge in favor of analytical and problem-solving skills, a shift that we had already established in our academic program at RACU. His desire for substantial reform in education emphasized the need to "eliminate the remaining ideological baggage and historical distortions from the Soviet period." Regarding funding for education, he proposed increasing the share of education spending from 3.5 percent of the federal budget to 6 percent over the following fifteen years. He knew that Russia's investment in education was one-third to one-half of that spent on education by any country in Western Europe or North America, and more was needed for significant improvement. RACU's leadership was enthusiastic about his appointment and strongly supported his commitment to investing in Russia's human capital, essential to the rebuilding of Russian society.[7]

A fourth key friendship developed over the years with the rector of Nizhni Novgorod State University, Alexander Khokhlov, who was also considered at one time for the position of minister of education. Khokhlov, another member of the original delegation of Soviet educators who visited the States in September 1990, had stayed in our home. As a result of this burgeoning friendship, he had invited Marge and me to spend a sabbatical at his university in the spring of 1992, as mentioned early in this book, and we became close family friends in the years that followed. We had no idea at the time that RACU, a small private school, would be so fortunate to have friendships like those with Khohklov, Trofimov, Filippov, and Kinelev, all educational leaders at the highest levels of Russia's government.

In Moscow a friendship that grew out of the National Prayer Breakfast in Washington, DC, in 1996, also resulted in a close personal relationship with Vladimir Platonov, chairman of the Moscow City Council. He became a member of RACU's board of advisers, and his position proved to be helpful when RACU faced opposition from other government officials. Our periodic luncheons and dinners were always fascinating experiences as Platonov openly shared stories of his struggles to build a progressive city council and his competition with officials in the Kremlin, who often interfered with the city's governance. When we faced tough issues regarding city permits, he was willing to intervene on RACU's behalf and over time became a reliable and invaluable supporter of our school.

By RACU's fifth year, my role as president also involved spending considerable time in Moscow with business leaders, especially American businessmen, who I hoped would value the school's graduates as possible employees. Dick Weden, general director of American Express in Russia, became a friend and introduced me to other corporate leaders in the city. He also offered valuable advice on how to handle challenges, and we shared "war stories" of dealing with the Russian bureaucracy. Other business leaders also showed support, and these friendships soon became essential parts of RACU's network. Karl Johansson, managing partner of Ernest and Young, and Michael Hancock, director of human resources at Mars Candy Company in Stupino, Russia, became donors as well as helpful

---

[7]"Revolutionizing Education," *The Moscow Times* (May 27, 2000).

advisers. I encouraged the Russian staff to invest in building friendships with these American business leaders and also with Russian corporate executives but was unsuccessful. Russian Christians generally assumed that business leaders in Russia were criminals who exploited Russia's transition to the free market for their own personal benefit. While this was true of the oligarchs who ran the country during Yeltsin's final years as president, such behavior was not the whole story.[8] Leaders of integrity worked in the marketplace, and we needed to invest in relationships with them.

BUILDING RACU'S BOARDS

One of the most crucial elements in RACU's development related to the composition of its board of trustees. When RACU began in the early 1990s, the first trustees were people with some connection and expertise related to Russia. Peter Deyneka Jr. and Mark Elliott, founders of RACU, brought considerable knowledge and understanding of Russia to the board. Deyneka's father had founded the Slavic Gospel Mission, and later his son created Peter Deyneka Russian Ministries, one of the most experienced Christian ministries operating in the former Soviet Union. Elliott, a professor at Wheaton College, played a key role in launching RACU in the early 1990s; his expertise in Russian history and religion made him a valuable member of the early board. In March 1998 Kent Hill, president of Eastern Nazarene College, joined the board; one of the few evangelical scholars with expertise in Russia and fluency in the Russian language, Hill earlier had helped to launch RACU as a member of the American Working Group in the early 1990s.

Phyllis Romkema, an international team staff member working in Moscow and later a consultant to US Agency for International Development, joined the board in 1996, and Stacie Schrader, the Russia country director for Opportunity International, was appointed a trustee in 1999. Both of these trustees had experience working in Russia, and their insights strengthened the board. However, the board faced major setbacks in 2000. Hill and Romkema both resigned: Hill when he was appointed to a leadership role in the US Agency for International Development, and Romkema because she moved back to the States and was no longer in a

---

[8]See David Hoffman's description of the six leading oligarchs in his book *The Oligarchs: Wealth and Power in the New Russia* (New York: Public Affairs, 2001).

position to travel to Moscow on a regular basis. In addition to these resignations, the death of Peter Deyneka in December 2000 after a battle with cancer left a huge void. Peter's vision laid the groundwork for RACU, and without his involvement and that of his wife, Anita, I would not have been involved in this adventure. By the close of 2000, the fifth year, only three American trustees remained.

With the counsel and assistance of numerous friends, five new trustees joined the board of trustees in May 2001, a month before RACU's first graduation, and their involvement began to transform the board's engagement. The five new trustees, leaders in business, law, and education, proved to be both generous donors and wise counselors with a vision for using their resources to build Christian communities in former communist states. Both Milt Kuyers and Dennis Kuester, Christian businessmen from Milwaukee I mentioned earlier in this book, had a passion for equipping Christian professionals to be witnesses in the marketplace. Howard Dahl, the president of Amity Technology, shared much in common with Kuester and Kuyers. A businessman who manufactured large-scale agricultural equipment that he sold in the States, Canada, Russia, and Ukraine, Dahl uniquely combined extensive business expertise about working in the former Soviet Union with theological training. Introduced to me by Peter Deyneka, Dahl quickly became a key partner in RACU.

Rich Dean, a lawyer who lived in Moscow and opened one of the first law offices in the Soviet Union, gained considerable experience in the late 1980s with Coudert Brothers and later Baker & McKenzie. He soon became an important adviser and a close friend. Dean knew Russia and its history and culture, so his counsel was greatly appreciated, and I leaned heavily on his advice over the years. Richard Gathro, my former colleague from the Coalition for Christian Colleges and Universities (formerly the Coalition for Christian Colleges), also became a trustee in 2001, although he had been involved in RACU from the beginning through our friendship. As an educator with considerable crosscultural experience, Gathro played a helpful role on the board with insight and encouragement. When these five new members joined Mark Elliott, Stacie Schrader, and me as American members of the board, its strength grew exponentially. For the first time, the board had not only strategic thinkers but also financial power.

One lesson learned during this period of board growth concerned the significance of the spouse of each trustee. Decisions made about gifts to RACU and other organizations resulted from discussions with these marriage partners. In subsequent years, the spouses of the trustees attended board dinners in both the States and in Moscow. Ann Dahl, Susan Dean, Darlene Elliott, Kathy Gathro, Sandy Kuester, and Carol Kuyers also became friends of Marge and mine as well as each other. During board meetings the spouses spent time together touring or taking part in joint activities. In this way over the years strong personal bonds developed.

The excitement of adding gifted American trustees to RACU's board was unfortunately matched by disappointment with our failure to identify and recruit Russians with similar talents. Alexander Zaichenko, one of the few Russian Christians with a PhD whom we knew in the early 1990s, had played an important role as a founder, along with Evgeny Goncharenko and Vladimir Obrovets. Goncharenko, well-known in Moscow's Christian community for his role as artistic director of the Moscow Cultural Center, had helped give RACU credibility with Protestant pastors in the city, and the same was true of Vladimir Obrovets, a scientist who was also associate pastor of Second Baptist Church in Moscow and had extensive contacts in the evangelical community in Russia. Obrovets helped recruit Yuri Apatov, executive secretary of the Euro-Asiatic Federation of the Unions of Evangelical Christians-Baptists. These four Russians served as trustees with no new Russian additions until 2001, when Ekaterina Smyslova, an attorney with experience helping Christian organizations become legally registered in Russia, was appointed. Smyslova, a very energetic board member, showed that Russian Christians with quality leadership skills could be found, but no additional Russian appointments were made until 2007.

The inability to build Russian ownership of the school proved to be one of RACU's greatest failures. This issue, repeatedly discussed in board meetings, was a problem without resolution. RACU's Russian trustees were constantly urged by the American trustees to nominate others to the board, but very few potential candidates emerged. In addition, these four trustees, struggling financially in Moscow's turbulent economy, never became major financial donors to the university. Over time this created an uncomfortable distance between them and the American trustees who had a considerable financial stake in RACU.

What we experienced with RACU's Russian trustees was also true of the churches that sent us their students. Church leaders proved unwilling to provide any support for scholarships and assumed that Christians from the States would provide this funding. Our Russian trustees warned us about this "culture of dependency" that characterized Christians in their country, based on the assumption that rich Christians in the West owed them this because of the persecution they experienced under the Soviet regime.

The trustees' attention also focused on RACU's board of advisers, especially as the school gained a higher profile in Moscow, highlighted by its first graduation in May 2001. Shortly after the charter and bylaws of RACU were registered, the first appointments to the board of advisers were made. By 2001, twenty Americans and Russians joined the board of advisers, including Kinelev, two young Russian businessmen, and a Russian attorney.[9] These appointments greatly elevated the prestige of RACU and opened doors to leaders in Moscow and at the US Embassy that previously proved hard to enter.

BUILDING RACU'S INFRASTRUCTURE

Within two years of the arrival of Hannes Furter as RACU's new leader in Moscow in 1998, it became clear that Furter's experience with Bible college education did not prepare him for working with a faith-based liberal arts curriculum, and he recognized this. In spring 2000 Furter told the board that his administrative team needed a vice president for academic affairs.[10] Fortunately for RACU, Larry Ort of Spring Arbor College was spending a sabbatical in Moscow during spring semester 2000. When he read the announcement advertising the need for an academic dean, he submitted his application. Ort had a long history of interest in Russia going back to his high school days, plus teaching experience in Russia at St. Petersburg Technological Institute, so his credentials were impressive. The board enthusiastically approved of his appointment in August 2000.[11] By this time, the RACU staff had grown to thirteen members, of which eleven were Russian.

In addition to the growing staff and the change in leadership from Hannes Furter to Larry Ort, the other key infrastructure priorities related to computers and library resources. Through gifts of used computers from the Council for

---

[9]See appendix C for a list of members of RACU's board of advisers.
[10]RACU Board of Trustees Meeting, "Minutes—May 12, 2000," May 12, 2000, 1, RBM 2000.
[11]John A. Bernbaum, "RACU Support Letter," August 21, 2000, 1, SL.

Christian Colleges and Universities, arranged by Kyle Royer, as well as the work of Don Mulder, a vice president from USRobotics and a member of RACU's board of advisers, who was able to convince his company to make a donation of seven new computers and software for both office and classroom use, RACU was able to equip its computer labs.

RACU's library, located in the Center for Christian Ministry in a shared room with New Life Bible College, also received numerous donations when the school opened. A donation of four thousand volumes from Peter Deyneka Russian Ministries, funded by Overseas Council International, included a unique collection of Russian-language theological volumes and numerous English-language reference works.[12] Within the first few years of RACU, this collection quickly increased through donations from numerous RACU faculty and board members. In a surprisingly short period of time, RACU's library housed valuable resources not available elsewhere in the country.

RACU BECOMES A LAND OWNER

After searching Moscow for a potential campus facility and visiting more than forty-five different sites, another surprising event happened—one of many in RACU's short history. For the previous several years, RACU staff had worked with several real estate agencies to locate potential campus facilities and had conducted their own independent research since these agencies did not prove to be particularly helpful, in part because of RACU's limited resources in a rapidly growing real estate market. In March 2001 the staff decided to change companies and instructed our two new agencies to search for existing buildings that could be renovated or for vacant land on which RACU could build a new facility. Within three weeks, Neil Lessman and Vasili Terekhov informed the staff that they had examined documents on one hundred buildings in Moscow, with none fitting RACU's needs and price range. Their conclusion: RACU must buy land and build, and they believed they had found the spot. The vacant land plot, located adjacent to beautiful park property within two blocks of a metro station (Babushkinskaya metro station) in the northern quadrant of the city, was about to be auctioned off by the Moscow city government. The auction price of $90,000, very reasonable by Moscow standards, included a long-term lease of forty-nine years.

---

[12]John A. Bernbaum, "Thursday Night Report," September 19, 1996, 1, RACU Chron File 1996, RA.

This land plot was one of the last pieces of land on the market since the mayor had put a hold on additional land sales in the capital city.[13]

I was in Moscow when this land plot was discovered and visited the site with Lessman and Terekhov. The three of us agreed that RACU should pursue this option. A conference call with the board of trustees concluded with agreement that a letter of intention expressing an interest in the land would be submitted to the city government.[14] In the week that followed, we learned that the principal competitor for this land was the Small Business Committee of the Moscow city government, which wanted to develop small retail businesses on the property. The regional administrators decided they preferred an educational institution over retail shops, so they contacted Terekhov and Lessman and gave them the full packet of land documents (totaling over four hundred pages) and the deposit slips needed to submit a bid. They told them that if RACU submitted a bid on April 16, it would be accepted, and they would announce the winner shortly thereafter. That is exactly what happened. After submitting an initial deposit of $18,000, the staff took the four hundred pages of documents to RACU's lawyers at Coudert Brothers, established by board member Richard Dean, and in forty-eight hours received a comprehensive report that "all was in order" with no "surprises."[15]

The board of trustees of RACU's US corporation agreed on April 9, 2001, to submit an offer of "up to $150,000" to the Moscow Land Commission for the purchase of this land, and the following day RACU's Russian trustees concurred.[16] Ten days later RACU learned that it won the tender for the land plot of 0.32 hectares (3,200 square meters) for $100,000. The land documents allowed the lessee to build up to a five-story building of forty-six hundred square meters, larger than we specified in our planning documents. When we received the news that the deal was signed and sealed, we were gratified that the negotiations had proceeded to completion cleanly, transparently, and according to the law, in an environment where corruption was a dominant feature, particularly in real estate

---

[13]John A. Bernbaum, "Need for Counsel on Moscow Property Option," March 28, 2001, 1-3, New Campus Facility, RA.

[14]John A. Bernbaum, "Next Steps: Babushkinskaya Land Plot," March 30, 2001, 1, New Campus Facility, RA.

[15]John A. Bernbaum, "RACU Is a Land Owner in Moscow," April 27, 2001, 1, RACU Chron Files 2001, RA.

[16]RACU/U.S. Inc. Board of Trustees Meeting, "Board Action—April 9, 2001 by Conference Call," 1; and RACU Board of Trustees Meeting, "Board Action—April 10, 2001 by E-Mail," 1, RACU Board of Trustee Meetings, RA.

negotiations.[17] These extraordinary events, which transpired so quickly in April
and May 2001, right before RACU's first graduation on May 19, could not have
been more dramatically timed.

When we learned about securing the land lease in Moscow, Art DeFehr, a
trusted member of RACU's board of advisers, told us about Harry Giesbrecht and
his construction company, Central Canadian Structures. Giesbrecht had built a
number of facilities in Canada for DeFehr's company, Palliser Furniture, and the
deals were all consummated with a simple shake of hands. He also said that the
construction company had building experience in the former Soviet Union and
that Giesbrecht was a trustworthy Mennonite. The board quickly agreed to
contact him as our contractor and his staff visited the site and reported that the
vacant lot had never been built on before, that it appeared easily accessible with
a gentle slope to the nearby Yauza River, and that its convenient location near the
metro and a major city highway were all "very good for Moscow." Giesbrecht
agreed to prepare a construction budget for a new five-story building once the

Figure 14.1. Informal groundbreaking ceremony. Pictured: Larry Ort, Vladimir Obrovets, Alexander Zaichenko, and John Bernbaum (May 2001).

---

[17]Bernbaum, "RACU Is a Land Owner in Moscow."

building design was approved by the board.[18] After years of moving to various campus locations, the staff and faculty got an enormous boost from finally having land where RACU's future campus would be built. We also knew that property ownership played a major role in securing accreditation, since Ministry of Education officials emphasized the importance of owning property as proof of the school's long-term viability.

RACU'S FIRST GRADUATION

The excitement about the purchase of the land lease spilled over to the events surrounding the first graduation, and together they resulted in an extraordinary climax to RACU's first five years. The staff successfully negotiated a contract with Russian Peoples' Friendship University to hold the graduation ceremonies and receptions on their campus, negotiations that took months of tough bargaining.[19]

In most Russian universities, graduation involved students reporting to the main office of their academic department, picking up their diplomas, and having a piece of cake. No speeches, no processionals and recessionals, and no musical presentations took place. RACU's leadership decided that our graduation would be done American style, and this was enthusiastically supported by the faculty and graduates.[20]

The two-day weekend began with a board of trustees' meeting on Friday morning, May 18, 2001. A private party for the graduates, their families, and visiting international guests followed on Friday evening, ending at 9 p.m. The next morning, a worship service was held in an auditorium at Russian Peoples' Fellowship University, where many Communist Party activities had taken place. This worship service on Saturday morning was designed to be a special time for the graduates and their families.[21] An informal luncheon for the graduates, their families, RACU staff, and overseas guests followed, enabling all to stay on campus for the graduation ceremony to follow.

Promptly at 2 p.m., the grand strains of Modest Mussorgsky's "Promenade" from his much-loved musical masterpiece, "Pictures at the Exhibition," could be

---

[18]RACU Board of Trustees Meeting, "Minutes—May 18, 2001," 5, RBM.
[19]RACU Management Team meeting, "Minutes—March 23, 2001," 1, MC—January–June 2001.
[20]Ralph Veerman played a key role in organizing the two days of events surrounding RACU's first graduation. His rich experience in planning major events proved to be an extraordinary contribution.
[21]"Worship Service—Program Protocol" in "Worship Service Script," RACU Graduation—May 1, 2001, RA.

heard. It was time for RACU's first graduation processional to begin. Leading the line into the auditorium, I was filled with excitement and gratitude, emotions I have felt each time I hear that powerful and regal piece, which became the signature processional for all future RACU graduations. As they followed, many faculty members, especially Russians, also dressed in academic regalia, walked down the aisle with tears of joy on their faces. Some wore brightly colored academic robes, signifying the institution from which they received their advanced degrees. Platform speakers and board members processed in black robes. The graduates wore signature US graduation robes and the unusual caps, with tassels streaming from them. At the end of the ceremony, these would be moved in unison to the other side of the cap—graduates at last.

After the graduates were invited to the platform to receive their diplomas and academic robe cords, a new experience in Russia, the recessional began with Mussorgsky's "Gates of Kiev," and the students were mobbed by their families and friends. The reception, well-stocked with beautifully presented, delicious food, also proved to be a highlight everyone enjoyed.

For the RACU staff, these events were clearly the most complicated and challenging that they had ever organized. The musical groups were outstanding, and the two translators who moved back and forth from Russian to English were extraordinary.[22] The *Moscow Times* did a major news story on the graduation and highlighted that eleven of the nineteen graduates were business majors; it also emphasized that RACU's education program was "morally and ethically grounded in the Judeo-Christian tradition."[23]

One of the graduation sponsors, Dick Weden, general manager of American Express in Moscow, sent an email the next day expressing his congratulations. He concluded his message with these words: "Congratulations to you all for this truly outstanding accomplishment, both for the students that you have and will produce for generations to come, but more importantly for Russia." I wept as I read his words and thought about how far we had come since September 1996, when we accepted these students as our first freshmen class.

On Sunday morning, before some of our international guests departed for home, a groundbreaking ceremony took place at the Babushkinskaya land plot.

---

[22]Nina Koryakina translated the worship service, and Konstantin Lysakov translated the graduation ceremony.
[23]"Christian University Celebrates First Graduation," *Moscow Times*, May 22, 2001, 10.

Figure 14.2. RACU's first graduation ceremony (May 19, 2001).

These events marked the climax of two dramatic milestones in the history of RACU at the end of the first five years: the possession of land on which to build RACU's campus and the first commencement service for its graduates, with the promise of many more to follow. Although the struggle to build RACU proved to be challenging and stressful, these events demonstrated that it was possible to get things done in Russia's tumultuous environment, often with miraculous intervention and surprises.

PRESIDENT PUTIN TAKES CHARGE

The excitement about RACU's first graduation and the prospects of building a new campus facility were enhanced by the positive response to Russia's new president, Vladimir Putin. No one knew for sure what he stood for and where he would lead the country, but his youth and energy made him an attractive contrast to the sick and feeble Yeltsin. He pledged to build a new, rule-abiding Russia, secure and prosperous.[24]

---

[24]Steven Lee Myers, *The New Tsar: The Rise and Reign of Vladimir Putin* (New York: Alfred A. Knopf, 2015), 180-81.

Following President George W. Bush's election in November 1999, the Kremlin hoped that the new Republican administration would be a more congenial partner than the previous Clinton administration. The new American president, in a speech at the National Defense University on May 1, 2001, the same month as RACU's first graduation and purchase of its land lease, declared that the Cold War was over: "Today's Russia is not our enemy."[25] Like many of our Russian friends, the RACU staff felt optimistic about the school's future and what appeared to be increased stability in Russia.

Part of the optimism was based on the remarkable economic growth of the Russian economy under Putin. Russia was essentially bankrupt when Putin became president, yet within five years after he took power, all of Russia's foreign debts had been repaid and its foreign exchange rates built up. Between 1999 and 2008, because of major increases in the global price of oil and natural gas, Russia went from the twenty-third-largest economy to the ninth-largest. Its growth rate over these years was twice that of China.[26]

In my conversation with the university's board of trustees, both Americans and Russians, as well as with corporate leaders in Moscow, the consensus was that Russia was finally under control and had the leadership in place to move it forward on the path of reform. No one expected improvement to be dramatic and without periodic setbacks, but most anticipated Russia would now become a "normal country." These encouraging developments bolstered the views of RACU's leadership that the school's successful first five years offered hope for the future.[27]

---

[25]Lilia Shevtsova, *Putin's Russia* (Washington, DC: Carnegie Endowment for International Peace, 2003), 197-98.

[26]Fiona Hill and Clifford G. Gaddy, *Mr. Putin: Operative in the Kremlin* (Washington, DC: Brookings Institution Press, 2013), 133-34.

[27]John A. Bernbaum, "A New Leader and a New Attitude," *Reflections on Russia*, January 2001, 1-2, Reflections on Russia file, RA.

15

STABILITY BEARS FRUIT

THE EXCITEMENT GENERATED BY RACU's first graduation and the purchase of a land plot for a new campus facility created momentum that fired up the staff and faculty. RACU's fifth year ended with a budget surplus for the first time, and gifts for scholarships proved to be the largest to that point. While many high-profile Western universities set up shop in Russia in the early 1990s, many left when large federal subsidies from the US government were radically reduced. RACU made the opposite statement by its management and behavior, saying in essence that we were there to stay, and our plans to build a new campus in Moscow provided evidence of that commitment. Our nineteen graduates, the first from a private Christian liberal arts college in the history of Russia, exemplified the quality RACU envisioned. The leadership wanted to keep building on the foundation laid the first five years.

The sixth year of the university began with the largest freshman class in the school's history: sixty-four students were admitted from a pool of more than one hundred applicants. With the enrollment of 135 full-time students in the fall 2001 semester, and 140 in the spring semester that followed, RACU exceeded our expectations. Thirteen professors, including one RACU graduate, taught at RACU for the first time during this school year; four new American faculty and nine Russians taught over one hundred courses in the fall and spring semesters along with spring modules in May and June 2002.[1] RACU's provost, Larry Ort, noted that the year was off and running with only a few minor glitches, amazing in Russia. Just before the students arrived, the staff and faculty gathered for a retreat

---

[1]John A. Bernbaum, "RACU Support Letter," October 12, 2001, 1, SL. See also Larry Ort's "Report on Campus Life and Programs," October 15, 2001, 1-4, ProvR.

outside Moscow in a rustic conference facility. Under Ort's leadership, we tackled diverse topics ranging from accountability to handling cultural differences.[2]

While the school year began with much enthusiasm, the pain of not being able to admit additional qualified applicants because of space constraints continued to weigh heavily on the admissions committee. Perry Glanzer, one of RACU's professors, shared this description of his experience on the committee:

> They both sat there crying. All of us on the committee felt an uncomfortable sadness. The stories had already been the same for the past few days as we sat interviewing applicants to RACU. Many students had high marks, wonderful recommendations, and potential to be Christian leaders. Of course, few had money or even the present possibility of paying the $1,000 annual tuition without help from RACU.
>
> This particular student sat crying with her pensioner mother who was forced to explain that because she made $60 per month, she would not be able to pay the $250 fee that RACU requires everyone to pay when they enroll. My head told me, "Perry, this is how most of the world lives. Few in the world get a chance to go to college," while my heart told me, "It's not supposed to be like this." And I couldn't help shed tears with them.[3]

Stories like this were heartbreaking; I attended these interviews and knew how painful it was to witness the disappointment. But stories like this also energized me because I was convinced that young Russian Christians just needed a break, a chance for quality Christian education that could change their lives, the lives of their families, and the ministry of their churches. When we shared Glanzer's comments with our supporters, the response was generous, and we were able to admit this student and others who simply did not have the funds to cover even some of the basic costs because of their families' poverty. But we were unable to make room for all of them.

SEPTEMBER 11, 2001: A NEW PARTNERSHIP EMERGES

At the beginning of each school year, I traveled to Moscow for several weeks to participate in the fall retreat for faculty and staff and to greet the students during their orientation sessions. In September 2001, I also wanted to support Larry Ort as he began his second year as RACU's provost. On the day of the attacks in New

---

[2]John A. Bernbaum, "Mid-Trip Report," September 4, 2001, 1-2, President's Trip files, RA.
[3]Perry Glanzer's description was included in my "RACU Support Letter," August 24, 2001, 1, SL.

York and Washington, I had gone out for dinner with Larry and Judy Ort and returned to their apartment for dessert. Galina Muravskaya, a friend from Nizhni Novgorod, somehow got the Orts' phone number and called me. She said, "Something terrible has happened to your country, and I am concerned for your family and friends in New York and Washington, DC." We immediately turned on CNN and saw repeated footage of the planes hitting the twin towers. It was incredibly painful to watch these attacks from Moscow because we wanted to be with our families, to be sure they were safe. We sat glued to the television, horrified and speechless. The next morning, after reading emails expressing loving concerns from friends, both Russian and American, I baptized my laptop with tears. I was ticketed to return to the States the following day, September 12, but all flights were canceled for an unknown period of time. I decided to use the time to practice what I had just shared with RACU's faculty and staff on the retreat—to be an agent of hope, despite the horrendous evil of these attacks.[4]

Overwhelming sympathy and affection kept coming from my Russian friends, students, and staff, as well as from Russians I did not know who, when they recognized that I was an American, would bow their heads and put their right hand over their heart as a sign of support. I went to the US Embassy and saw the piles of flowers left there by Russians and was deeply touched by all the acts of kindness.

On the day of the attack on the World Trade Towers and the Pentagon, the first foreign leader to call President George W. Bush was Russia's President, Vladimir Putin. In addition to expressing his condolences, Putin made it clear that the Russian army would not mobilize to match the mobilization of US forces— marking the first time since World War II that one of the competing forces of the Cold War stood down. The next day, the two leaders spoke again. Putin informed Bush that he had declared a moment of silence across Russia and the lowering of flags to half-staff. The two men agreed to work together to defeat the terrorist threat, a threat that put everyone in fear.

Both presidents were newly elected in 2000 and were trying to figure out how to relate to each other. Bush took a pragmatic approach toward his Russian counterpart, and during their first meeting in Slovenia in June 2001, he made the now-famous statement: "I looked the man in the eye. I found him to be very

---

[4]John A. Bernbaum, "Travel Plans: Coming Home," September 12, 2001, 1-2, President's Trip files, RA.

straightforward and trustworthy. . . . I was able to get a sense of his soul: a man deeply committed to his country and the best interests of his country."[5] The bond between the two presidents grew even stronger after September 11, and in Bush's view Russia had now become a partner, a friend, and even an ally of the United States in its battle against terrorism. This surprising development provided a great encouragement to RACU's leadership. The increased stability of Russia since Putin's election and now his willingness to work together with the American president added to the hopefulness of the new school year.

RACU'S ACADEMIC GROWTH AND UNEXPECTED CHALLENGES

In the early planning stages of RACU, the word *American* was not in the title because the original goal was to assist Russians in the development of a faith-based liberal arts university and then withdraw from the project once it was launched. However, in discussions with Russian leaders about the concept of a new private university in Moscow, the Russian trustees strongly urged us to reconsider our proposal and to build instead a binational institution, one that would be a permanent bridge between the two societies. While the university would, in its early stages, closely resemble faith-based liberal arts colleges in the United States, all agreed that over time it would be adapted to appropriately fit the Russian context. Once agreement was reached on these founding principles, the proposed mission statement and institutional charter were redrafted to include the binational structure. This founding vision appeared to be a good match for the emerging partnership between the two presidents of Russia and the United States and their leadership teams.[6]

As Russian-American trust grew, the opposite took place between RACU and its landlord, leading to an unexpected upheaval. The Center for International Education, a part of Moscow State University, leased RACU ample space for its program, but by spring semester 2002, the board of trustees became concerned when it learned from staff that the receipts for our rental payments were not official Moscow State documents but appeared to be personal receipts from the center's director. When the staff raised questions about the receipts, the director

---

[5]Steven Lee Myers, *The New Tsar: The Rise and Reign of Vladimir Putin* (New York: Alfred A. Knopf, 2015), 206.
[6]John A. Bernbaum, "RACU Support Letters," December 5, 2001, and January 11, 2002, 1, SL.

repeatedly postponed the discussions. At the instruction of the board, the staff made it clear to the director that RACU would withhold any future rental payments until a legal lease agreement was signed with Moscow State. The next day, the locks on RACU's classrooms were changed, and our staff was told to vacate immediately its leased space, just before final examinations and two three-week spring modules. Learning of our plight, New Life Bible College generously provided classrooms in the Center for Christian Ministry on a short-term basis for the examinations and modules.

This crisis became one of the few times the board of trustees members were not united in their decision. The Russian trustees opposed confronting the director of the center unless we had another lease option, since they fully expected we would be forced out of the Center for International Education in Moscow's volatile real estate market. The American trustees insisted on a legal lease and refused to accommodate any illegal rental payments that appeared to be going to the director and not Moscow State. The Russian trustees insisted that the board do things "the Russian way," but the Americans strongly disagreed. When the board of trustees voted to support the position of the Americans, most of the Russian trustees reluctantly agreed. Fortunately this disagreement was a rare occurrence between trustees.[7]

During the summer of 2002, RACU was homeless and faced another time of testing for the staff and faculty. After a difficult and frustrating time of searching that began in May, RACU found a new rental facility in August in, of all places, the former location of the Moscow Silk Factory. RACU signed a four-year lease for 640 square meters (6,400 square feet) on the second floor of the facility, with a separate entrance; the monthly rental was $13,802, higher than we paid previously, but the location near center-city Moscow warranted the increase.[8] The building needed considerable renovation to get it ready for the start of the school year in September to meet Ministry of Education facility requirements, estimated to cost $150,000. Once again, RACU had unexpected expenses that we had to supply in order to continue its program.[9]

[7]RACU Board of Trustees Meeting, "Minutes—May 17, 2002," 3, RBM.
[8]"RACU's New Home," August 2, 2002, 1, RACU Campus Locations, RA.
[9]John A. Bernbaum, "New Lease: Celebrate!," August 8, 2002, 1, PresR.

The staff decided to turn this challenge into a positive experience, so we invited the students to join all of us in painting and cleaning our leased space. We bought pizzas and sandwiches each day and worked together with the students, which proved to be a unique and valuable experience. The students had never seen university leaders and faculty members in old paint clothes working next to them, with music blaring in the background and pizza boxes spread out on the floor. When I arrived at the school one morning, five students were working in the entryway, laughing and having a great time together. What a joy to see the students refer to this facility as "theirs," since they had completely renovated it. As a result, classes started several weeks late, but the faculty made early assignments reasonable in light of the students' physical labors for the school. An unexpected challenge proved to be a positive community-building experience.[10]

With the completion of RACU's sixth year and its second graduation, of twenty-five students, the university had forty-one alumni. The seventh year began with Provost Ort's report that, in his judgment, "RACU has never been stronger in terms of its academic program and departmental leadership." For the first time RACU had qualified faculty serving as chairs and deputy chairs of each department. The sad news was the decision of Larry and Judy Ort to complete their service in Moscow after three years to return to the States. Ort had originally agreed to a two-year contract and extended it to a third year but decided to return to Michigan at the end of June 2003. He gave RACU exceptional leadership as an experienced Christian educator. Judy also used her skills to help strengthen RACU's academic and administrative program.[11]

By the end of the spring semester in June 2003, another sixteen students marched across the stage to get their RACU diplomas in front of an auditorium packed to overflowing. Fortunately the selection of a successor for Larry Ort as provost was easily made when David Broersma agreed to accept the offer. After his years of experience at RACU as chair of the English-language department and dean of the faculty, the faculty, staff, and students enthusiastically supported his appointment.[12]

---

[10]John A. Bernbaum, "Report from Moscow," September 5, 2002, 1, PresR.

[11]John A. Bernbaum, "President's Report (July–December 2002)," 1-2, PresR.

[12]John A. Bernbaum, "President's Report (April–June 2003), 1-2," PresR.

THE LAST BIG ACADEMIC HURDLE: ACCREDITATION

During the first few years of RACU's existence, one of the biggest challenges was all the legal work required in Russia. Part of the difficulties related to the fact that private colleges and universities had not existed in the Soviet Union, so new laws had to be passed after the failed coup in August 1991 to regulate these new educational institutions. This legal work created many opportunities for requests for bribes by government officials promising to facilitate RACU's paperwork, but only if cash was paid to help them "prioritize their work." The first step involved becoming registered as a legal entity in Russia, and it had finally been completed on July 25, 1997; the second step required securing a license to operate as a school that offered specific degrees, and RACU had received its license on December 3, 1997. The third and final step involved getting accredited, and we knew this was the most difficult, in part because the processes for recognizing private universities were slowly being developed, with opposition from state universities. Accreditation was essential for RACU's future because it meant graduates would receive diplomas recognized by the state and males could get deferments from military service while attending. Up to this time RACU student population had been largely female as a result.

While we knew that many private colleges and universities had been established in Russia in the 1990s, we also knew that only five had been accredited out of two hundred that had a license, so the challenge presented a big hurdle.[13] RACU's work on this process was led by Erna Abramyan and her student assistant, Olga Boytsova, aided by RACU's vice president, Vladimir Obrovets. Many hours were spent by faculty preparing notebooks of materials on their department's requirements.

November 12, 2003, was an exciting day. RACU learned that it had been granted full accreditation by the Russian Ministry of Education, the first private faith-based liberal arts university to be accredited in Russia's entire history. After years of hard work, the testing of RACU graduates, and the preparation of hundreds of pages of material, the Accreditation Collegium, made up of forty-two members, including officials from the Ministry of Education, nine presidents of Russian universities in Moscow, ten presidents from Russian universities from across the Russian Federation, and other education experts,

---

[13]"Higher Education in Russia," *Kennan Institute for Advanced Russian Studies Report* 14, no. 4 (1996).

Figure 15.1. Celebrating RACU's accreditation. Pictured left to right: Alexander Zaichenko, John Bernbaum, Erna Abramyam, and Kathy and David Broersma.

announced its decision. The report submitted to them by ministry officials documented the quality of RACU's programs and presented data indicating that the university had met or exceeded all of the required standards.[14]

GROWTH AND LEADERSHIP CHALLENGES ON CAMPUS

The news about RACU's accreditation added momentum, and the number of male students grew the following school year when males could be assured of draft deferments while they attended an accredited university. During the 2003–2004 academic year, the full-time student enrollment remained about 130, the limit allowed by RACU's educational license based on square meters per student in our facility. Under Provost Broersma's leadership, fifty-eight classes were offered during the fall and spring terms, with nineteen courses offered in May and June, fifteen of which were taught by Americans and four by Russians. This was the only way the university could come close to balancing out course offerings by faculty from the States and Russia. The addition of RACU graduates to the staff of the university was a positive development because of the immediate bonding with students who knew them.

The addition of three new executives, who together had more than one hundred years of experience in higher education, added considerable strength to RACU when they agreed to joined the leadership team. All three were recruited by

---

[14]John A. Bernbaum, "RACU Support Letter," November 25, 2003, 1, SL.

RACU board members and agreed to join our team as volunteers after distinguished academic careers. Anthony J. Diekema, who had served as president of
Calvin College for twenty years, agreed to serve as an adviser to the president and
to assist me in development and fundraising. He also accepted a nomination to
serve on the board of trustees and, when elected, was immediately made board
chair. He became my mentor, and I sought his counsel on numerous occasions
when facing crises for which I was unprepared. Robert DeBruin, recently retired
vice president for administration at Central Michigan University, had already
contributed to RACU by developing a new budget-reporting system. He agreed
to serve as a liaison to Central Canadian Structures, the contractor building
RACU's new campus facility in Moscow, a position for which he was well prepared,
having served as project manager for a number of new campus facilities at Central
Michigan. The third new addition was Clyde Vollmers, a recently retired professor
of business at Northwestern College. He became RACU's MBA director, with the
challenge of strengthening RACU's professional business-training program and
exploring the possibility of RACU opening an MBA program.[15]

By fall 2004, the enrollment at RACU jumped to 156 students; because the
intensive English program was listed as a part-time program, the thirty-four
students participating in it did not violate the legal limit set by RACU's license.
Although the enrollment in the social work program was only half that of the
business and economics program, the number of students in the English language and literature department almost matched that of business. The hunger to
learn English continued to escalate. As RACU's staff grew, it became the leadership's long-term strategy to "grow our own" faculty and staff members in order
to build a foundation for the university's future development. Fortunately, RACU
had some exceptional students in the early years of the school's existence, and
our American faculty often commented on the quality of the students. As a result,
some of our brightest graduates joined the staff or continued their education in
graduate programs, with the goal of returning to RACU as faculty members.

PLANNING RACU'S NEW CAMPUS FACILITY

While the academic program kept the Moscow staff and faculty busy, the purchase of the land plot in May 2001 caused the board of trustees to focus on the

---

[15]John A. Bernbaum, "RACU Support Letter," May 14, 2004, 1, SL.

planning of RACU's new campus facility and the related challenge of raising the necessary funding from RACU's small donor base. When the land plot was purchased, the board knew that permits and approvals were in place for a five-story building. The capital campaign initially had a goal of $4.5 million, of which $2.5 million had been received in gifts and commitments. The board questioned how to move forward on the construction project with only half of the estimated funds needed.[16] In May 2001 the board formed a task force on facilities, chaired by Dennis Kuester, together with Milt Kuyers and Howard Dahl. Meanwhile, Tom Ventulett, one of Atlanta's leading architects and designer of many of the buildings in downtown Atlanta, Chicago, and other major urban centers, prepared the first drawings of the new campus facility and submitted it to the staff and trustees in June. The miraculous partnership between the A Team (the consultants who assisted earlier) and the construction company was remarkable, enabling RACU to have access to the expertise of professionals in the construction field who did considerable work on drawings and detailed plans as a gift to the school.[17] Not only was the multiplicity of approvals by government agencies a major obstacle, but also the constant pressure for bribes was unending, and our refusal to make these payments further delayed progress on the building project.

On June 29, 2004, a meeting took place in Atlanta that provided the needed breakthrough on the building and capital campaign, meticulously planned by Ralph Veerman, RACU's marketing and development adviser. Tom Ventulett and Billy Mitchell, the leaders of the A Team, were the hosts, and they invited the two leaders of the construction company as well as the RACU facilities task force, which included Dahl, Kuester, and Kuyers, plus Diekema and me. In the impressive offices of Thompson, Ventulett, and Stainback, one of Atlanta's leading architectural firms, the members of RACU facilities task force met the A Team for the first time.

---

[16]RACU Board of Trustees Meeting, "Minutes—May 18, 2001," 5, RBM.

[17]The A Team was made up of the following members: architectural consultant—Tom Ventulett III, a principal of Thompson, Ventulett, Stainback and Associates (TVS) of Atlanta; real estate adviser—William A. (Billy) Mitchell, chairman and CEO of Carter & Associates, one of the largest real estate developers in the southeastern United States; construction design adviser—Chris Humphreys of Atlanta, with over forty years of construction experience in the Southeast; digital and print marketing materials—Bob Allen, president and cofounder of New South, Inc., a marketing communication firm; capital campaign counsel—Ralph Veerman, president of Veerman & Associates, a major gift-development network.

After reviewing design plans developed by Central Canadian Structures in dialogue with Ventulett and the A Team, Diekema and I met separately with the three RACU trustees and presented an updated plan to them, which expanded the capital campaign to the goal of $10 million; $7 million for the new campus facility and $3 million for an endowment for scholarships and faculty support. The proposal was Diekema's, but he told me that I had to be the one to ask these three trustees to contribute $1 million each to launch this second phase of RACU's capital campaign, which he believed was necessary to reenergize the campaign. Never in my life had I made such a request, but after the two of us prayed together, I did. "Let us talk privately," was their response. After fifteen minutes, which seemed like fifteen hours as we waited, we were invited back into the room and told that they had agreed to our contribution request. What an amazing experience! After reporting to the A Team and the construction company leaders, as well as the full board, about these major gifts, we immediately headed for the nearest restaurant to celebrate over dinner together, paid for by the A Team.[18]

RACU had much to celebrate as it opened its doors for the ninth year on September 1, 2004. We welcomed forty-four new students, half from the Moscow region and the other half from cities spread across the eleven time zones of Russia. Other exciting news came with knowing construction on our new campus was scheduled to begin soon now that several major gifts had been received over the last two months.[19] However, disappointment soon followed, an experience that we repeatedly witnessed during our work in Russia. In October we learned that the city had added a requirement that RACU construct an electrical substation at a cost of between $600,000 and $1.3 million, a totally unexpected expense. In addition, a special sprinkler system was needed at the cost of $122,500, as well as an "authorities fee and technical supervision charge" of $250,000—another unique Russian "surprise." In response, the board's executive committee put the construction project on hold.[20] The emotional roller-coaster ride was painful but became something we had to learn to live with in Russia. These were the mysteries of working in an authoritarian context where rules were unclear, graft was pervasive, and legal recourses unreliable. We had raised over $7.7 million in

---

[18]Executive Committee Meeting, "Memorandum for the Record—June 29, 2004," 1-2, RBM.
[19]John A. Bernbaum, "RACU Support Letter," August 27, 2004, 1, SL.
[20]Executive Committee Meeting, "Memorandum for the Record—October 18, 2004," 1-2, RBM.

RACU's capital campaign, a total hardly imaginable only a year earlier, but we were still unable to start building three years after the 2001 land purchase.

CAMPUS LIFE BLOSSOMS

After the five-year launch phase of RACU, the second period of growth, which stretched over the next four years, was a time of maturation and stability, although it required one more campus relocation. The momentum of the first graduation in May 2001 and the four graduations that followed were highlights in May of each year. The purchase of the land plot also was an exciting development, although the repeated delays due to complications caused by the city government were discouraging. But the students anticipated the exciting prospect of a new campus in RACU's future. Accreditation was another key step forward, making RACU one of the few private universities to achieve this goal. Students now graduated with state-approved diplomas, and males had deferments from military service while enrolled.

RACU's future looked bright by the conclusion of its first nine years, although constant pressure to raise more financial support for the school to cover both the capital campaign and student scholarships was unrelenting. However, less encouraging were the changing dynamics of Russia's political and economic life. Earlier signs of a possible growing partnership with the West, especially with the United States, were slowly diminishing. Increased hostility toward the West was on the rise, poisoning the environment in which the school operated. We continued to build constructive relationships with Russian political and education leaders but noticed that some of our Russian allies were backing away. While troubled by these signs, we remained committed to building RACU as a cultural bridge between our two countries as we headed into RACU's tenth year.

16

TERRORISM, ECONOMIC COLLAPSE, AND GROWING OPPOSITION

THE INSTABILITY OF RUSSIA'S POLITICAL and economic life and the cyclical nature of US-Russian relations throughout the 1990s and early 2000s were a constant concern compounding our work. Presidential primary seasons in Russia and the United States, something we witnessed every four years, were not times for constructive debate of our bilateral relationship. We soon learned that when Russia's president was on friendly terms with US leaders, the spirit of cooperation trickled down through the bureaucracy in Moscow, and leaders in the Kremlin and the Moscow government actively cooperated with RACU. But when relationships soured, this was quickly reflected by officials up and down the chain of command in the Kremlin. When terrorism reignited in Russia and multiplied during Putin's first term as president (2000–2004), the impact was felt throughout Russian society.

RUSSIA'S BATTLE WITH TERRORISM

On October 13, 2002, little more than one year after the attack on the World Trade Towers in New York, terrorists stormed the Nord Ost Theatre in Moscow, and the confrontation between police and Chechnyan terrorists resulted in 130 deaths. This attack hardened Putin and convinced him that Russia faced a dangerous threat from terrorists that required a strong response.[1] The war in Chechnya had

---

[1]Lilia Shevtsova, *Putin's Russia* (Washington, DC: Carnegie Endowment for International Peace, 2003), 254; Steven Lee Myers, *The New Tsar: The Rise and Reign of Vladimir Putin* (New York: Alfred A. Knopf, 2015), 217.

now spread to other parts of Russia as well as to its capital city. Like President Bush, Putin made the war against terrorism a top priority. The harshness of the Russian response to the theater attack in Moscow did little to end the threat. In 2004 Russians experienced a horrible series of violent terrorist attacks. On August 21, terrorists from Chechnya killed more than fifty people in an attack similar to one two months earlier in which they crossed the border into neighboring Ingushetia, a former part of Chechnya, and murdered more than one hundred people. Three days later, two passenger planes took off from Domodedovo Airport in Moscow and simultaneously exploded in midair, killing eighty-nine people. A few days later a woman blew herself up at the entrance to Rizhskaya metro station, just three miles north of the Kremlin, killing herself and nine others and injuring more than fifty innocent victims.[2]

The terrorism that plagued Russia in August continued by striking an unexpected target on the opening day of school on September 1, the so-called Day of Knowledge. Following a longstanding Russian tradition, parents and grandparents joined their children at School No. 1 in Beslan, a small city in North Ossetia, a predominantly Orthodox region in the center of the Russian Caucasus. More than twelve hundred people were gathered in the courtyard outside the school at nine o'clock that morning when a military truck pulled up and terrorists leaped out and herded everyone into the school's gymnasium. By the time this tragic hostage scene ended, 334 hostages had died, 186 of them children; ten Russian commandos gave up their lives trying to free them, and thirty Chechnyan terrorists were killed.[3]

Putin responded to these terrorist attacks by dramatically increasing the Kremlin's control of domestic life in Russia. In his post-Beslan speech to the nation, Putin declared, "The weak get beaten," and he made clear there would be no negotiations with terrorists but rather only a violent response from Russian security forces.

RACU FACES ITS FIRST OPEN OPPOSITION

The terrorism and resulting political chaos in Russia profoundly affected RACU, and the third phase of the school's development, from 2005 to 2008, was fraught

---

[2]Myers, New Tsar, 243.

[3]Myers, New Tsar, 254-58. See also Peter Baker and Susan Glasser, Kremlin Rising: Vladimir Putin's Russia and the End of the Revolution (Washington, DC: Potomac Books, 2005), "Epilogue: After Beslan," 371-82.

with struggle and conflict. The possibility of a constructive partnership between Russia and the United States, which had seemed possible in 2001, had largely evaporated in the years that followed. The expansion of NATO into countries bordering Russia, despite promises by President Clinton not to engage in this activity, was one major irritant. For Russians, NATO became a "four-letter word."[4] President George W. Bush's decision to attack Iraq in 2003 without the United Nations' approval further strained relations. The American action, vehemently opposed by Putin and his Kremlin advisers as well as by the French government under Jacques Chirac and the German government under Gerhard Schroder, caused further alienation. The Iraq attack served as a turning point in Putin's relationship with President Bush, convincing Putin that the United States was out to run the world as a unipolar power committed to isolate and weaken Russia in the process. In response Putin ended the work of the Peace Corps in Russia, stripped Radio Free Europe of its license to operate in his country, and expelled an AFL-CIO union organizer considered a threat to Russia's domestic stability.[5]

Putin's growing opposition to the United States quickly translated into increasing hostility in Russian society toward Americans. RACU soon felt the shift. In October 2004 we published a brief article in a local free newspaper at the suggestion of district officials who wanted us to introduce RACU to our new neighbors. Within two months, a group of individuals from the northeastern district where our land plot was located sent a letter of complaint to Moscow Mayor Yuri Luzhkov protesting the construction of RACU's campus in their area. They argued that RACU was a "Western Protestant missionary center" committed to "undermining traditional Russian values." The mayor forwarded this letter of complaint to the office of the local prefecture, one of the nine administrative units in Moscow. One month later, a local district official responsible for investigating the complaint contacted us. She told us that she had scheduled a public hearing for February 1 at the local municipal building, convinced that the complaint had "no judicial ground whatsoever." She recommended that our staff make a presentation at this public meeting that described the university and its educational goals.[6]

---

[4]James M. Goldgeier and Michael McFaul, *Power and Purpose: U.S. Policy toward Russia after the Cold War* (Washington, DC: Brookings Institution, 2003), 208-10.

[5]Myers, *New Tsar*, 229-30.

[6]John A. Bernbaum, "Opposition Efforts to Obstruct New Campus Construction: Chronology," January 26, 2006, 1, ARO.

Approximately fifty people showed up at the public hearing. The local district official opened the meeting by reading from the Russian constitution, which guarantees freedom of religion in Russia, and urged attendees to treat each other with respect. After a brief presentation by RACU's vice president, Vladimir Obrovets, angry attendees shouted out a barrage of questions, revealing that the unruly crowd had no particular interest in our responses. RACU's staff realized that the audience was divided into two groups. The first group expressed anger because they had been denied a permit to build an Orthodox church in the area and opposed any other group they considered non-Russian to receive one. The second group, residents of the apartment building adjacent to the campus land, simply wanted more detail about the plans. They rarely got a chance to speak. After a difficult two-hour session, the official chairing the hearing made this concluding statement: "I have spent all this time with you people and I have yet to hear a single serious argument which would substantiate your case."[7] Unfortunately, this did little to placate the opposition, as we soon learned.

The next day a petition with fifteen hundred signatures arrived at the Moscow City Council protesting the construction of RACU's new campus. *Kommersant* (*The Businessman*), a daily Moscow newspaper, highlighted the petition in an article with the subhead: "The cultural traditions of the Babushkinsky region are in jeopardy." The article quoted the comment of the local district official responsible for overseeing the construction of our school, who said, "We don't share their [the protestors'] opinion. . . . All the needed approvals have been obtained." Irina Raber, the prefect of the Northeastern Administrative District, in an interview about this petition, noted that the signatures were collected by a priest of a local Orthodox church and that the people who signed it did not know what they were signing. She concluded: "It's much ado about nothing," and went on to argue that the university would bring a "big advantage" to the local community.

The pressure continued to escalate and each petition or complaint meant we had to halt construction until the issue was adjudicated. In April 2005, while RACU staff was hosting an open house for new students and their families, a small group of protestors arrived on campus and kept interrupting staff with provocative questions. A television crew filmed the proceedings and made it

---

[7] Alexander Smirnov, "Comprehensive Report on the Meeting at Babushkinsky District Municipal Administration Headquarters—February 1, 2004," 1-5, ARO.

appear that the group of protestors was much larger than it was. A five-minute story covering the event later appeared on a television program called *The Russian Home.* Three days later, the Ecology Department of the city government notified RACU that it wanted to investigate environmental concerns about our building related to the protestors' complaints, and a hearing would be needed. The next month, at another public hearing, fifty protestors showed up and tried to block RACU staff from entering the building. The meeting lasted two hours, and once again the protestors' behavior was unruly despite the calming efforts of the local official who presided. At the end of the meeting, one of the commissioners who led the investigation into our case told our staff that RACU's documents were "irreproachable."[8]

Despite the encouraging support of local government officials, the opposition and obvious anti-American and anti-Protestant sentiments of the protestors continued. The situation became even more threatening the following month. On June 22, 2005, RACU staff received notification from the regional branch of the Rodina (Homeland) political party that they planned to organize a "full-scale protest campaign" against "your institution's subversive educational activities. . . . We will not allow the propaganda of an ideology alien to our nation on the site adjacent to our homes. This is going to be just the first sign of our protest. It is just the beginning." The following day a crowd estimated to be two hundred and fifty people gathered for a ninety-minute demonstration at the campus site. Most of the banners related to the Rodina political party, urging the audience to become members. I asked RACU staff members to attend the demonstration and take photos. They told me later that they decided not to get too close to the protestors because of the presence of intimidating young men with shaved heads, dressed in black T-shirts that read "Be Orthodox or Die," who were patrolling the crowd. Shortly thereafter we received another message from the office of the prosecutor from the Northeastern District with an "unofficial request" to see the documentation on the rezoning changes made for RACU's property. Meanwhile, other protestors contacted the vice mayor of Moscow to voice their opposition to RACU's construction, and we learned about this from the local prefect's office.[9]

---

[8]Bernbaum, "Opposition Efforts," 1-2. On May 19, 2005, the *Moscow Times* ran a short article on the protest titled "Christian Campus Protested."
[9]Bernbaum, "Opposition Efforts," 1-2.

In late July I received a message from my staff informing me that Prefect Irina Raber was instructing me to come to Moscow for an "emergency meeting." When I responded that I would gladly send one of RACU's vice presidents in my place since I was in the States, she insisted that I come and come immediately. When I arrived in Moscow and went to her office, accompanied by several of my staff, I faced an unexpected challenge. In my previous contacts with Prefect Raber, she had been gracious and supportive, but the environment was different now. She began the meeting with a forty-five minute harangue about how RACU's construction had created the most difficult situation she had faced in her fifteen years as a city leader. As her message was translated for me, I broke into a sweat because of the heat in the room and the pressure of this crisis. I remember sweat running down my neck and back.

Figure 16.1. Large opposition protest at RACU construction site (June 2005).

When she finished, I sat in silence trying to collect my thoughts and praying for wisdom. After a brief pause, I told her that I appreciated her support since the beginning of this construction project and reminded her that she had signed all the necessary approvals for our building; we had completed all of the requirements legally and had not paid any bribes. I continued by noting that we had invested $1.5 million in the property to date and we had no intention of moving somewhere else. She listened to my reply and said we needed to find a compromise. After a brief pause, she proposed the following solution: if we stayed away from the construction site until after the December 4 parliamentary elections, since the Rodina political party was using this as a recruitment tool, we could continue construction work once the scramble for votes was over. I agreed to her proposal after she clearly stated that she would be totally behind our construction project after December 4, as she had been earlier. I left the room totally soaked in sweat but encouraged that RACU could continue to build and not lose our substantial investment in the foundation and other site preparations. In the years that followed, Prefect Raber became a supporter and a friend.[10]

The opposition continued unabated throughout 2006 and 2007. An investigation by the public prosecutor, conducted at the request of a radical right-wing member of the parliament in January 2006, took six weeks. Once again RACU's record proved to be clean, and the criminal charges were dismissed. In November a lawsuit was filed against the city government and RACU, stating that the land sale was illegal. This suit was dismissed by a lower court, but in March 2007, two hearings were held with no new witnesses and no new evidence; the panel of three judges overturned the decision of the lower court. Our lawyers at Baker & McKenzie told us that obviously the opposition had gotten to these judges. This ruling meant that RACU no longer had a legal title to the property, and the thought of losing the property and all of the money already spent on construction was frightening. However, with the expert guidance of Baker & McKenzie's legal team, this negative ruling was subsequently overturned by a higher court, and the title was restored to RACU in May 2007.[11]

CAMPUS LIFE IN THE MIDDLE OF THE STORM

While RACU's staff and board of trustees dealt with the continuing conflict with opposition groups, endless lawsuits, and investigations, life on RACU's campus continued in an upbeat spirit. While students and faculty expressed disappointment that construction on the new campus kept getting blocked by petitions and demonstrations, they chose not to be drawn into the public confrontations. David Broersma reported that the ninth school year (2004–2005) was "an excellent one for RACU" from his perspective as provost. Course offerings expanded to sixty-four for 156 students; another highlight in May and June involved thirteen Americans and five Russians as faculty.[12]

In February 2005 a new, unexpected complication cropped up without warning—something not unusual for us. The owners of our rented campus facility, the Moscow Silk Factory, instructed us to vacate the property at the end of

---

[10]Alexander Smirnov, "Minutes of the Meeting with Prefect Irina Raber," August 3, 2005, 1-2, ARO.
[11]John A. Bernbaum, "Updated Information on RACU's Legal Challenge," April 3, 2007, 1-2, ARO. See also Alexander Smirnov, "Update & Memorandum," November 3, 2006, 1-14, ARO, and John A. Bernbaum, "President's Report," May 8, 2007, 1, RBM.
[12]David Broersma, "Academic Programs and Campus Life," May 2005, 1-3, ProvR.

June 2005, despite our four-year lease, due to a major renovation of the entire property to convert it into class A commercial space. A few months later, as we unsuccessfully searched for new space, good news arrived; in an unexpected change, the owners told us RACU could stay one more year. This highlighted the fragility of our school's existence in a city where leases and contracts were not binding.

In the midst of this instability, RACU's social work program, a key distinctive of the university, continued to grow in quality. Students took four years of rigorous coursework and served in internships, an academic requirement largely developed by American faculty. Internships provided practical, hands-on exposure to the social work profession. In the spring 2005 semester, students served as interns with Refuge for Children, an organization working with street children who maintained nomad lifestyles in Moscow; Agape Medical Clinic, which provided medical care to low-income families and individuals; Sister Lily, a charitable Catholic relief agency working with mentally challenged children abandoned by their parents; and the Gagarinsky Social Welfare Center, an official government operation that RACU students opened on their own initiative with promised government support that never materialized.[13]

Each fall, when students returned to campus for the beginning of another school year, staff heard stories of how they spent their summer months. For the first time, at the beginning of RACU's tenth year (2005–2006), Peter Smirnov, RACU's director of student development, conducted a survey, and the results clearly demonstrated the difference between our students and Generation *Nyet*.[14] Out of a student population of 160 students, 42 participated in summer church camps as leaders, helpers, interpreters, and musicians; 18 participated in various evangelization efforts; 10 worked with young people in church programs; and 14 volunteered in orphanages. In addition, three students helped build or rebuild churches, five went on mission trips to isolated regions of the Russian Federation, three worked with people with disabilities, six taught in Sunday schools, and two worked in homes for the elderly. Smirnov estimated that over fifty-eight hundred people had been positively affected by our students during the summer. RACU students were living out their faith in a culture where concern for others outside one's family and close friends rarely occurred.[15]

---

[13]John A. Bernbaum, "RACU Support Letter," March 21, 2005, 1, SL.
[14]See chap. 12.
[15]John A. Bernbaum, "RACU Support Letter," September 28, 2005, 1, SL.

The Moscow winter of 2005–2006, one of the coldest in recorded history, led the staff to consider closing the school for several days as temperatures plummeted to −34°C (−29°F). The doors stayed open, but I was delighted plans had me miss that January in Moscow. Enrollment remained in the 150 to 170 range for the next three years (2005–2008), with multiple summer modules offered by a steady stream of highly qualified Americans volunteering as short-term faculty.

At the end of the fourth year in the former Moscow Silk Factory, in June 2006, RACU prepared to vacate the premises. Unfortunately, the constant harassment and lawsuits by radical opposition groups had seriously delayed construction of our new campus, slowed the securing of needed permits, and this meant another temporary home was needed. The fourth campus turned out to be the best arrangement to date. Tushino Evangelical Church had recently purchased a large former House of Culture, which needed substantial renovation. When we approached the church leaders about leasing space, both parties realized that this was a win-win situation. RACU would invest in remodeling parts of the building, and when we departed the church would benefit from the renovation. The contract allowed RACU to lease fifteen thousand square feet, the largest space to date for our school. The leased space included rooms with large windows and an impressive auditorium and cafeteria. Although not conveniently located, with a fifteen-minute bus commute from the nearest metro station, the facility had curb presence resembling an institute or academic building.

Forty-nine freshmen entered RACU in the fall semester of 2006, thirty-eight in the fall of 2007, and forty in the fall of 2008.[16] The academic quality of the entering freshman classes continued to improve, and by 2008 the majority of students were Muscovites for the first time. In addition, children of RACU's Russian faculty also enrolled, and the spiritual life on campus blossomed through the efforts of staff and faculty who wanted to spend additional time nurturing the students. Patrick Black, a gifted American language teacher and accomplished musician, launched musical groups to lead in worship services and also held concerts for students and friends of RACU. Other small groups, organized by staff and students themselves, directed book studies and published a school newspaper.

---

[16]John A. Bernbaum, "RACU Support Letter," August 23, 2006; August 31, 2007; and August 26, 2008, 1, SL.

RACU'S CHALLENGE AS A PRIVATE UNIVERSITY

Several key contextual factors continued to be threats to RACU's survivability. The first was the uniqueness of private education in Russia after centuries of state-controlled higher education designed to serve the nation's employment needs. Free education was viewed as a right by Russians, and having to pay for it was a difficult adjustment to make, especially in unstable economic times. Government officials, whose entire experience had been working with state universities, were not supportive of the dynamic growth of private schools, and many resisted the reforms advocated by Gorbachev and Yeltsin. While some academic leaders appointed by President Yeltsin welcomed American and European educators in the 1990s, the majority had no interest in changing their system, and our Russian colleagues who supported the establishment of RACU from the early 1990s communicated this clearly to us.

In addition, private education required an entirely new set of laws to regulate it, which meant a succession of regulations, each of them leading to an unending requirement for mandatory government permits. Gaining the permits became especially important since many of the new schools were diploma mills or mechanisms used to conceal funds illegally gained. While we recognized this, we had no choice but to endure constant bribery requests from unsupportive officials. With little experience navigating our way through these numerous Moscow bureaucracies, part of our challenge related to knowing where to turn for counsel on licensing and accreditation issues. RACU also lacked funding to hire more experienced, high-priced experts who could help us, especially in the early years of the school's foundation.

The other shocking reality was the profound corruption of educational institutions in Russia, particularly universities. In 2007 a study by the Independent Fund for Public Opinion and the Higher School of Economics in Moscow described higher education as "the most corrupt sector of Russian society." Their research concluded that at least half of all Russian families paid bribes to instructors and college admission officials on behalf of their children. The rector of Moscow State University, Viktor Sadovnichy, commented that corruption was a "systemic illness" in the educational system and noted that he saw an advertisement for a service guaranteeing a perfect score on entrance exams to his university—for a hefty price.[17]

---

[17]Maria Danilova, "Russia to Fight Corruption in Education," *Washington Post*, February 2, 2007. See also John A. Bernbaum, "RACU Support Letter," February 16, 2007, 1, SL.

In this context, the leadership at RACU placed a high value on integrity and the character development of our students, concepts that did not seem to be valued at state universities. The mission of RACU was to equip students for leadership in their communities, churches, and workplace, and a key to leadership was being an honest person who kept commitments. With corruption evident in all facets of Russian society, our faculty and staff worked hard to teach students that there was another, better way to live.

THE GLOBAL ECONOMIC CRISIS OF 2008

As Putin neared the end of his second term as president in 2008, a global economic crisis ravaged Russia and compounded the political tensions generated by fears of terrorism and domestic upheaval. The economic crisis, triggered by mortgage defaults in the United States in September, did not seem at first to be much of a threat to Russia. But bankruptcies in the States, together with a drop in global oil prices, reverberated around the world and hit Russia harder than most. The Russian stock market dropped 17 percent in one day, after Lehman Brothers declared bankruptcy on September 15, and from June 2008 to January 2009 it lost nearly 80 percent of its value. In addition, between October and December, $130 billion in capital flooded out of the country. With a dramatic drop in disposable income, the crisis hit Russians hard from the richest to the poorest. Russia's booming economy went bust so swiftly that it brought back memories of the similar financial disaster in 1998. The two crises seemed like bookends to a decade of prosperity. In 2009 the Russian economy shrank 8 percent, the worst performance among the world's twenty largest economies. From Putin's perspective, the cause of Russia's woes was obviously the United States.[18]

This economic crisis affected RACU in two ways. First, it increased the financial adversity of many students whose families were living on subsistence-level salaries and ratcheted up the needs for scholarship support when many American donors also struggled with the economic downturn caused by the mortgage market collapse. RACU, like many US nonprofit organizations, saw a dramatic decrease in donations in the fall semester of 2008, which meant that staff and faculty salary payments had to be delayed as well as monthly lease

---

[18]Myers, *New Tsar*, 354-56; Fiona Hill and Clifford G. Gaddy, *Mr. Putin: Operative in the Kremlin* (Washington, DC: Brookings Institution, 2013), 87.

payments to our landlord. The second impact was equally painful. The crisis contributed to growing anti-American hostility, and this negative attitude encouraged more open opposition to the school and even less willingness on the part of government officials to assist RACU in securing needed permits and approvals, which seemed to be an unending challenge when building a major facility in Moscow.

BEGINNING CONSTRUCTION OF THE NEW CAMPUS

After five years of delay caused by RACU's unwillingness to pay bribes, and the constant work stoppages required when complaints and lawsuits were filed with government authorities, construction of the new campus finally began in summer 2006. Our real estate advisers informed us that securing building permits in Moscow normally took eighteen months, but in RACU's case it took five years! Finally, in July 2006, the site preparation phase was completed. The next phase involved driving the pilings into the ground for the foundation. Our contractor told us that he thought the building would be completed in one year.[19] We did not know then that it would take another four years!

Political protests and demonstrations continued through 2006 into 2007, with animosity toward the United States driven by Putin and his Kremlin advisers, but the support of local government officials provided some protection for RACU. Meanwhile, because RACU's land lease involved vacant space and was unofficially considered a "green zone," with park land sloping down to the river, there were protests from neighbors who did not want to lose even a part of it.

Compounding these objections were new building complications. Moscow architectural authorities insisted on eleven iterations of the architectural plans designed by one of American's leading architects, Tom Ventulett; our contractor thought they wanted to send a message that Russians have lessons to teach American designers, even the best ones. Even more troubling, when the ground was excavated in preparation for the foundation pilings, underground streams were unexpectedly discovered as well as buried pollutants that had to be removed and disposed of in distant locations because of their risks to the health of the neighborhood. All of this added substantially more cost and slowed the construction process.

---

[19]John A. Bernbaum, "RACU Support Letter," July 26, 2006, 1, SL.

The additions to the board of trustees of Marty Ozinga III, Bob Foresman, and Ren Broekhuizen in November 2005 brought more strength and financial power, just when we needed it. After Ozinga, the owner of a large concrete company based in Chicago, attended one of RACU's graduations, he thanked me for inviting him to join the board. This was a rare experience—getting thanked for asking someone for their financial support and voluntary board service.

The same was true of Foresman, a young and well-known American in Russia's financial world, who brought considerable expertise to the board through his extensive experience working with some of the most powerful leaders in the Kremlin. When I first met him, he told me he was considering leaving his position at a major bank in Moscow in order attend seminary. At the risk of alienating my new friend, I told him that this was a bad idea and that he needed to stay where he was because of his strategic access to key Russian leaders; he was also facilitating back-channel communications between Presidents Putin and Bush. Fortunately, he accepted my advice and played an important role in RACU's development and in encouraging US-Russian cooperation while officials on both sides were becoming increasingly hostile. Bob and his wife, Luda, became dear friends and important additions to our leadership team.

Broekhuizen, a former missionary and pastor, also brought strength to the board with his wise counsel and experience working with a number of other major nonprofit organizations. A number of RACU trustees served on other college boards, and they told me they had never seen a board so committed in terms of sharing their time, talent, and treasure over many years.

The American trustees became helpful partners in recruiting potential donors to join the five Volga River cruises Marge and I hosted between 1999 and 2006, designed to give in-depth exposure to life in Russia and the mission of RACU. Several of these were combined with groups from Peter Deyneka Russian Ministries. Approximately half of the time was spent in St. Petersburg and Moscow, while the remaining time was spent cruising Russia's numerous channels and lakes, with stops in beautiful places such as Kizhi Island in the middle of Lake Onega.

One trip is particularly memorable, our second Volga River cruise in June 2000, when we had only two guests, Doug and Florida Ellis, from Atlanta. We were disappointed that we could not recruit more participants, but we decided to proceed as planned. As a result of our time together on this trip, Doug and

Florida became dear friends and generous supporters of our ministry. When I asked them and other guests what they enjoyed most about their trip, I expected comments about the amazing palaces of the Russian czars, the beauty of the Kremlin and St. Basel's, or the magnificent forests, especially the birch trees, which seemed endless. Invariably the time in Moscow with RACU students, staff, and faculty proved to be the highlight of their experience.[20]

By early 2008, substantial progress was finally being made on the new campus facility. The concrete work was finished, the roof completed, windows installed, and the heating system was operational.[21] While we experienced some vandalism and a number of broken windows reportedly caused by rock-throwing youth in the neighborhood, the local police department helped stop this destruction. We did not know whether this vandalism was due to anti-American sentiments, possibly encouraged by some of the protest groups or unhappy neighbors, but the residents in the apartment building adjacent to our facility gradually became more friendly. In fact, a number of them asked about possible jobs in the school once it opened at the new site.

PUTIN'S CHALLENGE: MANAGING HIS SUCCESSION

Tensions with the Bush administration grew in 2007 as the United States criticized Russia for the assassination of leading journalists, such as Anna Polikovskaya. At the same time, the decision by the American president to establish American military bases in Poland and the Czech Republic alarmed Putin and his military commanders, who viewed these as a direct threat to their country's deterrent strategy. Putin used the occasion of the annual Munich Security Conference in February 2007 to give a public dressing-down of the West for a list of grievances. From his perspective, the United States was out to dominate the world on its own terms. This speech became a landmark in Russia's relations with the West. Steven Lee Myers, a *New York Times* writer, poignantly observed: "It was as if the bear that was the Soviet Union had awoken from two decades of hibernation."[22]

Through summer and fall 2007, concern existed among Putin's leadership team that Russia would lose the gains it had made if he stepped down, since the

---

[20]For further information about RACU's Volga river cruises, see the trip files in RACU Marketing & Capital Campaign Files.

[21]John A. Bernbaum, "RACU Support Letter," January 11, 2008, 1-2, SL.

[22]Myers, *New Tsar*, 318-22.

Russian constitution only allowed the president to serve for two consecutive terms and his second term was coming to an end. Three months before the election, Putin arranged a meeting in the Kremlin with the leaders of the four principal political parties, who nominated Dmitri Medvedev, his longtime colleague from St. Petersburg, as his successor. This preserved the pretense of pluralistic choice, not an act of dictatorial manipulation. The next day, Medvedev said he would nominate Putin as his prime minister if he were elected, with his principal goal being stability.[23]

In March 2008, the predictable election of Russia's new president, Dmitri Medvedev, brought with it the hope of RACU's leadership and many others that the new administration would be less confrontational toward the West and more committed to democratic reform in Russia. However, the opposition RACU had faced from 2005 to 2008 seemed to indicate otherwise. The events that unfolded in the following three years caught us by surprise. Medvedev's presidency looked hopeful at first, but the Kremlin's policies, largely directed by Putin as prime minister, became serious threats to the future of RACU.

---

[23]Myers, *New Tsar*, 326-33.

17

THE STRUGGLE FOR SURVIVAL

FOUR GIANTS AND A NAME CHANGE

AT THE BEGINNING OF RACU'S THIRTEENTH YEAR (2008–2009), Provost Broersma reported to the board of trustees that the school faced four giants, each one a formidable foe. The first giant involved the impending battle over relicensing and reaccreditation, both of which grew more complicated because of repeated moves; each time RACU relocated to another campus, numerous approvals and permits had to be filed with government authorities, particularly the Ministry of Education. The second giant related to the recruitment of students in light of the declining university-age population and changes made by the Kremlin to protect state universities from any further loss of applicants by increasing financial support for them from the government. The third and fourth giants were closely linked. The third was the increased funding in order to complete the campus facility due to dramatically escalating construction costs. The final giant came with increased need for essential scholarship monies due to the global financial crisis of 2008–2009.[1]

An additional factor involved the decision by the staff and the trustees to change RACU's name. When the board, after much discussion, decided to explore a name change, no one realized that the timing could not have been worse for this action, complicating the challenges relating to the four giants. From the early years of RACU, we experienced problems because of our name and misunderstanding about its unique identity. For many in Russia, the name immediately suggested a Bible college or seminary, even though RACU did not offer degrees

---

[1]RACU Board of Trustees Meeting, "Minutes—November 7-8, 2008," 2, RBM.

in Bible or theology. In addition, to most Russians the word *Christian* meant "Protestant" or "Baptist." Many Russians assumed that RACU was an American Protestant seminary.

RACU never operated as an exclusively Protestant educational institution. From the beginning, we welcomed students from the full range of Protestant denominations, as well as Orthodox and Catholic believers. The same was true of our staff and faculty. Since Protestants in Russia made up less than 1 percent of the population, we did not want to further minimize their presence by building a small denominational school.

Our vision emphasized cooperation among all Christians in the country, because the pressing issues involved in the rebuilding of the country after seventy years of communism required their unity.

The board asked Nancy Low, who had built a successful marketing company based in Washington, DC, to assist the staff in determining a new name for the school. As a marketing professional, she believed intensely that the name change should be done

Figure 17.1. Dr. David Broersma, RACU's campus leader.

in the context of a larger marketing strategy so that the school could be repositioned in the market.[2] Nancy and her husband, David, traveled to Moscow in fall 2007 and organized focus groups made up of RACU students, alumni, and friends. After extended discussion, the board approved a new name similar to the original name: the Russian-American Institute (RAI). The tag line, "Character, Competence, and Christian Worldview," words often heard in the focus groups, highlighted the distinctive faith basis of the Institute. The phrase affirmed the mission of RAI to nurture the moral and spiritual character of the

---

[2]Nancy Low, memorandum to RACU board, July 12. 2006, Name Change—2006–2009, RA.

students, to give them the skills and abilities to be professionally competent, and to ground them in a historic Christian worldview. Retaining the term "Russian-American" in the title affirmed the bicultural character of the school and that our students learned English and took almost half of their courses in English, which still had great appeal in Russia.[3]

THE FIRST TWO GIANTS

The principal priority for RACU's academic growth centered on preparing for the second round of approvals by the Russian Ministry of Education in order to maintain its educational license and accreditation. Like the American educational system, universities and institutes in Russia faced requirements to be periodically reviewed in order to ensure they met the country's quality standards. Unlike in the United States, the approval process in Russia operated under the control of government agencies rather than by peer reviews, and this worried us, especially as US-Russian relations deteriorated during Putin's second term as president (2004–2008).

RACU's provost, David Broersma, orchestrated the work of applying for a renewed educational license and reaccreditation. Because many new private colleges and institutes operated as storefront businesses or diploma mills, or in some cases money-laundering vehicles, we knew that the second round might be more demanding than the first, in 2003. Making an investment in Russia by building our own campus would set us apart from most private schools, which rented facilities and had little institutional strength.

When the fall term began in 2008 with forty new freshmen, sixty-nine courses, and 141 students, spirits were high because the new campus appeared to be nearly complete, and students often traveled to the construction site in anticipation of being able to move in. The staff knew that this school year would be a watershed year in RACU's history because of the new campus and the challenges of securing government approvals for RACU's diplomas. When it became clear that the new campus would not be ready for occupancy for another year or so, we faced several difficult complications. Our initial lease with the Tushino Church in 2006 covered

---

[3]Nancy Low's "RACU Board Presentation," dated November 2, 2007, was approved by the trustees at their meeting on November 9-10, 2007, Name Change—2006–2009, RA. See John A. Bernbaum, "RACU Support Letter," July 22, 2009, 1-2, SL. As mentioned below, the name change did not take effect until near the end of 2009, so I will continue to use RACU in discussing events up until then.

eleven months, and we renewed it each year that followed, since short-term leases like this did not have to be registered with the Moscow government. In order to get reaccredited, the government required RACU to have an officially registered five-year lease. The leadership of the church agreed, but we soon found out that many of their legal documents were outdated, a common reality in Moscow. We had no idea how difficult and time consuming this process would be, since the pressure for bribes factored into almost every needed approval.

The second complication resulted from the poor timing of our decision to rename our school. This involved revising the school's charter and securing approval of the revised charter by the Ministry of Justice, which proved to be a tortuous process. We learned that the Ministry of Justice had moved to a new location, which meant indefinite delays for all business with their staff, including approvals for new or revised charters.[4]

While facing these challenges, another surprise awaited us. Because of the delays in getting the lease agreement with the Tushino Church registered with the government, RACU's educational license expired on December 12, 2008. Once we received our registered lease agreement on January 11, 2009, and tried to quickly get relicensed, we learned that RACU could not be relicensed until we changed our legal address to the Tushino Church, rather than Russian Peoples' Friendship University, which had served as our legal address since the school opened in 1996. This setback became a crippling wound when authorities in the Ministry of Education told us that we could not apply for relicensing but had to apply as a new school with a new name and a new location.[5]

Rumors circulated in Moscow that the Kremlin wanted to eliminate one-third of all private institutes and universities in Russia, and without warning the Ministry of Education began to change the regulations for accreditation so that small colleges and institutes could not possibly meet the standards required. When we submitted documentation for accreditation, which highlighted that over 120 American faculty had taught at RACU to date, 90 percent of whom had doctorates from leading graduates schools in the States, ministry officials said they did not recognize American PhDs. This meant RACU could not meet the standards for the number of doctorates required by Russian regulations.[6]

[4]David Broersma, "Academic Programs and Campus Life," November 2008, 1, 10-11, ProvR.
[5]David Broersma, "Academic Programs and Campus Life," June 2009, 1-2, 12-16, ProvR.
[6]John A. Bernbaum, "RACU Support Letter," June 10, 2009, 2, SL.

While the changing requirements created difficulties for all small schools, part of the reason for our struggles related to inadequate preparation and the lack of adequate reporting systems within our school. Data required by the Ministry of Education had not been collected by our staff, and we did not have the expert leadership we needed to direct this effort. While our staff developed new reporting systems, the effort was too little and too late to prevent the loss of RACU's license to operate as an educational institution.[7] We were unsuccessful in slaying giant number one.

The second giant was intimately related to the first. In the turmoil that surrounded the end of the Soviet empire and the disintegration of the USSR from 1989 to 1991, parents had no desire to have children until their country's future became more clear. New births severely declined in the years that followed, and the population of the Russian Federation fell nearly seven million by 2010. Demographers described this as "the largest single episode of depopulation yet registered in the postwar era."[8] The resulting dramatic drop in university-age students, a reduction by 50 percent, proved to be an unprecedented development that startled everyone.

State universities lobbied the Kremlin for protection from this radical drop in students and focused their attention on the threat posed by the large number of new private institutes and universities. Though there was no public notification of these issues (particularly challenging when operating in an authoritarian context), RACU's leadership soon perceived a change in attitude from Ministry of Education officials. The growing hostility did not appear to be directed at RACU because of its faith-based academic program or its American ties, but rather because as one of many private schools it could not be controlled like the state universities and was perceived as harmful competition.

The culmination of these combined issues hit RACU hard in December 2008, six months after the election of Russia's new president, Dmitri Medvedev, when hopes were high for an improved US-Russian relationship. Because the school's educational license had expired, RACU could no longer legally offer regular classes in spring semester 2009. The staff made a decision, with the board's approval, to offer free seminars and free noncredit lectures for our students. The

---

[7]John A. Bernbaum, "President's Report," November 20, 2009, 2, PresR.
[8]Nicholas Eberstadt, "The Enigma of Russian Mortality," *Current History* (October 2010): 288.

loss of the license also meant that we could not collect tuition and fees from our students, and the resulting deficit in the operating budget, together with more unexpected construction costs, put the school's future in jeopardy. We also had to cancel the graduation ceremony planned for June 6, even though RACU's new campus neared completion and the staff had hoped to hold the next graduation in the new building.[9]

The pressures on RACU's Moscow leadership escalated as the school faced all of these new hurdles. When I came to Moscow after the end of the school year in 2008, then again in 2009, and met with David Broersma, he shared with me the considerable stress he was under. After discussing this ongoing situation with Anthony Diekema, RACU's board chair, the decision was made to decrease the stress by appointing him dean of the faculty and retaining his considerable strengths in the classroom. Fortunately, Clyde Vollmers, who taught at RACU in its business program, and his wife, Kathy, accepted the board's invitation to step in as RACU's provost for the 2009–2010 school year. During summer 2009, difficult decisions had to be made about dismissing staff and faculty, and this proved to be one of the most painful parts of my responsibility as president.

Though we were successful in completing construction of the new facility by September 2009 and moved staff and faculty into their new offices, we had to cancel the fall program because of RACU's expired education license. No one knew whether or when it might be renewed.[10] Finally, on December 3, 2009, exactly one year after the license expired, RACU received its new license and began using its new name, the Russian-American Institute. With the new license secured, RAI announced classes beginning on January 18, 2010, and fifty-eight of our students, a little less than half of the previous full term, returned for the spring semester; most of the remaining students had enrolled in other schools, and many told us they planned to reenroll in the fall. RAI's twenty-member faculty offered a reduced number of courses, and five additional instructors taught in RAI's intensive English-language program.[11] Seven American faculty came to Moscow during the summer to offer classes in business, of which three

---

[9]John A. Bernbaum, "RACU Support Letter," May 15, 2009, 1, SL.

[10]John A. Bernbaum, "President's Report," November 20, 2009, 1-2, PresR; John A. Bernbaum, "RACU Support Letter," October 21, 2009, 1, SL.

[11]John A. Bernbaum, "RAI Support Letter," March 30, 2010, 1, SL; Clyde Vollmers, "Provost's Report," March 10, 2010, 1-2, ProvR.

were first-time teachers, and although the class sizes were small, these courses appeared at the time to mark a turnaround in the school's future. Despite the setbacks, the staff and faculty were hopeful that the new license and new facility would begin a resurgence of the institute, to be highlighted by the dedication of the new building in May 2010.[12]

BATTLING THE OTHER TWO GIANTS

The continuing financial inflation in Russia, especially in Moscow's rapidly developing real estate market, meant that any delays in construction caused by public protests and demonstrations increased construction costs. Between 2006, when construction finally began on the new campus facility, and 2009, when largely completed, the annual inflation rate averaged 10.7 percent. The wife of Moscow's mayor, Yelena Baturina, had a monopoly on concrete, and this was another source of high prices and unpredictable shifts in costs.[13] One of RAI's trustees, Marty Ozinga III, who owned a large concrete company in the Midwest, commented how difficult it was to build in this city, although he smiled and said he would not mind having a similar monopoly in Chicago!

By the beginning of President Medvedev's term in 2008, RACU had raised $15 million for its capital campaign, most of it from a handful of trustees and their friends whom they recruited to render monetary assistance to the school. The executive committee had no idea it could raise this amount, since a few years before its members felt a goal of $10 million might be beyond their reach. Major new gifts came in, sometimes demonstrating that God answers prayers "just after the nick of time," as our pastor used to say, and in some cases these were unsolicited gifts. Such miraculous signs of support proved to be a great encouragement as we struggled with opposition groups in Moscow. However, increasing costs meant we still needed another $5 million by fall 2008. This giant appeared to be impossible to conquer. The board investigated the option of a bridge loan, from either a Russian or an American bank, but these efforts failed. The executive committee of the board of trustees faced the harsh reality that it might have to sell the building since the shortage of funds seemed overwhelming.[14]

---

[12]Clyde Vollmer, "Provost's Report," May 28, 2010, 1-3, 6-7, ProvR.

[13]Yelena Baturina was reported to be Russia's richest woman by *Forbes Russia*, with her estimated worth at $1 billion; Baturina and her husband, Yuri Luzhkov, moved overseas when he was removed as Moscow's mayor in 2010 ("Russia's Richest Woman Is Ex-Moscow Mayor's Wife," *Moscow Times*, August 21, 2014).

[14]Executive Committee Meeting, "Memorandum for the Record—July 31, 2008," 1-2, RBM.

Unexpected demands from city authorities continued, even in the final stages of construction. When the school's staff applied for an occupancy permit, which we had been warned might become another primary opportunity for bribe requests from inspectors, government officials told us we had to make changes to accommodate the handicapped, which had already been a part of our building design, but they wanted more changes even though they admitted that the laws on handicapped rights were still being written. As far as we knew, we were being forced to make changes for handicapped accessibility that no government building in Moscow had in place.[15]

RAI's fourth giant—the school's increasing financial deficits—grew dramatically with the economic crisis in Russia in 2008–2009, which increased the need for more scholarship support, and this pressure never let up. With the dismissal of staff and faculty in summer 2009, the board offered generous compensation and severance payments that also required more funding. The amazing willingness of trustees and a small number of major donors to make loans to RAI in order to complete construction of the new facility and to make salary and severance payments proved to be the resolution that defeated the third and fourth giants. By the time the building was completed and we moved in, RAI's construction loans totaled $8.5 million, provided by fewer than ten families. These construction loans, plus gifts to the annual fund for scholarships and severance payments, exceeded anything I had ever experienced or imagined possible.

RAI'S BUILDING DEDICATION

After an eight-year struggle, the new forty-six-thousand-square-foot campus facility was completed, and by January 2010 RAI faculty offered courses in the new building, one of the few owned by any private university in Russia. The leadership of RAI had great expectations about future developments, and the building offered many new opportunities for education and service in the Moscow community. For example, faculty-initiated English-language classes held in the evening for adult learners as well as new seminars in counseling for professionals started. Since the institute had a renewed five-year educational license, the undergraduate programs in business and economics, social work and counseling, and English language and literature restarted. Although only fifty-eight former

---

[15]Executive Committee Meeting, "Memorandum for the Record—December 23, 2009," 1-2, RBM.

RAI students enrolled in the spring semester, we expected a full complement of students in September 2010 because many of our former students had already paid for a full year's tuition at other schools for the 2009–2010 school year.[16]

On May 27, 2010, the dedication of RAI's new building took place amid heavy security due to the attendance of Russian and American government officials.[17] The audience of over four hundred, including more than forty RAI supporters from the States, attended the dedication ceremony and the graduation the following day. The Moscow news service *Protestant* reported on the dedication ceremony and called the building "the most beautiful and representative building in all of Russian Protestantism." There were several inspiring messages: speeches by Vladimir Platonov, chair of Moscow's City Council (Duma) and a longtime supporter of RAI; greetings from Metropolitan Hilarion (Alfeyev), the newly appointed head of the Russian Orthodox Church's Department of External

Figure 17.2. RACU Board of Trustees at the building dedication (May 2010).

[16]John A. Bernbaum, "RACU Support Letter," January 11, 2010, 1, SL.

[17]A video of the building dedication on May 27, 2010, is accessible on BEAM's website, http://beam-inc .org/a-visual-history-of-the-russian-american-christian-university/.

Relations, read by one of his staff; and words of support from Irina Raber, the prefect of Moscow's Northeastern District. Support from Moscow leaders, as well as a presentation by Eric Rubin, deputy chief of mission at the US Embassy, was encouraging, despite the current difficulties in US-Russian relations.

On May 28, RAI's ninth graduation took place in the new facility. Eighteen students received their diplomas and heard Anthony Diekema, chair of the board of trustees, share with the audience his thoughts on this important milestone in the school's development.[18]

Figure 17.3. 2010 graduates at the new campus (May 2010).

THE PERFECT STORM: SUMMER 2010

The impressive new campus facility gave the institute stability and credibility, two important factors in the Russian context, but the challenge remained to discover and implement a plan for recovering from the forced closure of its semester program in fall 2009 and the low enrollment with the renewed license in the spring. As expected, the 2009–2010 academic year turned out to be one of the most difficult in the institute's history. The recruitment of students for the fall semester became the highest priority. The full reality of Russia's catastrophic demographic decline hit RAI with full force. Not only were we experiencing, with

---

[18]RAI Marketing Staff, "The Institute's First Graduation in the New Campus Facility," n.d., 1-2, RAI Building Dedication, RA.

all of Russian educational institutions, the 50 percent drop in university-age students, but we also witnessed firsthand how Russian state universities handled the same challenge by offering free tuition to half of Russia's first-year students and admitting many who did not pass the minimum requirements of Russia's new national entrance exams. RAI hired additional student recruiters, who worked hard in the spring and summer, but they reported that many potential students, including some of RAI's former students, confessed they wanted to return but had received free tuition offers from state schools that they could not afford to turn down. Many male students at RAI also chose to attend accredited universities and institutes in Moscow or their home cities in order to be sure they could evade service in the Russian military.[19]

In addition to these challenges, the unexpected and eventful weather that summer in Moscow compounded RAI's struggle for survival. A record-breaking heat wave, a severe drought, and forest fires that filled the city of Moscow with smoke made daily living in the city almost unbearable, and many families fled. All of this added to the frustrations of our staff recruiters. By the time the institute began classes in September 2010, only eighty-four students enrolled. This low enrollment threatened the institute's viability. The mountaintop experience of May 2010 gave way to a valley of deep disappointment four months later.

Two other major crises followed the storm and threatened RAI. Our lawyers at Baker & McKenzie notified the board that the institute had to pay over $2 million in valued-added taxes, in part because RAI's contractor and subcontractors could not provide proof that these taxes were paid from funds paid to them by RAI for this purpose; in addition, the school no longer had a tax exemption on its property, because of changes in laws pursued by the Kremlin. The estimated annual property tax on RAI's new building went from $2,000 to $500,000 per year, or more than $41,000 per month. We understood clearly that the Kremlin's decision to remove tax exemption from property owned by private institutes and universities, together with the refusal to recognize the doctoral degrees of American faculty, raised serious questions about the school's future.[20]

---

[19]John A. Bernbaum, "President's Report," July 13, 2010, 1-2, PresR.
[20]Executive Committee Meeting, "Memorandum for the Record—October 4, 2010," 1, RBM.

THE FINAL BIG DECISION

By fall 2010, the board of trustees was fully aware of the serious financial, en-rollment, and accreditation challenges facing RAI.[21] RAI staff estimated that the budget for operations in Moscow would result in a projected net loss of $1.25 million during the next fiscal year. Provost Clyde Vollmers and vice president Alexander Smirnov prepared a recommendation that RAI "stop this bleeding" by phasing out RAI's undergraduate academic program, offering classes only to seniors who could graduate by the end of summer 2011, and immediately renting out classrooms and office space on the second floor as well as the remainder of the third and fourth floors to small companies. For students currently enrolled at RAI, they proposed that tuition be refunded to first-year students, financial assistance be provided for second- and third-year students to transfer to other schools, and special effort be made for fourth-year students to complete their program with the use of independent studies, if needed.[22]

At a trustees' meeting held in Oak Brook, Illinois, on November 12-13, 2010, the board made two momentous decisions. The first determined to gain title to the building for the purpose of monetizing it in order to pay construction debts. A re-lated discussion involved the use of the net assets from the sale of the building for further ministry of RAI in Russia, to be defined at a later date. The second decision suspended the undergraduate program by August 2011, following the recom-mended steps outlined by Vollmers and Smirnov. Only one American trustee was absent from this historic meeting, but two of the four Russian trustees chose not to participate, which reflected their much lower level of commitment and financial investment in RAI. Before the meeting concluded, most board members remained for a luncheon meeting, during which they brainstormed about future possibilities for RAI. This time proved to be a stimulating discussion about many new future prospects. Before they departed, the board asked me to continue in my role as president through June 2013. They also asked the same of Vollmers and Smirnov in order to preserve a team of three they wanted to keep in place at least through 2013.[23]

While the closure of the undergraduate program indicated a major change of mission, the trustees felt convinced that they were not closing down the institute

---

[21]John A. Bernbaum, "RAI's Current Financial Challenges: Key Factors," October 25, 2010, 1, RAI's Pro-gram Closure, RA.

[22]Clyde Vollmers and Alexander Smirnov, "Tourniquet Strategy," November 13, 2010, 1-4, RBM.

[23]RACU Board of Trustees Meeting, "Minutes—November 12-13, 2010," 1-37, RBM.

but rather starting a new stage in its development without owning a major piece of property in Moscow. Difficult decisions had been made, yet an expectancy remained of new opportunities ahead. That resiliency on the part of the trustees demonstrated the character and quality of these leaders, who easily could have decided to close down the school and leave Russia after so many painful battles.

The question of how to use the institute's twenty years of experience and financial investment became the central focus of board discussions. A related concern focused on finding ways to support programs that trained young Russians to be citizens of integrity and agents of justice, grounded in the rule of law. The school closed, but work in Russia remained to be done. The challenge was figuring out how to do it.

18

CHANGING COURSE

FOUR DAYS AFTER THE BOARD OF TRUSTEES decided to suspend RAI's undergraduate program, sell the new campus facility, and investigate new opportunities for educational programs in Russia, the students learned about this change of course. This was the most painful period in the university's entire history. On November 17, 2010, Provost Clyde Vollmers asked faculty and staff to attend the student assembly to help them through the trauma of these dramatic changes. After Vollmers told the students that the undergraduate program would be suspended in August 2011, he explained that fourth-year students would be able to complete their programs, while second- and third-year students would be assisted as they arranged to transfer to other schools. In addition, first-year students would receive full refunds for their tuition payments. Vollmers shared this information with tears in his eyes, and many students cried when they realized what lay ahead.

Vollmers reported that while the students were disappointed, even though they suspected this might happen, there were no negative comments or criticism. Everyone focused on encouraging others around them rather than on their own sorrow. The students amazed the Americans with their attitude and once again showed how they dealt with setbacks and disappointments, which they had learned to expect from life. No one expressed any sense of entitlement or asked, "Why did this happen to me?"

Vladimir Obrovets, RAI's vice president, stood up after Vollmers finished his comments and tried to put the suspension of operations into an historical context. He told the students that in 1995, a partnership between Russians and Americans started with the intention that American financing would wind down and Russian financing would ramp up within ten years. He concluded his remarks by stressing that "the Americans did their part and, in fact, did more than they promised, but the Russians have not kept their part of the agreement." This was a hard truth but was not the reason the school was forced to close.

When the meeting ended, students embraced faculty and staff and thanked them for the privilege of having studied at RAI. Mark Currie, one of RAI's American faculty members, commented that "the day went as well as possible." Just like when we were forced to dismiss faculty and staff in summer 2009, after RAI lost its educational license, the Russians showed no bitterness or anger at all and thanked us for allowing them to be a part of the school, which they considered a gift.[1]

THE DIASPORA

The undergraduate program for fall semester 2010 had seventy undergraduate students, with an additional twenty students in the intensive English program and forty-four students in the English language school offered in the evenings and on weekends, for a total of 134 students. All of these numbers were substantially lower than we had hoped, and they contributed to the board's decision to suspend the undergraduate program. For the faculty and staff, the primary focus of the 2010–2011 academic year became assisting all fourth-year and some third-year students in completing their degree requirements so they could graduate in spring 2011, with others projected to complete their programs by December. This pool of approximately forty students included several from earlier years who reenrolled in order to quickly complete missing courses for their degree. The second priority was to help second-year and the remaining third-year students transfer to other schools, either faith-based or state institutions. RAI faculty worked hard to assist these students, logging many additional hours helping them locate and apply to schools that best fit their courses of study. They also accompanied them as they visited other schools of interest. Fourteen business majors successfully transferred, with two enrolling in Calvin College and four in Lithuania Christian College, while

---

[1] Clyde Vollmers, "Wednesday Report," November 19, 2010, 1, RAI's Program Closure, RA.

the remainder entered state schools, including some with Moscow's best business programs. Fifteen third- and fourth-year language majors completed their undergraduate programs, and six second-year students transferred to the prestigious Russian Academy of Education. Provost Vollmers reported to the board of trustees that as far as we knew, not one academic hour of credit granted at RAI was lost in the transfer to other educational institutions, including several in the United States. The care and commitment of faculty for their students that was a hallmark of RAI throughout its history remained firm until the very end.

The undergraduate program at RAI closed on June 2, 2011, as forty-two students walked across the stage and received their diplomas, with tears of both joy and sadness and many hugs of faculty and family members. The graduation celebration was only the second held in our new campus facility, and it was the last. RAI's eleventh graduating class had twenty-five students from Moscow or the larger Moscow region, and seventeen students from across the Russian Federation, Uzbekistan, and Moldova.[2]

At the conclusion of the school year, the RAI staff had only fourteen members—five administrators, five faculty, and four building-related staff. Vollmers announced on January 25, 2011, that he was resigning following the June graduation, so the leadership of the school by the summer of 2011 was now in the hands of Alexander Smirnov, RAI's chief operating officer; Vladimir Obrovets, RAI's Russian vice president; and me, with my time divided between Moscow and the States. Fortunately the board of trustees made a tactical decision to create a task force of the executive committee, chaired by Dennis Kuester, which included Howard Dahl, Bob Foresman, Sid Jansma Jr., Milt Kuyers, and Marty Ozinga III. The focus of the task force, through discussions by phone and email on a biweekly basis, was to secure the title of ownership of RAI's new building, address tax issues, and determine how to repay RAI's substantial construction loans. With no expertise in any of these areas, I was grateful when the board asked me to focus on overseeing the remaining programs of the evening English-language school and the social work program while shaping a new mission for the institute.[3]

---

[2]RAI Commencement Program, June 2, 2011, RACU Graduation files, RA.

[3]John A. Bernbaum, "President's Report," July 8, 2011, PresR.

PURSUING A NEW MISSION

One month after RAI's last graduation, I submitted a report to the board that itemized four essential principles for any future institute program. It must

1. be one that Russians value and willingly support financially;

2. be led by Russians and, when possible, be in partnership with Americans to insure a binational character;

3. be available to Orthodox, Catholic, and Protestants by design; and

4. be funded from both Russian and American sources, with no more than 50 percent provided by American donors.[4]

These were not new principles; they were goals from the beginning of the institute's history, but they had not been achieved. Restating them made it clear that the institute had no future in Russia unless things changed and Russian support was forthcoming.

For the next school year, the board agreed to allow RAI's social work undergraduate program to continue in an evening format because of its interdependency with RAI's new graduate-level Christian counseling program, which was successfully recruiting new students, mostly professionals in the field who wanted additional certification. The eighty-hour lay-counseling short courses quickly became popular, and fifty-two applicants enrolled, because it was the only faith-based program for social work in Russia. In addition, RAI faculty held the first international Christian Counseling Conference at RAI in May 2011, with sixty attendees from a broad range of cities and churches. A week later, Lanny Endicott, a professor of social work from Oral Roberts University and a frequent guest faculty member at RAI over the years, directed a seminar in Moscow for seven hundred church leaders about Christian care and counseling. The future of the social work program, with its counseling specialty, looked bright.

The second program that showed promise was RAI's English-language school, which Tim Hange and Tamara Kozlovskaya reshaped and expanded for the 2011–2012 school year. By appealing to residents of RAI's immediate neighborhood, the institute gained access to businesspeople who worked in Moscow and wanted to improve their English-language skills. Utilizing the skills of qualified language

---

[4]John A. Bernbaum, "A Report to the Board of Trustees—Pursuing a New Mission for the Russian-American Institute," July 8, 2011, 2-3, RAI's New Mission, RA.

teachers who were Christians, the institute positively affected these adult learners, who were attracted to the program by the supportive relationships they discovered among the faculty and staff. The board agreed that both the social work and English-language programs should be set up as separate profit centers so their financial progress could be carefully monitored.[5]

The other new priority that emerged from discussions with board members and RAI's supporters in Moscow became deepening the institute's relationship with the leadership of the Russian Orthodox Church. Through a personal friendship developed between Bob Foresman, RAI trustee and well-known Barclays investment banker in Moscow, and Metropolitan Hilarion Alfeyev, the Russian Orthodox Church's chairman of the Department of External Church Relations, new, unexpected opportunities emerged. With Foresman's encouragement, Metropolitan Hilarion met with me on several occasions, and in February 2011 Foresman and I hosted him on a ten-day visit to the States, during which he met with evangelical and Catholic leaders.[6] As a result of this remarkable friendship with the impressive metropolitan, a young, well-educated leader with two doctorates and fluency in multiple languages, the institute's trustees and staff became increasingly convinced that the moral and ethical foundation needed for a healthy, vibrant Russia could be built on religious values. In addition, they shared the conviction that no substantive changes could be made in Russia toward building a free, just, and secure society without the joint partnership of the historic Christian communities (Orthodox, Catholic, and Protestant). We were committed to fanning the flame of cooperation in any way possible.

Until the title of ownership of the new campus facility was secured, the trustees were not in a position to make any firm strategic decisions about future programs. In summer 2011, an incremental plan was approved by the board that affirmed the staff's recommendation that the Christian counseling initiative and the English-language school be developed and expanded as the principal ongoing educational programs of the university. In addition, the board encouraged the

---

[5]Bernbaum, "Report to the Board of Trustees—Pursuing a New Mission," 3-4.

[6]John A. Bernbaum, "Metropolitan Hilarion's Trip to the States (February 2011)," 1-6, Trip Report—Russian Orthodox Church Records, RA. For his interview with *Christianity Today*, see Timothy C. Morgan, "From Russia with Love: Orthodox Metropolitan Hilarion Offers Evangelicals More than an Olive Branch," May 2011, 38-41, www.christianitytoday.com/ct/2011/may/fromrussialove.html.

staff to explore networking opportunities with other nonprofit organizations committed to strengthening the family and bringing dignity and integrity to the Russian marketplace. The third goal centered on the further nurture of RAI's relationship with Metropolitan Hilarion.[7]

Amazingly, in the fall 2011 semester, the new campus facility was once again full, with more students enrolled than at any time in the school's history. Between the social work evening program for undergraduates and its certificate programs for professionals, along with the burgeoning size of the English-language school, more than two hundred students, both university age and adult learners, were enrolled, with the expectation of more growth in the spring semester. While the institute could no longer offer an accredited undergraduate program, these specialized programs appeared to provide valuable training, and early signs indicated that they did not require financial subsidies as the undergraduate program did.[8] By the spring semester, the institute's School of Social Work and Counseling added an expanded training program for orphanage workers and volunteers. While care for orphans had been a focus of the social work program from its inception in the mid-1990s, aided by both American and Russian specialists, who developed one of Russia's first international social work departments, this new expansion raised the profile of the program.[9]

ROLE REVERSAL IN THE KREMLIN

While RAI trustees and staff were wrestling with decisions about the future mission of the school, new educational programs, and monetizing the assets of the campus building, the political context in Russia entered a new period of uncertainty. Moscow became filled with tension following the surprise announcement by Medvedev in September 2011 that he supported the candidacy of Putin for president in the election scheduled for the following spring. Putin mentioned to reporters that this decision had been made several years earlier—an admission that angered many Russians, who thought there would be open

---

[7]Bernbaum, "Report to the Board of Trustees—Pursuing a New Mission," 5-6.

[8]John A. Bernbaum, "Support Letter," October 14, 2011, 1, SL.

[9]Anthony J. Diekema, "Support Letter," February 17, 2012, 1, SL. Two American faculty with expertise in this field played key roles in helping the institute develop its special focus on the care of orphans and the equipping of families to adopt them: Beryl Hugen, a professor of social work at Calvin College, and Lanny Endicott, a professor of social work at Oral Roberts University. Both did extensive comparative studies of child-welfare systems in the United States and Russia.

competition for the presidency. The decision and subsequent comments made clear that from Putin's perspective the people had no role to play in deciding who would lead the country; their only part in the election would be ratifying the ones chosen by current leadership.[10] The strategy of Putin was shaping up to be a Soviet-style election reminiscent of the past.

The December 4, 2011, parliamentary elections took place in a country where the mood had darkened considerably. Medvedev and Putin were aware of the public outcry against electoral abuses in the local elections of 2008 and 2010 and knew that election fraud had been the catalyst that spawned the Arab Spring, which had resulted in the populist overthrow of several Middle East governments in 2010. Despite this, election abuse was again rampant. Ballot-box stuffing captured on video and shown on the internet and television revealed the scale of the corruption and mobilized thousands of formerly apathetic Russians to fill the streets in protest. Antigovernment demonstrations grew to be the largest since August 1991.[11] The anger spilled over into the presidential elections, only three months away, and Putin's plan to return to power was less popular than he had hoped.

In response to this negative buildup to the election, Putin expressed his conviction that the United States wanted a regime change in Russia and was working to undermine his support base. He needed an enemy to unite the country behind him, and the United States became that enemy. Putin's election strategy comprised declaring himself the protector of Russia's social and cultural values and staunchly opposing the decadent values of the West, thereby launching a cultural war against his opponents inside and outside Russia.[12]

As everyone expected, Putin won the presidential election in March 2012, with 63 percent of the vote in the first round. Although his election critics knew that millions of votes were illegally counted, there was no question he had the support of most Russians. He won every region in the country except Moscow, the capital city. Most Russians simply shrugged their shoulders and accepted the election results with resignation.[13]

---

[10]Steven Lee Myers, *The New Tsar: The Rise and Reign of Vladimir Putin* (New York: Alfred A. Knopf, 2015), 388.

[11]Timothy J. Colton, "New Uncertainties Enliven Russia's Election Season," *Current History* (October 2011): 260-61; Myers, *New Tsar*, 388-98.

[12]Myers, *New Tsar*, 403-14.

[13]Myers, *New Tsar*, 406-7.

WHAT ABOUT RAI'S NEW CAMPUS FACILITY?

In the middle of the electoral drama and street protests, RAI finally received its title of ownership for the new campus in January 2012, after a drawn-out process of more than a year in which the trustees and staff refused to pay bribes to get proof of the building's ownership. By the summer the board focused on resolving its financial obligations to donors, the payment of taxes, and the management of the building, in which 50 percent of the space was now leased and occupied by small businesses.

Because the board had a strong moral obligation to repay all construction loans from private individuals that enabled RAI to complete the campus building, selling it in order to do so was a top priority. In April 2012, with the title of ownership secured, the board of trustees approved the sale of the building and authorized the executive committee, under the leadership of Dennis Kuester, whose experience as a bank president equipped him for the task, to conduct negotiations and complete the sale.

The board's top priority involved offering the building to Protestant churches or denominations at a discounted price—a price that covered the construction

Figure 18.1. RACU's new campus facility.

loans and taxes, with a small net asset to be used for the future mission of RAI.[14] One Pentecostal pastor contacted the board of trustees and asked that the facility be given to him "free of charge," while a small number of other Protestant leaders entered into negotiations but were unable to offer a purchase price that covered RAI's liabilities.

The only offer that emerged during the early months of 2012 came from the Church of Latter-Day Saints, and the board initially had reservations about considering this offer. A number of American trustees and most of the Russian trustees were opposed to a sale to Mormons, but when no acceptable offer was made by any Protestant group, the board chose to accept the offer with an "option agreement" that allowed the Mormons to conduct extensive "due diligence" on the campus facility. After numerous discussions with Mormon leadership over seven months, the option agreement expired because the trustees were unwilling to meet a complex series of demands by the buyer, and in January 2013 the facility was listed for sale on the Moscow commercial real estate market. Over the following twelve months, the executive committee reengaged in negotiations with several Protestant groups, but they again proved unsuccessful. After these efforts failed, the executive committee signed agreements in October 2013 with four real estate companies in Russia, and in December 2013 the board began intense negotiations with IPG Photonics, a large, international private company started by Russians that was interested in purchasing the building for administrative offices and educational purposes. They offered to pay the asking price, and a sale and purchase agreement was approved by the board of trustees on March 21, 2014.[15]

SHIFTING GROUND IN AN INCREASINGLY HOSTILE ENVIRONMENT

During the three long years that RAI's leadership devoted to selling the campus facility, the board had approved a staff proposal that the institute spin off its two principal educational programs and set them up as Russian legal entities. The English-language school was the easiest to convert, and it rented space in the new campus facility until the space was subsequently sold in 2014. The Institute of Social Work and Counseling was similarly set up in January 2013 and moved into

---

[14]Board of Trustees, "Minutes—April 6, 2012," 1-2, RBM.
[15]These negotiations related to the sale of the campus facility are summarized in the meetings of the executive committee and the board of trustees between March 18 and November 16, 2013, RBM.

two facilities in Moscow, one for its evening undergraduate program and another for its certificate program for professional counselors.[16] To our great surprise, the undergraduate social work program was later invited to become a part of an Orthodox university in Moscow; because of its reputation and the development of its program by both American and Russian social work experts, it proved to be an attractive addition despite its decidedly evangelical character. Meanwhile, RAI trustee Mark Elliott was asked by the board to form a task force with responsibility for finding a home for the institute's library collection and its archival records. He eventually arranged for the library to be donated to St. Petersburg Christian University and, together with RAI's president, agreed to house the institute's files at Asbury Theological Seminary in Wilmore, Kentucky.[17]

When the institute's academic program moved off campus, the staff was further reduced in size and provided with generous severance agreements. The board approved my proposal that I shift to a half-time position beginning on July 1, 2013, an arrangement that remained in place for the next eighteen months. My responsibilities largely focused on managing the operations of the school, especially its US office, with oversight of the Moscow office, and preparing proposals for the board on the institute's future mission.[18] With the sale of the campus facility, earlier discussions about possibly using part of the facility for RAI's educational programs came to an abrupt halt. Dennis Kuester encouraged the RAI trustees not to let a "little thing" like the sale of the building stand in the way of future programs supported by RAI, based on its twenty years of experience and commitment to Russia's future welfare.[19]

The board's discussion of the institute's future took place in the midst of a continuing downturn in US-Russia relations. Headlines in international news coverage highlighted a meeting between President Obama and President Putin on the Baja California coast during the G20 summit in June 2012, during which neither president made any effort conceal his disdain for the other. Following this negative encounter, Putin began to use language that echoed the worst periods

---

[16]John A. Bernbaum and Alexander Smirnov, "Future of RAI's School of Social Work & Counseling," which included the budget for 2012–2013, was approved by the board of trustees, "Minutes—November 2-3, 2012," 3, RBM.

[17]Board of Trustees, "Minutes—November 2-3, 2012," 5, RBM.

[18]John A. Bernbaum, memorandum to the executive committee, "RAI's Transitional Leadership," April 11, 2013, 1-2, RBM.

[19]Dennis Kuester to the board of trustees, "Future Ministry," December 19, 2012, 1, Russia's New Mission, RA.

of the Cold War.[20] The following month the reelected president signed into law a proposal from the governing United Russia party requiring nonprofit organizations receiving foreign donations and engaging in political activity to register and declare themselves foreign agents. RAI got caught in this trap. By October 2012, the US Agency for International Development was forced out of Russia, followed by several democracy-promotion groups, including the International Republican Institute and the National Democratic Institute.[21]

Shortly after the ban on US organizations became law, Russian federal-security officers visited the RAI campus without any advance warning and copied hundreds of pages of the organization's files, searching for materials and weapons that supported Kremlin opposition. Our staff informed them RAI was an educational institution, not a terrorist organization, and that it was not engaged in political activities. Their explanation was disregarded, and the search continued for five hours. Ultimately the security services notified RAI's staff that they had determined that RAI was not engaged in any underground resistance but fined the institution for several minor legal infractions. Actions such as this sent an unmistakable message: Russian citizens should keep away from foreigners if they did not want personal trouble with the government. While this made no impact on RAI's students and faculty, it did make working with government officials much more difficult. Unlike the 1990s, when RACU was openly welcomed by Russian educators and government officials, the attitude toward Americans operating in Russia by the mid-2000s was increasingly hostile.

Once the offer to purchase the building by IPG Photonics was accepted by the board in March 2014, the trustees were warned that it might be impossible to move the proceeds from the sale of the campus out of Russia. Deteriorating bilateral relations and sanctions instituted by the United States and the European Union in response to Russia's annexation of the Crimea and its involvement in conflict in eastern Ukraine raised the possibility that RAI's substantial construction debts, mostly to its trustees, might never get repaid. Fortunately, with the help of the institute's excellent accounting team at KPMG, the staff was thrilled to report that taxes owed to the Russian government had been paid, and a wire transfer of the balance of the funds was successfully completed to RAI's US bank account. I think

---

[20]Myers, *New Tsar*, 420-21.
[21]Fiona Hill and Clifford G. Gaddy, *Mr. Putin: Operative in the Kremlin* (Washington, DC: Brookings Institution Press, 2015), 347-48.

the trustees all across the country heard my shout of celebration from the RAI office when my laptop computer indicated that the funds had arrived in RAI's US account. By the next day, all construction debts were fully paid. The pressure of these debts had weighed heavily on me, and I had felt a burden to get them repaid to donors and trustees who had done so much to build the institute. August 2014 was a time of rejoicing. With debts repaid, the trustees could focus on the future of the institute, using the remaining assets from the campus sale.[22]

BILATERAL RELATIONS WORSEN

While RAI trustees continued to search for ways to stay involved in Russia, the relationship between the two countries dramatically worsened in 2014. The Sochi Winter Olympics in February 2014 became a major source of tension between the West and Russia when Western leaders refused to attend in order not to endorse Putin's regime. Putin authorized the funding of the largest construction project on the planet, originally estimated at $12 billion, and it grew to an estimated $51 billion, making it the most expensive Olympics ever.[23]

At the same time as the Olympics drama, antigovernment demonstrations in Ukraine led to the removal of its Russian-backed president, partially overshadowing Putin's moment of glory. When Putin decided to annex the Crimea, part of Ukraine, in reaction to these revolutionary events, and subsequently ordered military involvement in eastern Ukraine, the war mode between Russia and the West became evident. In the words of two leading Western analysts, "Putin's actions in 2014 alienated the world outside Russia more than any other set of actions in the decades since the collapse of the USSR."[24]

The pragmatism of Putin's first two terms as president had slowly given way to a confrontational approach toward perceived enemies, and the events in Crimea and Ukraine in 2014 illustrated this dramatic break from earlier policies. Putin intended to reassert Russia's power with or without the recognition of the West, shunning its "universal values," its democracy and the related rule of law, because he was convinced they were alien to Russia.[25]

---

[22]"Chronology of the Building Sale," 2014, RACU Building Sale Files, RA.
[23]For a detailed analysis of Putin and his Sochi Olympics projects, see Myers, *New Tsar*, chap. 24, "Putingrad," 434-56.
[24]Hill and Gaddy, *Mr. Putin*, 380.
[25]Myers, *New Tsar*, 475.

BEING FLEXIBLE

In this context I was amazed by the institute's trustees, who refused to give up or walk away from the risky undertaking in Russia. While the institutional partnership had ended when the school shut its doors in 2013, the trustees continued to search for ways to be a constructive force in Russia and particularly to support educational programs run by Russians and Ukrainians. When Anthony Diekema stepped down as chair of the board of trustees in January 2014, after providing remarkable leadership through difficult times, Dennis Kuester was chosen to succeed him. He accepted the appointment with great enthusiasm, despite the obvious challenges of working in a hostile Russian environment.[26]

By mid-2014, our formal partnership with our Russian colleagues, including RAI's Russian trustees, practically came to an end. The financial stake at risk during the three years seeking to sell the campus was that of the American trustees, because their resources and those of other major American supporters paid for it. Russian financial contributions were never substantial, even from Russian members of the board of trustees or advisers, so the struggles during the closure stage primarily resided with the American trustees. The role of the board of trustees diminished in importance as the executive committee increasingly carried the weight of decision making concerning the campus sale, payment of taxes, and repayment of construction debts; it also wrestled with plans about the future, with almost no input from its Russian members. The executive committee met by phone or in person weekly or biweekly during the transition, and the shift to American leadership became the new reality.

The new mission for RAI emerged from discussions among the staff and trustees throughout 2014. In November, current and former US board of trustees members and spouses came together for two days in Washington, DC. The opening dinner celebrated the achievements of the institute and the friendships and cooperation that had developed during the school's twenty-year history, with many sharing stories of personal reasons for thankfulness. The following day the trustees' meeting included lively discussions and frank assessments of future possibilities for the institute. In the weeks that followed, the trustees enthusiastically endorsed a confidential proposal that described the establishment of a

---

[26]Executive committee, "Meeting—December 14, 2013," 1-2, RBM; John A. Bernbaum to the board, "Electing New Board Officers," December 21, 2013, 1, RBM.

private foundation using the net assets of the sale of the Moscow campus. Its funding priorities would be the following:

> Educational programs in Russia for Christian professionals to help them relate their faith to their work and that train them to be leaders of integrity and sound character;

> Programs that encourage reconciliation and cooperation among Protestant, Orthodox, and Catholic communities in Russia; and

> Programs that help build constructive relations between the Russian Federation and the United States, primarily through the sharing of common Christian values.[27]

When the meeting concluded, the board decided to keep RAI's Russian corporation alive legally, but it was no longer used as the primary vehicle for the institute's work. RAI's remaining Moscow staff, who had managed the campus facility prior to its sale, were hired by IPG Photonics with a substantial salary increase, so their transition proved to be positive. As the sole remaining RAI employee, working part time, I was tasked with the job of establishing a private foundation, which was a new experience for me.

The proposal to create a private foundation began a new stage in RACU/RAI's development. It became the guiding document for RAI's US corporation, and the only subsequent change was to include programs in Ukraine as well as Russia. By 2015, the board was excited to see that the story of the RACU and RAI was continuing with some surprising consequences.

---

[27]John A. Bernbaum, "The Russian-American Institute's New Mission," December 6, 2014, 1, RAI's New Mission, RA.

19

LESSONS AND LEGACIES

THOSE WHO DEVELOP AN INTEREST in Russia soon come across Winston Churchill's famous judgment about this large and largely misunderstood country: it is a "riddle, wrapped in a mystery, inside an enigma." Martin Malia, a scholar of Soviet Russia, noted that Churchill's verdict was later modified by an American ambassador to Moscow, who said "Soviet Russia is not a mystery; it is only a secret." Malia added that with the collapse of 1989–1991, the world of Lenin and Stalin is no longer even a secret, since the archives of the Communist Party are now open.[1] When I began traveling to Russia in 1990, I thought Churchill's judgment was accurate, but after more than twenty-five years of work there, I know this is no longer true. Russia can be understood. No special expertise or theory is required. Like any other nation, it requires that people desiring to acquire understanding discard preconceptions and prejudices and explore Russia's past and present as much as possible. Such a pursuit requires patience.[2]

THE TRAUMA OF RUSSIA'S POSTCOMMUNIST TRANSITION

When Mikhail Gorbachev was chosen as general secretary of the Communist Party in 1985, he gradually introduced reform initiatives that dramatically changed the USSR and eventually brought about its collapse in December 1991. Russia went through radical political reforms, comprehensive economic changes, unimaginable military reductions, social crises that affected families when the

---

[1]Martin Malia, *The Soviet Tragedy: A History of Socialism in Russia, 1917–1991* (New York: Free Press, 1994), ix.

[2]I agree with this judgment by Stephen F. Cohen, *Failed Crusade: America and the Tragedy of Post-Communist Russia* (New York: Norton, 2000), 69.

Soviet support systems collapsed, and a moral crisis in which Marxism-Leninism was recognized to be a complete failure and its atheistic, materialistic view of life to be a fraud. For a country to experience five massive transitions at the same time is unique in modern history.

Like many Western observers, I described these radical changes as revolutions, rather than transitions, when they were underway. Reflecting back on this period from 1989 through 1991, a more accurate assessment for these developments would refer to them as transitional stages rather than revolutions. With little bloodshed and only a modest amount of popular support for the radical changes that took place under both Gorbachev and Yeltsin, *revolution* does not correctly describe the movements. When I was in Moscow during the August 1991 coup, it appeared to be a dramatic overthrow of the Communist Party from the bottom up. However, it soon became evident that these events signaled another top-down upheaval, not unlike the Bolshevik takeover in 1917.

Unlike the American Revolution of 1776, in which George Washington, John Adams, Thomas Jefferson, and many other colonial leaders encouraged and mobilized opposition to British rule, in Russia many of Yeltsin's advisers who were given leadership roles in his government after the failed coup in August 1991 were former Communist Party leaders who rejected their previous political allegiances and reconstituted themselves as "democrats." They were equivalent to eighteenth-century British Tories (Loyalists) who saw an opportunity to take over the revolution and shape it to their benefit. Although they were willing to help Yeltsin dismantle the Communist Party's monopoly on power, they had no serious commitment to democratic capitalism.

The board of trustees and the American staff of RACU did not fully comprehend the tumultuous developments in Russia in the 1990s and were hopeful that democratic change would take place. Through the lives of our students, who shared their families' struggles with RACU staff and faculty, we increasingly gained a sense that the Russian people were suffering from the radical economic policies of the Yeltsin government and were viewing democracy and capitalism as destructive systems leading to their impoverishment. Understandably, American outsiders had a hard time discerning what was happening in Russia when many Russians were also at a loss to fathom the complexities of contemporary events.

No blueprint or model existed to help decision makers in Russia or its Western advisers figure out how to dismantle a communist regime and replace it with a democratic capitalist system. Some of the key Americans involved in shaping US policy during this period, such as President Bill Clinton's principal adviser on Russia, Strobe Talbott, admitted, "We, like the [Russian] reformers, had a far clearer notion of where we wanted to see Russia go than how it could get there, how long it would take, and what we could do to help."[3] Ambassador Jack Matlock Jr., who served in Moscow from 1987 to 1991, confessed that most of the advice "that Gorbachev got when he was seeking help consisted of theory devoid of the engineering required to put it into practice." He compared the challenge of managing the transition to that of converting "a submarine to an aircraft while keeping it functioning with the same crew throughout the process."[4]

Reflecting on Russia's experience in the 1990s, former Secretary of State Condoleezza Rice observed that "those who advised the Russians, not to mention the Russians themselves, had no earthly idea how to break up and reconstitute the deeply dysfunctional economy. . . . The speed of change clearly outpaced the development of the rules of the game and institutions to contain the new forces." She explained, "America's Founding Fathers worried about creating a state that would be too strong and thus a threat to democratic values. But they understood that the state had to be strong enough to carry out certain functions. . . . Russia did not find that sweet spot."[5]

The struggles and cries of the poor and vulnerable in Russia were not being heard by Yeltsin's cabinet ministers or their Western advisers who were committed to "shock therapy." Hundreds of thousands of Russians were suffering from the total loss of their savings when currency was devalued and when food costs skyrocketed. For them democracy and the free market meant great pain, not an improvement in life. World Bank officials realized that their investment strategies in developing economies were not resulting in the progress that they had experienced with the Marshall Plan after World War II, so they initiated efforts in the 1990s to hear from "the true poverty experts, the poor themselves."[6]

---

[3]Strobe Talbott, *The Russia Hand: A Memoir of Presidential Diplomacy* (New York: Random House, 2002), 117.
[4]Jack F. Matlock Jr., *Superpower Illusions* (New Haven, CT: Yale University Press, 2010), 108.
[5]Condoleezza Rice, *Democracy: Stories from the Long Road to Freedom* (New York: Twelve Books, 2017), 90-91.
[6]Steve Corbett and Brian Fikkert, *When Helping Hurts* (Chicago: Moody, 2012), 49-51. See also Bryant Myert's *Walking with the Poor* (Maryknoll, NY: Orbis Books, 2011).

Yeltsin's ruling elite and their Western advisers ignored the lessons gleaned from this endeavor by the World Bank, and the cries of the poor met with little response in Russia, while oligarchs seized the country's assets, accumulated enormous fortunes, and moved their stolen assets overseas for safekeeping. Beginning during Yeltsin's regime and then continuing expansively under Putin, there were 2 Russian billionaire oligarchs in 1998, 36 in 2004, 87 in 2008, and 110 in 2013, third only to the United States and China, and they amassed $427 billion in capital. Not a single Russian would have been worth $1 billion in 1991.[7] This was not what the average Russian hoped for when the communist system collapsed. During the early 1990s, hundreds of old men and women were lined up on the streets of Moscow and other cities selling used clothes and family heirlooms so they could earn enough money to buy food.

Analysts have contended that Putin used corruption to sustain a kleptocratic authoritarian regime,[8] but a recent study argues that, with the help of liberal technocratic economists, Putin created a dual economy: one portion dominated by corrupt and inefficient state enterprises, the other powered by innovative private companies. Out of this struggle a "hierarchy of Putinomics" has emerged: "first, political control; second, social stability; third, efficiency and profit." The first two objectives were achievable, but not the third, which is why the country's healthcare and educational systems are underfunded and corruption persists.[9]

To expect Russia to become a democracy with a free-market economy in fewer than ten or twenty years shows little understanding of the complexity of change on the scale attempted. That attitude demonstrates a lack of sensitivity to the legacy of history and how characteristics and qualities in Russian culture must change before political, economic, social, and moral transformations can occur.

Rebuilding Russian society from the rubble of the Soviet regime was a difficult task made even more complex by the failure to understand the necessity to address the deep cultural and moral issues at stake and the financial impact on its people.

---

[7]Timothy J. Colton, *Russia: What Everyone Needs to Know* (New York: Oxford University Press, 2016), 162-63.
[8]Karen Dawisha, *Putin's Kleptocracy: Who Owns Russia?* (New York: Simon & Schuster, 2014).
[9]Chris Miller, *Putinomics: Power and Money in Resurgent Russia* (Charlotte: University of North Carolina Press, 2018).

THE CHALLENGE OF BUILDING A PARTNERSHIP

When the Yeltsin government invited the staff of the Christian College Coalition to establish a college in Moscow in October 1990, we knew the crosscultural challenges would be significant because of our experience in the long history of building faith-based liberal arts colleges and universities in the United States. However, the enthusiasm of both American and Russian educators involved in the undertaking was high, and leaders in both countries hoped that the collapse of the Soviet regime in Moscow in 1991 would bring an end to the Cold War and the beginning of a constructive relationship between the two countries. Both sides represented societies who "were among the very few great powers that never fought each other and cooperated more than they competed." With the end of the Cold War, it now appeared possible to return "to this historical norm," in the words of the Russian ambassador to the United States, Vladimir Lukin.[10] He was convinced that if Russians and Americans learned to live with ambiguities and avoided both illusions and cynicism, this would happen. The early planners of RACU agreed with Ambassador Lukin.

But our American leadership soon learned the devastating legacy of seventy years of communism. Our initial partners in the Russian Christian community, who had suffered severe persecution in the Communist Party's attempt to elim-inate religion in Russia, were traumatized by their experiences and carried the psychology of persecution into the new period of freedom. We expected to find people of faith from different traditions celebrating the collapse of Marxism-Leninism and embracing each other; instead, we found Christians who trusted no one outside their immediate community, even other Christians. This distrust was one of the biggest surprises of my twenty-five-year experience in Russia.

The low-trust culture of Russia, a direct product of the repressive legacy of the czarist and Soviet regimes, made it very difficult to build Russian ownership of RACU. The institute's administrative leadership and its board of trustees were both convinced that people of faith needed to work together to rebuild Russia after the devastation of the Soviet regime, but getting religious communities to see themselves as partners was extraordinarily difficult. Pastors and denomina-tional leaders were eager to send young people from their churches to RACU but were not willing to provide funding for them or the school. The "culture of

---

[10]Vladimir Lukin, "No More Delusions," *Washington Post*, April 3, 1994.

dependency" that RACU's Russian trustees described as particularly characteristic of Russian Protestants was accurate. Most Russians involved in the university believed that wealthy American Christians should support RACU because the hardships they had suffered under the communist regimes warranted this. Despite repeated efforts to gain partial financial ownership of RACU by the Russians who benefited from it, we experienced limited success and frankly had no idea how this reality could be changed.

A second challenge came in the effort to find educators and community leaders who were willing to serve as volunteers on RACU's boards. When we invited a number of religious leaders to become part of the university's leadership team, they made it clear that they would only do so if they were paid. The concept of voluntary community service was simply unknown to them, since private organizations of any kind were not permitted in the atomized Soviet culture. Despite knowing that the American members of RACU's board of trustees were business and education leaders who offered their time, talent, and treasure to support the founding of the new school, few Russian Christian leaders were willing to make a similar commitment.

The long history of free Soviet, state-controlled higher education created an obstacle in the establishment of any new private school, except those for children of the new Russian elite, who used their wealth to build schools for their children that were inaccessible to average Russians. Taking the initiative to build a private school like RACU appeared overwhelming to many Christian leaders, not only because of their total lack of knowledge and experience in such an effort but also because of the built-in expectation that all education was to be provided free by the state.

Another financial complication arose related to funding. The traditions of philanthropy and Christian tithing that were part of Russian life in the previous century disappeared during the Soviet era. As a result, many Protestant churches lacked the resources to pay their pastors—an issue that did not significantly improve even after the Russian economy began to recover in the early 2000s. Support remained abysmal for charities and benevolence agencies, and even their own churches.

For the original American working group and later the board of trustees, the idea of developing a private partnership between Russians and Americans using education as the vehicle for cooperative work seemed to be promising. Following the October 1990 invitation to establish a faith-based liberal arts college in Moscow, Americans with expertise in Russia, such as James Billington, the librarian of the US Congress, emphasized the importance of people-to-people initiatives such as this between our two countries. Billington was convinced that the United States had a special role to play in nurturing democracy in Russia, and he made a strong case for nongovernmental efforts, arguing, "What is needed is not another government program, but an all-American engagement of private and local organizations in helping all of the peoples of the Soviet Union build the infrastructure and absorb the ethos of modern, pluralistic democracy."[11]

A year later, when Billington met with coalition delegates to discuss their educational initiatives in Russia, he said,

> What you are doing is tremendously, seminally important. Thoughtful people in the Russian system know there is a better way to run a society . . . without it being a self-indulgent society. This is why they have come to you. We need to reach out to [the Russian people] in ways that accent their renewed interest in the spiritual dimension. This is something you are uniquely equipped to do.[12]

RACU's board of trustees, staff, and faculty, made up of both Americans and Russians, were convinced that building a private, binational school and working together to educate young Russians was an important undertaking that could contribute to the rebuilding of Russian society. The Americans were largely in agreement that our goal was not to make Russia into a Eurasian version of the United States but rather to deal with the country as a nation emerging from seventy years of atheism and forced collectivism; our challenge was to learn about its unique history and culture and to treat Russians with respect. The staff and American faculty also repeatedly cautioned our Russian students not to try to make Russia like the United States. We encouraged them to search their own cultural and spiritual heritage, to reject the Soviet mindset, and to rebuild the moral and ethical foundations of their country in ways that fit their context.

When I look back over these twenty-five years and our efforts to build a private partnership between Russians and Americans, I am constantly amazed at the incredible willingness of Americans to provide funding for the school,

---

[11]James H. Billington, "U.S.S.R.: The Birth of a Nation," *Washington Post*, September 8, 1991.
[12]Strategy Council Meeting, "Record of Meeting—September 1992," 1-2, Russian Initiative files, RA.

including annual scholarships year after year as well supporting a substantial capital campaign to build a campus facility in Moscow. In addition, 120 American and Canadian faculty traveled to Russia, sometimes for multiple years, to teach at RACU as volunteers. In some cases, their schools paid for their travel costs, while others raised support from friends or paid for the costs themselves. Repeatedly Russians would ask Americans, "Why are you doing this at your expense?" This provided the opportunity to talk about caring for each other despite the political tensions—a generosity not often witnessed by either our Russian students or faculty. It also showed how nongovernmental organizations can play important roles in building friendships.

RACU'S LEGACY

Deep friendships. I have often wondered what would have happened if the political relationship between the United States and Russia had not deteriorated so rapidly after President George W. Bush's emerging warm friendship with President Vladimir Putin following September 11 and Putin's dramatic, unexpected offers of assistance. From my perspective on the ground in Moscow, the breakdown in this bilateral relationship was initially caused by mistakes made by the leadership of both nations. While the media on both sides blamed the other for the new Cold War, they were acting as a mirror image of their opponent, just as they had for years during the height of the Cold War.

Despite the deteriorating relationship between the two governments in the first decade of the twenty-first century, amazingly, people-to-people friendships continued to blossom. Russians were increasingly critical of America's political leadership in the White House but had little hesitation about befriending Americans in Russia or holding positive views of the American people. A similar phenomena existed in the States. While critical of Putin and his KGB background, most Americans I knew had little, if any, hostility toward the Russian people.

One of the consequences of a low-trust society was the way Russians primarily formed deep and enduring friendships within their family and clan, but if a Russian became your friend, the decision resulted in a hospitality and loyalty rarely seen in America. While the formal Russian-American partnership collapsed in 2012 when the university was forced to close, the hospitality and friendships with Russians never let up, although Putin's increasing anti-American posture, especially after his foreign-policy speech in Munich in 2007 and the takeover of Crimea in 2014, made maintaining these friendships more difficult. Frank email exchanges with Russian friends and colleagues about life in Russia came to an end as Putin's security officials increased their monitoring of electronic communications.

Program spinoffs. With the realization that government officials were going to make RACU's future existence tenuous, the board decided to be proactive. Two of RACU's principal educational programs were spun off and reconstituted as Russian educational entities. The School of Social Work and Counseling, which was one of the first international social work programs in Russia, developed by Americans and Russians in partnership, was given funding by the board in diminishing amounts for three years in order for the department to become self-sustaining.[13] The program, directed by Ruslan Nadyuk in cooperation with his two American partners, Mark and Christine Currie, became a leader in this developing academic field.

The Moscow staff subsequently divided its program into two entities: the Institute for Social Work and Counseling, a nonprofit educational organization, and the Department of Social Work and Family Counseling at Moscow Orthodox Institute of St. John the Divine, where it was invited to relocate its undergraduate program. The principal attraction to the academic leaders of Moscow Orthodox Institute was the department's unique international character and its quality curriculum, developed by Russians and Americans in partnership.

RACU's social work program developed a unique focus on soul care, or more literally "trusteeship of the soul," which became well-known first in Moscow and then in outlying regions of the country, and now many seminaries and Bible colleges offer courses on soul care, modeled after its program. The institute also offered professional-development certificates for social workers who needed continuing-education credit, and this popular program continued after RACU closed its doors. In September 2014, the institute began the first professional degree program in church-related pastoral counseling at Moscow Evangelical Christian Seminary, which is located near RACU's former campus facility. The

---

[13]RACU was the recipient of a grant from the Shaw Fund, administered by my home church, National Presbyterian Church in Washington, DC, which provided the funding for this three-year transitional subsidy. The church also provided partial funding for my work at RACU for many years.

legacy of RACU lives on through these two outgrowths of the social work and counseling department and through hundreds of university-age students and adult learners who received degrees and certificates, including many in other cities through online courses.[14] In addition, Ruslan Nadyuk has worked with Christian counselors and psychologists in other post-Soviet republics, so its impact has spread beyond Russia's borders.

The Russian-American Language Institute, an outgrowth of RACU's Department of Literature and Linguistics, also became a separate legal entity and continues to offer courses in English in the evenings and weekends. Under the leadership of Tim Hange and then Bernard Jacobsen, the program began in September 2012 with a vision for small group language training that would open up the possibility of developing trust-based relationships. In addition to regular classroom instruction, the faculty also arranged special weekend language retreats that allowed them to deepen their friendships with the students.[15] Within a year after the school closed, these two programs in social work and English language were training several hundred university students and adult learners.

Both of these spinoffs have been negatively affected by Russia's increasing anti-Western policies, so participation by American faculty has been substantially reduced. While relationships with Western colleagues have not been completely cut off, the enthusiasm for international exchanges of the early 1990s has come to an end but can hopefully be regenerated if and when political relationships are improved.

Graduates. From RACU's beginning in fall 1996, its Department of Business and Economics attracted the largest number of applicants, and this continued for the remainder of the school's existence. In the first ten years, 150 students graduated with training in free-market values and institutions, computer skills linked to the world of commerce, English-language competence, and a solid grounding in moral and ethical values. Many of these graduates were immediately hired by major international corporations and a growing number of new Russian companies; some chose to start their own small companies, while others

---

[14]Mark Currie, "The Legacy of RACU's Social Work & Counseling Program," July 23, 2014, and Mark Currie, "RAI's Legacy," June 10, 2017, RACU's Legacy file, RA.

[15]Bernard Jacobsen, "The Legacy of RACU's English Language Program," September 10, 2014, RACU's Legacy file, RA.

went on to graduate school for advanced degrees, particularly MBAs.[16] The staff and faculty of RACU are still in contact with some of these alumni and are pleased to see them prosper but sense the challenges that they face in a market-place where corruption and bribery seem inescapable. If RACU were still in op-eration, we would have developed programs for our graduates to help them wrestle with the challenges they face—they were asking for this in the closing years of the school's existence.

The graduates of each department are RACU's most important legacy. The school's American supporters made immeasurable investments in the lives of hundreds of these young people, as did the faculty and staff. Unlike most Russian university students, RACU students did not reflect the self-centered, materialistic values of their generation. Many of them became actively engaged in programs working with orphans or disabled people, or assisting in summer youth camps for troubled teenagers on a full-time or part-time basis while attending RACU. Very few got involved in political engagement, like most of their generation, but they did find ways to reach out to those who were struggling.

To the leadership of the school, the majority of RACU's students showed they were people of character who cared deeply about their country, their families, and their local communities. While long-term friendships are hard to maintain with graduates who are on the move professionally and geographically, we be-lieve seeds have been planted and these young people have been equipped to be constructive citizens of Russia and potentially future civic leaders. Again, Putin's anti-Western policies have made it more difficult to communicate with our grad-uates because no one is willing to discuss the problems they face through the internet or over the phone. Perhaps some time in the future a Russian working group of RACU alumni will form to establish a faith-based liberal arts university like the one they attended!

A charitable business network. When the staff and faculty began to develop internship opportunities for its students, internships where they could gain ex-perience in a professional context, a number of substantial relationships resulted. These ties with leaders in the business community soon grew into networks that served the students well in opening up internship placements to match their

---

[16]John A. Bernbaum and Bob Foresman, "The Legacy of RACU's Business Program," September 18, 2014, RACU's Legacy file, RA.

career interests; the networks in business and social work also provided opportunities for the faculty to have their programs reviewed by professionals in the field, which had rarely happened in Moscow before this time. Linking business professionals to the university was a mutually beneficial phenomenon.

But an unanticipated legacy also emerged. In 2002 a Bible study and support group of ten young, senior business executives began to meet regularly, with leadership provided by several RACU trustees, me, and Bob Foresman, an American who lived and worked in Moscow and was well-known in the Russian business community. The group, made up of five Russian Orthodox believers and five American Protestants, called itself the 5-on-5 Group and had as its goal "building a bridge of friendship that can carry the weight of truth."[17] The legacy of low trust mentioned earlier meant building enough trust and confidence in each other was a difficult hurdle, especially for some of the Russian members who operated in a hostile business environment in which no one shared personal information with colleagues, who might use it against them in the future. However, over time, this became a close group in which everyone talked about their personal lives and provided support for each other as husbands, fathers, and employees.

As a result of Foresman's growing friendship with Metropolitan Hilarion of the Russian Orthodox Church, the 5-on-5 Group was converted into the Tuesday Group by Foresman, and it became a vibrant Russian businessmen's fellowship, with twenty-five Christians from a wide range of religious backgrounds. The group meets on a biweekly basis in Moscow and has two purposes: to strengthen the spiritual lives of its members and to affect Russia by its charitable activities. This business network, which among other projects has supported orphanages and the free distribution of 920,000 copies of the New Testament and Psalms since 2012, is an extraordinary outgrowth of RACU.[18]

Investment fund. Following the sale of RACU's Moscow campus, the net assets of the sale—less taxes owed to the Russian government—were successfully sent by wire transfer to RACU's bank account in the States. The American members of RACU's board of trustees were in agreement that the foundation created from the sale of the Moscow campus should be used to support

---

[17]This slogan was borrowed from the Haggai Institute.
[18]Bernbaum and Foresman, "Legacy of RACU's Business Program."

Russian-run educational programs and humanitarian projects, since Americans were no longer able to operate freely in Russia. They also decided to expand the territory covered by grants to include Ukraine, since many of RACU's graduates and friends were active there and the country was completely open to Western cooperation and support.

Since 2015 a substantial number of grants have been approved for Christian educational programs, especially those that work with university students. For the trustees of the new foundation, one of the top priorities is supporting the equipping of Russian and Ukrainian youth to be faithful disciples of Jesus and constructive citizens of their country, committed to building a just, peaceful, and secure society.

Major grants to Mission Eurasia's Next Generation Professional Leadership Initiative and School with Walls programs, as well as support for other programs for university students run by derivatives of InterVarsity Christian Fellowship and Campus Crusade in these two countries, are evidence of this commitment.

In addition, grants have been made to various nonprofit organizations created by RACU graduates, particularly those working with orphans and children with special needs. Priority has also been given to programs that encourage ecumenical cooperation between Christian communities (Protestant, Orthodox, and Catholic). The goal is to support local Christian leaders to carry on the goals of RACU, and this has led to deepened relationships with program leaders in both countries.

The foundation's trustees share the view that moral and spiritual renewal will provide a solid basis for Russia's emergence from the rubble of communism's collapse, a perspective that Peter Deyneka constantly articulated when the "red door" opened in the early 1990s. Looking to the free market as the cure for Russia's or Ukraine's plight was a failed strategy. It also became clear to the trustees that the deteriorating relationship with Putin's regime, especially after his return to the presidency in 2012, meant the foundation's name had to be changed and the Russian-American label removed, since it was not helpful for making grants either in Russia or Ukraine. In May 2016 the US nonprofit corporation was renamed BEAM, Inc. (standing for Business & Education as Mission).

Grants to Russian and Ukrainian programs increased in 2017 and 2018, and updates keep the board informed of developments with grant recipients. Grants have generated partnerships with civic leaders in Russia, Ukraine, and other post-Soviet countries. In addition, Christian educators in these countries are asking for advice on how to build Christian schools—elementary schools, high schools, and colleges—based on lessons we learned with RACU and our close association with Christian colleges and universities in the States. Repeatedly trustees have commented on how the foundation has allowed RACU's legacy to continue in some surprising ways.

WHAT LIES AHEAD FOR RUSSIA?

The heightened animosity between the United States and Russia, especially since the episodes of cyber-warfare related to the American presidential election of 2016 and accusations of possible collusion between the American president and Russian leaders, has generated a contentious debate about the future of Russian-American relations and Russia post-Putin. Our experience at the ground level in Russia taught us that we need a different perspective on Russia's future development and the bilateral relationship between our two countries. The secular mindset of Western journalists and policymakers who largely focused on political and economic issues resulted in the misdiagnosis of Russia's transition out of communism beginning with Gorbachev's radical reforms in 1987–1988 and continuing through Boris Yeltsin's presidency in the 1990s. Because they were tone-deaf and did not listen to what Gorbachev and his closest advisers were saying, or hear the cries of the Russian people who were struggling with economic decisions that did not offer a safety net for them, or pick up the prophetic insights from several decades of Russian writers who powerfully articulated the loss of identity and moral emptiness in Soviet life, their analyses were flawed.[19]

Beginning with Gorbachev's policies of *perestroika* (restructuring) and *glasnost* (openness) and especially after the failed coup of August 1991, Western journalists and politicians quickly predicted the birth of democracy in Russia and the development of a free-market economy. For many observers, there was a firm belief that the former Soviet Union would inevitably democratize if its leaders wanted to modernize their country, since there was no other path forward in the age of globalization. It was wishful thinking. When it became clear by the late 1990s that this was not going to happen, at least in the near future, then claims were made about Russians having a genetic disposition toward autocratic rule.[20]

---

[19]See this analysis in chap. 7, "Reading Russia Right."
[20]These helpful insights were drawn from David S. Foglesong's *The American Mission and the "Evil Empire"* (Cambridge: Cambridge University Press, 2007), 196-97.

This failure to integrate religious and ethical aspects of Russian life with its economics and politics, which I wrote about in the early 1990s, has been partially addressed by the emergence of a number of books in which authors highlight the connections between religion and foreign policy.[21] As a result of these resources and a number of international crises caused by armed religious organizations, the Foreign Service Institute now offers courses on religion and international diplomacy to its foreign service officers, although my off-the-record conversations with recently retired ambassadors indicate that the impact on their staff has been marginal and mostly helpful for those who already are religiously active. Much more needs to be done to alert policymakers about the importance of religion and its cultural impact, as well as its potential to be a force for peacemaking, particularly in Russia.

The failure to recognize and address the changes that were needed in Soviet culture and the pervasive Soviet mindset became evident in our work with RACU students and their families, as well as our Russian faculty and staff. Seventy-five years of insider privilege for elites and antimarket, antiprofitmaking, and antientrepreneurial attitudes were major obstacles to economic and political reform.[22] Even Federal Reserve Chairman Alan Greenspan admitted that he used to assume that capitalism was "human nature," but having witnessed the collapse of the Russian economy in the late 1990s, he concluded that "it was not human nature at all, but culture."[23]

A growing number of journalists and scholars are now focused on how cultural values and attitudes can facilitate or block progress in developing nations. Like the ideas of Alexis de Tocqueville, who understood that what made the American political system work was a culture congenial to democracy, and Max Weber, who explained the rise of capitalism as rooted in religion, these new insights are emerging and need to be applied to Russia.[24]

---

[21]Two significant studies were published that address this issue, and many more have followed. The first is Douglas Johnson and Cynthia Sampson, eds., *Religion: The Missing Dimension of Statecraft* (New York: Oxford University Press, 1994), and the second is Jonathan Fox and Shmuel Sandler, *Bringing Religion into International Relations* (New York: Palgrave MacMillan, 2006). See also *The Review of Faith and International Affairs*, issued by the Institute for Global Engagement.

[22]David Landes, "Culture Makes Almost All the Difference," in *Culture Matters: How Values Shape Human Progress*, ed. Lawrence E. Harrison and Samuel P. Huntington (New York: Basic Books, 2000), 3.

[23]Lawrence E. Harrison, *The Central Liberal Truth: How Politics Can Change a Culture and Save It from Itself* (New York: Oxford University Press, 2006), 13.

[24]Lawrence E. Harrison, introduction to *Culture Matters*, xxi.

The unprecedented multiple transitions that Russians experienced after the August 1991 coup and the collapse of the Soviet Union four months later brought back fears of instability and violence. The changes that are needed in the traditional culture of Russia—for example the affinity toward the rule of a czar, a strong man, and the lack of civic institutions that can be a constraint on national leadership and can hold political authorities responsible—will not take place quickly. Deep cultural change can happen, but this takes time. Democracy cannot be forced on a country that lacks the underlying ethical and moral qualities required to support it. The seeds of democracy and a free-market economy require fertile soil if they are to form deep roots and ultimately bear fruit.

By downplaying or ignoring the ways in which Russian culture can limit institutional change, many Western policy advisers in the late 1980s and 1990s, as well as young Russian reformers in Yeltsin's cabinet from secular Soviet families, ignored the Russian Orthodox Church and other religious communities, which they considered of marginal importance. While there are leaders in the Russian Orthodox Church who are hostile to the West and to its democratic and free-market values, there are others in leadership who welcome them. One analyst, Nikolas Grosdev, argued that the mainstream doctrines of the Russian Orthodox Church are not supportive of democratic institutions or market economics and are roughly comparable to the posture of Catholicism before it shifted its stance to full support of democracy in the second half of the twentieth century.[25] This could change when young, progressive Russian priests are elevated to top leadership positions.

It has been my experience that when Westerners describe the Russian Orthodox Church, they often make many broad generalizations that bear little relationship to reality. Russia has many "Orthodoxies," as there are many varying "Christianities" in the United States.[26] The Russian Orthodox Church is like a large tent with a wide variety of practices and groupings under its cover. When considering the size of the country, spread over eleven time zones, a great diversity of Orthodox churches and leaders becomes easily imaginable. Orthodox, Catholic, and Protestant institutions in Russia compose the country's largest

[25]Harrison, *Central Liberal Truth*, 107-9.

[26]John P. Burgess, *Holy Rus: The Rebirth of Orthodoxy in the New Russia* (New Haven, CT: Yale University Press, 2017), 195.

nongovernmental organization with a massive network of congregations and religious organizations that could have been mobilized to help the millions of Russians who suffered financially and emotionally during the radical reforms of the 1990s. In a time when the world is rapidly desecularizing (except in Western Europe) and in a country that has a deep-seated spirituality ingrained in its culture for one thousand years, ignoring the role of religion in Russia was and is a costly mistake.[27]

James Billington's insights on this subject proved to be most helpful in our work in the Russian Federation. RACU's board of trustees wholeheartedly agreed with his judgment that Russians need to tap their rich spiritual heritage, evident in the writings of some of the world's most famous literary figures, whose works have had a great impact on Russia and the world. Russia is not going to become a copy of the United States or the democratic countries of Western Europe. Its citizens have to work out their own institutional structures, legal system, and vibrant civil society. While Russians can learn some lessons from the West, its own history and culture will shape its destiny. We must not expect Russia to change its character quickly, any more than the painful process we as Americans are now going through to figure out who we are will happen rapidly. Our own country has gone through incredible internal upheaval and change in its 240-plus-year history, and this should make us hesitant critics of others.

Having lived in Russia through the tumultuous 1990s, when it became clear that President Yeltsin was not committed to building democratic institutions and the country became increasingly anarchical after the 1996 elections, Vladimir Putin's election to the presidency in March 2000 was a sign of hope for RACU and its staff. Putin was young, energetic, and clearly in charge; law and order were restored to the streets of Moscow. But our initial enthusiasm began to wane as the new president clamped down on the press and began bringing in his colleagues from the security services to serve in his cabinet. It appeared for a brief period of time that Putin and George W. Bush were going to become allies, but Putin became frustrated with what he perceived to be unilateral actions by the United States, especially the attack on Iraq.

---

[27]Evan Osnos, *Age of Ambition: Chasing Fortune, Trust and Faith in the New China* (New York: Farrar, Straus and Giroux, 2014), is a remarkable study of China's economy, politics, and religious life—a rare analysis that weaves together these three facets of the "new China." A book like this needs to be written about postcommunist Russia.

By 2004, when NATO absorbed seven new countries from Russia's former empire and Putin witnessed a series of revolutions from Ukraine to Georgia, he became resentful toward the West. His anger deepened with the attack on Libya. He now came to believe that the West, especially the United States, was acting unilaterally in global politics and was also fomenting internal opposition in his country. With each term in office, Putin cranked up his rhetoric against the United States, and the possible partnership many of us hoped for never solidified.

The hope for a constructive relationship between Moscow and Washington, DC, diminished during Barack Obama's presidency, but Russia's annexation of Crimea and its attacks on Ukraine in 2014 "pushed the two sides over a cliff. . . . Russia and the West were now adversaries." A new Cold War had begun, and although this new Cold War was fundamentally different from the original one, since the world was no longer bipolar and the new conflict did not pit one "ism" against another, the tensions between Russia and the United States affected nearly every important dimension of the international system. In addition, "Putin's emphasis on Russia's alienation from contemporary Western cultural values" added to the estrangement.[28]

Since his reelection to a second six-year term as president, and with no obvious succession plan in place, Putin faces a difficult dilemma. Because the Russian system is incapable of transforming itself, Putin's survival mechanism is the emphasis on an external enemy that is arousing political opposition and justifies his domestic repression. A "Western threat" is his only source of legitimacy. In addition, the days of a booming economy from the first eight years of his presidency are over, and the Russian economy is stalled with a vanishing budget, a trade surplus, and dramatic cuts needed because of the low price of oil on the global market. On the other hand, Russian elites know that the future health of their economy depends heavily on Western financing and technology. Recent polls in Russia indicate that the Russian people are tired of endless wars with the West and want a "normal country."[29]

What is hard for Westerners to understand is how Putin continues to have the support of so many Russians, a phenomenon that populist autocrats have

---

[28]Robert Legvold, "Managing the New Cold War," *Foreign Affairs* (July/August 2014): 74-75.
[29]Lilia Shevtsova, "Putin Beware: Russians Are Changing Their View of the West," *Financial Times*, August 29, 2018.

successfully nurtured by stroking nationalist impulses. With a press that is largely under the control of the Kremlin, and with little popular dissent allowed, Putin has found ways to appeal to something deep in the psychology of the Russian people. Putin understands their grievances, based on their disorientation after decades of Soviet rule and communist ideology, animosity toward the oligarchs who purchased state enterprises at bargain-basement prices, and the sense of humiliation after the collapse of the USSR. When he refuses to cooperate with the West and criticizes its leaders for their moral bankruptcy and political hypocrisies, this bravado appeals to Russians because he appears to be restoring Russian self-respect.[30]

Because Putin has no obvious challenge to this presidential power, the fate of Russia is now intimately connected with his own. To Steven Lee Myers, author of *The New Tsar*, Russia is rushing forward as the troika (a carriage drawn by three horses) in Gogol's *Dead Souls* to an unknown destiny.[31] What is particularly troublesome is "how dangerously little Putin understands about us [Americans]—our motives, our mentality, and, also, our values."[32]

I agree with former ambassador to Moscow Michael McFaul: "As long as Putin remains in power, changing Russia will be close to impossible." McFaul argues that "real political change will likely begin only after Putin steps down," and maybe not even then, depending on who succeeds him. I also agree with him that Americans need to continue to develop ties with Russian society, including student and cultural exchanges and dialogues between nongovernmental organizations from both countries.[33]

MY PERSONAL RUSSIAN JOURNEY

Though I studied Russian history in my doctoral program and worked on US-Russian relations during my four years at the Department of State in the early

---

[30]These insights are based on Svetlana Alexievich's *Secondhand Time: The Last of the Soviets* (New York: Random House, 2017), for which she won the Nobel Prize in Literature in 2015.

[31]Myers, *New Tsar*, 480-81.

[32]Fiona Hill and Clifford G. Gaddy, *Mr. Putin: Operative in the Kremlin* (Washington, DC: Brookings Institution, 2015), 385.

[33]Michael McFaul, "Russia as It Is," *Foreign Affairs* (July/August 2018): 82-91. For Ambassador McFaul's perspective on his years in Moscow, see his book *From Cold War to Hot Peace: An American Ambassador in Putin's Russia* (New York: Houghton, Mifflin, Harcourt, 2018).

1970s, I never had any intention of living and working in the USSR. When my wife, Marge, and I agreed to give leadership to the Christian College Coalition's USSR Initiative in 1990, and later when I agreed to serve as chair of the American working group formed to establish a faith-based liberal arts college in Moscow, our original commitment was for seven years. Twenty-five years later, we stand amazed by what has developed.

The most difficult challenges came with the daily struggles of working in a country where nothing is as it seems, where bribery was pervasive, and where no one trusted anyone else. As a person with my type-A personality, who likes to carefully plan a schedule and set goals with specific targets in mind, working in Russia changed me and my work patterns. The need to be flexible and to tolerate sudden changes without any advance warning framed each day. I experienced fear when robbed by the police at a metro stop, and also when I was surrounded by four young Russian youth in a crowded subway car, as they began pushing me back and forth while searching my pockets and briefcase. They stole some paperwork but fortunately did not discover my airplane tickets and passport, hidden in my inside suit-coat pocket. While I often felt Moscow was safer than my hometown of Chicago or than Washington, DC, where we had a home during this period, these experiences, among others, were unsettling.

By far the most important lesson learned through this experience in Russia was to follow God's call, which I heard so clearly in 1990 when the Russian minister of science and higher education extended the amazing invitation to start a Christian liberal arts college in Moscow. This request became my Macedonian call, not unlike the apostle Paul's call to visit Macedonia on one of his missionary journeys, which was not a part of his planned itinerary (Acts 16:9-10). Many times during these decades, I wanted to quit and leave Russia for good. But the title of Eugene Peterson's book *A Long Obedience in the Same Direction* was taped on my desk, where every day I was reminded that I had been called to this task that required a steadfastness of purpose. Although I do not fully understand what we achieved by establishing RACU, I am convinced that the board of trustees' vision and faithfulness is being used by God for his purposes. We planted seeds in Russian soil, and I believe those seeds are growing, first beneath the surface, and then slowly they will emerge to bear fruit.

In September 1990 a journalist asked me to summarize the significance of our meetings with the delegation of Soviet educators from the USSR, which we hosted at the Christian College Coalition's offices in Washington, DC. I responded:

> This is truly one of those rare moments of truth in a nation's history when basic decisions are being made that will set the future course for millions of people. Our desire is to be witnesses of Jesus Christ to our Soviet friends and to help them restructure their educational system so that moral and spiritual values are integrated into all facets of their educational programs. The roots of Russian spirituality lie deep in their collective history and must be rediscovered. We also hope to challenge our own students to gain a vision for their lives that might include building bridges between our two cultures.

Looking back on these twenty-five years of work in Russia, our hopes for significant educational reform of state universities never had a chance, because of the tumultuous political, economic, and social upheaval during the years of Yeltsin's presidency; by the time he resigned, the educational reformers we worked with were no longer in charge. During Putin's presidency, education was rarely discussed, and the emerging private educational institutions, which were creating competition for the state universities, were increasingly under pressure from the Kremlin. Educational reform was and still is a low priority in Russia.

The legacies of RACU, summarized earlier in this chapter, were what came out of this partnership. The shared faith between American and Russian Christians was what generated these legacies, and it also planted in the hearts and minds of Russian and American students who traveled to the States or to Russia a continuing desire to build friendships and to find ways to work together to build healthy societies. Many American students who studied in Russia on exchange programs had their view of the world expanded; a number "caught the Volga bug" and went on to pursue graduate degrees in Russian studies and language. Many Russian students who decided to emigrate to the States or Canada, because they saw little opportunity in their own country, have become leaders in their new countries.

Peter Deyneka had a sense of urgency about our mission in Russia and in particular about the potential impact of RACU. He constantly reminded me and our Russian colleagues that the rebuilding of Russia after communism needed to be grounded in spiritual renewal and nurtured by quality Christian educational institutions. He also warned that the red door might not stay open, so we needed to work diligently while we had the chance. The doors have started to close, especially under Putin following his return to the presidency in 2012. But they are not yet shut, and I believe they will open again, when new leadership in our two nations decides to pursue the common interests we share and begin working together on the global challenges we face.

HISTORIC MILESTONES IN RACU'S DEVELOPMENT (1990–2016)

October 26, 1990	Initial request by the Russian minister of education to build a "faith-based liberal arts university" in Moscow
September 28, 1992	Formation of the American working group to develop a faith-based liberal arts college in Moscow
July 25, 1994	First meeting of the board of trustees of Russia-American Christian University in Moscow
March–May 1995	RACU offers its first four classes in the evenings at Russian Peoples' Friendship University's downtown campus
June 14, 1995	Incorporation of RACU/US, Inc., as a nonprofit organization
April 2, 1996	Signing of the foundation agreement of RACU by the board of trustees in Moscow
June 1995 and June 1996	RACU offers four-week summer English-language institute on the main campus of Russian Peoples' Friendship University
July 10, 1996	IRS grants tax-exempt status to RACU/US, Inc.
September 1996	RACU accepts its first class of full-time undergraduate students
October 1996	RACU moves into its new campus location at the Center for Christian Ministry
May 27, 1997	Approval of RACU's charter by the board of trustees in Moscow

December 3, 1997	The Russian Ministry of Education awards RACU an operational license with the right to grant undergraduate and graduate degrees
September 1999	RACU moves some of its academic operations to Moscow State University's Center for International Education
May 2001	RACU purchases a land lease in northeastern Moscow on which to build a new academic facility
May 19, 2001	RACU's first commencement celebration for nineteen graduates
September 28, 2001	The board of trustees for RACU/US, Inc., approves the building plans and capital-campaign budget for a new campus facility in Moscow
August 2002	RACU moves to its third campus location, at the former Moscow Silk Factory
November 12, 2003	The Russian Ministry of Education grants RACU full accreditation for five years—the first school of its kind to receive state approval
December 2005	RACU is granted permission to build its new campus facility by the Moscow city government
August 2006	RACU moves to its fourth campus location, at Tushino Evangelical Church
November 2007	RACU changes its legal name to the Russian-American Institute
December 12, 2008	RAI's five-year education license expires and needs to be renewed
Spring 2009	RAI's regular undergraduate courses are temporarily suspended for the spring semester due to its expired license
January 18, 2010	RAI receives its renewed education license and offers its first classes in the new campus facility
May 15, 2010	RAI receives its occupancy permit for the new facility
May 28, 2010	RAI's ninth graduation
May 29, 2010	The institute dedicates its newly completed forty-six-thousand-square-foot academic facility

Summer 2010	A perfect storm: new tax regulations result in the loss of tax exemption for the new facility, and annual property taxes are nearing $500,000; reaccreditation appears impossible due to Russian Ministry of Education's refusal to recognize any PhDs granted by American universities; and a major government scholarship program for state universities results in a substantial decrease in potential RAI student enrollment
November 12-13, 2010	The board of trustees unanimously votes to suspend RAI's undergraduate program at the end of the 2010–2011 academic year and monetize the Moscow campus with the goal of using net assets from the sale of the building for future work in Russia
June 2, 2011	RAI's tenth and final graduation (forty students)
January 27, 2012	RAI receives the title of ownership for its new facility in Moscow
April 6, 2012	The board of trustees authorizes the executive committee to sell RAI's new campus facility
March 18, 2014	The board signs a sales agreement with a large multinational corporation to purchase its Moscow campus facility
November 8, 2014	The board votes to use the net assets from the sale of RAI's Moscow campus facility to support Christian ministries in Russia and Ukraine
January 2015 to present	RAI makes grants to Christian ministries in Russia and Ukraine
May 2016	RAI changes its name to Business & Education as Mission (BEAM), Inc., and registers the name change with the IRS and the state of Oklahoma, where it is legally based

RACU'S BOARD OF TRUSTEES

AMERICAN MEMBERS

John A. Bernbaum
January 1994–present; chair January 1994–May 2004
RACU founder and president, Wheaton, Maryland

Ren Broekhuizen
November 2005–December 2012
educator and speaker, Holland, Michigan

Howard Dahl
Term: May 2001–present
president, Amity Technology, Fargo, North Dakota

Richard N. Dean
May 2001–present
partner, Baker & McKenzie LLP, Washington, DC

Robert L. DeBruin
November 2010–December 2013
vice provost (retired), Central Michigan University, Mount Pleasant, Michigan

Peter Deyneka
January 1994–December 2000 (RACU founder; died December 23, 2000)
president, Russian Ministries, Wheaton, Illinois

Anthony J. Diekema
May 2004–December 2013; chair May 2004–December 2013
president emeritus, Calvin College, Grand Rapids, Michigan

Mark Elliott
January 1995–present (RACU founder)
professor of history, Wheaton College, Wheaton, Illinois, and Asbury University, Wilmore, Kentucky; editor, *East-West Church & Ministry Report*

Bob Foresman
November 2005–present
Barclays country head for Russia (2009–2016), Moscow/New York City

Richard L. Gathro
May 2001–December 2013
director, Washington campus (retired), Pepperdine University, Washington, DC

Kent R. Hill
March 1998–2000
President, Eastern Nazarene College, Quincy, Massachusetts

Sidney J. Jansma Jr.
May 2008–present; vice chair December 2013–present
chairman of the board, Wolverine Gas & Oil Corporation, Grand Rapids, Michigan

Dennis J. Kuester
May 2001–present; chair January 2014–present
retired chairman/CEO, Marshall & Ilsley Corporation, Milwaukee, Wisconsin

Milton H. Kuyers
May 2001–present
chairman, GMK Companies, Inc., Milwaukee, Wisconsin

Marty Ozinga III
November 2005–present
president, Ozinga Brothers, Inc., Chicago, Illinois

Pricilla Young Romkema
January 1996–May 2000
International Teams, Moscow

Stacie Schrader
January 1999–December 2004 (appointed to board of advisers January 2005)
Russia country director, Opportunity International, Nizhni Novgorod, Russia

RACU'S BOARD OF ADVISERS

Alexander M. Abramov
president, Institute for the Development of Educational Systems, Moscow

John Ashcroft
former US Attorney General, Washington, DC

Alexei E. Bodrov
rector, St. Andrews Biblical Theological College (Orthodox), Moscow

Sam Brownback
US senator from Kansas, Washington, DC

Howard Dahl
president, Amity Technology, Fargo, North Dakota

Arthur DeFehr
president, Palliser Furniture Company, Palliser, Canada

George V. Denisenko
head of credit card sales, ZAO Citibank, Moscow

Max DePree
chairman emeritus, Herman Miller, Inc., Zeeland, Michigan

Anita Deyneka
president, Russian Ministries, Wheaton, Illinois

Sergei Drojin
chief financial officer, Integrated Energy Systems, Moscow

Vernon Ehlers
US representative from Michigan, Washington, DC

Andrei Gaidamaka
director of strategic development, Lukoil Oil Company, Moscow

C. William Pollard
chairman emeritus, The ServiceMaster Company, Wheaton, Illinois

James T. Priest
partner, Whitten, Nelson & McGuire, Oklahoma City, Oklahoma

Peter Reddaway
professor of international affairs, George Washington University, Washington, DC

Kyle H. Royer
vice president for finance, Council for Christian Colleges & Universities, Washington, DC

Charles E. Ryan
chairman, UGF Asset Management, Moscow

Stacie D. Schrader
country director for Russia, Opportunity International, Nizhni Novgorod, Russia

Ekaterina Smyslova
president, Esther Legal Information Center, Moscow

Mark Souder
US representative from Indiana, Washington, DC

Andrew Steer
president and CEO, World Bank, Washington, DC

Clyde Taylor
ambassador (retired), US Foreign Service, Washington, DC

Mikhail Timin
president, TALIS Holding Company, Nizhni Novgorod

Nicolai Trofimov
academician, Russian Peoples' Friendship University, Moscow

Ralph Veerman
president, Veerman & Associates, Orlando, Florida

Bob Wallingford
partner—tax department, KPMG, Moscow

Alexander Zaichenko
economist, Moscow

Appendix D

RACU/RAI PROVOSTS

Jay Shanor (administrator 1994–1995)

Stanley Clark (fall 1995–spring 1998)

Johannes Furter (fall 1998–spring 2000)

Larry Ort (fall 2000–spring 2003)

David Broersma (fall 2003–spring 2009)

Clyde Vollmers (fall 2009–spring 2011)

RACU FACULTY AND STAFF (AMERICAN AND RUSSIAN)

DISCIPLINE ABBREVIATIONS

BE	Business and Economics
ELI	English Language Institutes
GE	General Education
IT	Information Technology
LL	Languages and Literature
SW	Social Work

AMERICAN FACULTY

Name	Discipline	Name	Discipline
Joyce Arkebauer	LL	Pamela Indahl	SW
Patrick Black	LL/GE	Carin Lambert	LL
David Broersma	LL	Matt Miller	GE
Stanley Clark	SW	Cynthia Moody	BE
Mark Currie	SW	Josh Nunez	LL
Donoso Escobar	SW	Larry Ort	BE/GE
Sarah Fluegge	LL	Krister Sairsingh	GE
Annalies Galletta	LL	Cathy Thornberg Sheets	LL
Perry Glanzer	GE	Eric Van Genderen	BE
Tim Hange	LL	Carol VanDerHeyden	SW
Makinzie Heard	LL	Clyde Vollmers	BE
Matt Heard	LL	Karly Watson	LL
Sherie Henderson	LL		

RUSSIAN FACULTY

Name	Discipline	Name	Discipline
Boris Abdurakhmanov	SW	Nadezhda Grubaya	SW
Erna Abramyan	SW	Mikhail Gruby	LL
Nadezhda Abydenova	SW	Svetlana Grushina	LL
Nadezhda Agafonova	BE	Svetlana Horosheva	GE
Igor Alenin	LL	Maria Kainova	LL
Elena N. Antonova	LL	Irina Kargina	SW
Yuri Apatov	IT	Nonna Khaoustova	GE
Sergey Bagrov	GE	Natalya Kondrashova	LL
Olga Balaeva	SW	Nikolay Kornilov	GE
Zhanna Belotelova	BE	Nina Koryakina	LL
Valeri Bespalov	BE	Igor Koshelev	LL
Alla Bocharova	BE	Tamara Kozlovskaya	LL
Olga Bogdanova	LL	Alexander Krotov	IT
Pavel Bulgin	BE	Elena Kudinova	LL
Igor Burykin	GE	Zhenya Kulaga	LL
Oleg Chernishov	GE	Oksana Kuropatkina	LL
Galina Cherviakova	SW	Lidia Kustareva	SW
Vladimir V. Chuyev	GE	Antoni Lakirev	GE
Oleg Druzhbinsky	GE	I. A. Lapkina	BE
Vyacheslav Fatukhin	LL	Dina V. Liakhova	SW
Georgy Gambarov	BE	Elena Litskevich	LL
Ludmila Girko	SW	Tatyana Lobacheva	SW
Tatyana Golubeva	BE	Tatyana Makarova	SW
M. Goryacheva	SW	Anton Malkov	BE
Ilya Grits	GE	Evgeny Malkov	IT
Sergey Gromov	BE	Elena Malkova	SW

Name	Discipline	Name	Discipline
Yelena Matvechuk	SW	Natalia Smirnova	LL
Vyacheslav Mikheev	SW	Yana Smirnova	BE
Elena Miroshnikova	GE	Ekaterina Smyslova	BE
Elena Morozova	GE	Vladimir Solodovnikov	GE
Dmitri Motrenko	IT	Elena Studyonova	SW
Ruslan Nadyuk	SW	Olga Sukhareva	LL
Irina Namestnikova	SW	Andrei Timofeev	BE
Valentina V. Naumova	BE	Vladimir Torokhty	SW
Michael Nosov	GE	Alexander Tsuterov	GE
Vladimir Obrovets	GE	Irina Tubyanskaya	BE
Svetlana Y. Orlova	BE	Pavel Usishev	SW
Alexander Pestryakov	GE	Alexander Vaprov	GE
Nelly Roslyakova	LL	Leonid Vasilenko	GE
Julia Rybochkina	LL	Alexander Vasiliev	IT
Sergey Sanatko	BE	Sergei Vdovin	IT
Olga Savenkova	GE	Zoya Venetsyanova	BE
Gennady Savin	LL	Ludmila Voskanyan	LL
Vladislav Selivanov	BE	Nadya Vyshegorodtseva	LL
Elena Serebrennikova	LL	Tanya Yaskova	LL
Gennady Sergienko	GE	Alexander Zaichenko	BE
Elena Shapoval	BE	Ekaterina Zapolnaya	LL
Mikhail Sherbakov	GE	Nadezhda Zheltuhina	LL
Oleg Shevkun	LL	Tatyana Zhukova	BE
Tamara Shilov	GE	Olga N. Zotikova	BE
Peter Smirnov	SW		

ADJUNCT AMERICAN FACULTY

Name	Affiliation or Occupation	Discipline
Ike Adams	Asbury College	SW
Beulah Baker	Taylor University	LL
Gary Baugher	Iowa Public Schools	GE
Joan Borst	Grand Valley State University	SW
Tim Boyd	Roberts Wesleyan College	GE
Majel Braden	NOVA University	SW
James Brownlee	Malone College	LL
Marilyn Cain	Calvin College	BE
Robert Cubillos	church business administrator	GE
LaRaine Dail	youth consultant	LL
Susan DeHaan	Wheaton College	ELI
Janet DeLay	Southwestern College	ELI
Fred DeJong	Calvin College	SW
Peter DeJong	Calvin College	SW
Lonna Dickerson	Wheaton College/University of Illinois	ELI
Stephanie Diepstra	Calvin College	SW
Carolyn Dirksen	Lee College	ELI
Murl Dirksen	Lee College	ELI
Donna Drake	Shelby State Community College	GE
Henry Dueck	Canada/Lithuania Christian College	ELI
Mary Dueck	Canada/Lithuania Christian College	ELI
Bob Eames	Calvin College	BE
Mark Elliott	Asbury College	GE
Lanny Endicott	Oral Roberts University	SW
Rodney Fitzgerald	Calvin College	ELI
Tat Fong	Geneva College	BE
Eugene Grossman	Deyneka Russian Ministries	GE
Svetlana Grushina	Kent State University	LL
Virgo Handojo		SW
Pat Hargis	Judson College	LL
Cathy J. Harner	Taylor University	SW
T. Harner	Businessman	BE

Name	Affiliation or Occupation	Discipline
James Heizer	Georgetown College	GE
Ruth Heizer	Georgetown College	GE
Stephen Hoffmann	Taylor University	GE
Jessica Hooten	Baylor University	
Richard Hornbeck	management consultant	ELI
Beryl Hugen	Calvin College	SW
Joseph Iadonisi	Wheaton College	ELI
Kelly Jensen	Samford University	LL
Joyce Johnson	Wheaton College	ELI
Tom Kay	Wheaton College	GE
Paul Kilpatrick	Geneva College	LL
Suzanna Kok	Dordt College	ELI
Timothy Kowalik	Northwestern College	ELI/GE
Jeff Lehman	Huntington College	IT
Randall Lewis	Spring Arbor College	BE
Billy Lewter	Palm Beach Atlantic College	SW
Enedina Martinez	Point Loma Nazarene College	ELI
Becky Matthews	Columbus State University	GE
Elroy Miller	Eastern Mennonite College	SW
George Monsma	Calvin College	BE
Mark Motluck	Anderson University	BE
Don Mulder	Businessman	BE
William Nettles	Mississippi College	ELI
Richard Newkirk	Des Moines Public Schools	SW
Deborah H. Nikolaeva	Indiana University	GE
Amy Obrist	Biola University	LL
Caryn Pederson	Wheaton College	ELI
JoAnne Powell	Taylor University	SW
Larry Powell	Businessman	BE
John Primus	Calvin College	GE
Dave Radius	Christian Reformed World Missions	BE
Marlene M. Reed	Baylor University	BE
Lawrence Ressler	Taylor University	SW

Name	Affiliation or Occupation	Discipline
Don Reynolds	Ferris State University	BE
Joseph S. Ricke	Taylor University	LL
Frank Roberts	Calvin College	GE
Patricia Robertson	California Baptist University	SW
Mark Rodgers	Dominion University	SW
Shirley Roels	Calvin College	BE
Michael Rowley	Huntington University	LL
Kyle Royer	Coalition for Christian Colleges & Universities	ELI/BE
Carla Schemper	Counselor	SW
Lugene Schemper	Calvin College	GE
Robert Schoone-Jongen	Calvin College	GE
Brenda Schull	Businesswoman	BE
Ray Slager	Calvin College	BE
Pamela Smucker	Oral Roberts University	GE
Caren Sturgill	ESL China	ELI
Lowell Sturgill	Attorney	ELI
Jim Vanden Bosch	Calvin College	ELI/LL
Ray Vander Weele	Calvin College	BE
Gary VanderPlaats	Geneva College	BE
John Visser	Dordt College	BE
Stacy Vollmers	University of Minnesota	BE
Wendy Wakeman	Fresno State University	GE
Frank Walker	Lee University	BE
Darrell Warner	Elon College	SW
Jonathan Warner	Dordt College	BE
Richard Warner	Lehigh Carbon Community College	BE
Jeffrey Wetterman	Oral Roberts University	GE
James Wilkens	Calvin College	ELI
Judy Williams	Franklin High School	LL
Emily Wilson	social worker	LL
Pete Wozniuk	Businessman	BE
Mary Zwaanstra	Calvin College	SW

ADJUNCT RUSSIAN AND EUROPEAN FACULTY

Name	Affiliation or Occupation	Discipline
Vadim Babashkin	Finland	GE
Ron Brunson		GE
Brian Burnett	businessman—IT specialist	BE
David Challenger	Truro University (Moscow)	LL
William Clancy	Non-Profit Medical Center (St. Petersburg)	BE
Daniel Clendinin	International Institute for Christian Studies	GE
Christine Currie	psychological counselor (Moscow)	SW
Steve Dintaman	Lithuania Christian College	
Ruth Dowdey	Moscow State University graduate student	LL
Guaita Giovanni		GE
Mark Harris	Recovery Treatment Center (Ryazan)	BE
Eric Hinderliter	Lithuania Christian College	BE
Rebecca Hinderliter	Lithuania Christian College	BE
Pauline Jacobs	ESL instructor (Moscow)	LL
Teri Jones	London School of Economics	BE
Karin Krekeler	language instructor (Moscow)	LL
George Law	Deyneka Russian Ministries	BE
Neil Lessman	Integra Venture	BE
J. P. Manley	International Board of Missions	GE
Christopher Ohan	International Christian Foundation	GE
Alan Smith	Hinkson Christian Academy	GE
Albert Van Houwelingen	Netherlands	BE
Diana Vermillion	Agape Medical Clinic	GE
William Vermillion	Moscow Evangelical Theological Seminary	GE
Brad Wathen	International Federation of Evangelical Students	GE
Daniel Weston	businessman	BE

INDEX